Readings in

Special Olympics

by
Robert E. Cipriano
Chairman, Department of
Recreation and Leisure
Studies, Southern Connecticut
State College

Special Learning Corporation

42 Boston Post Rd. Guilford, Connecticut 06437

Special Learning Corporation

Publisher's Message:

The Special Education Series is the first comprehensive series designed for special education courses of study. It is also the first series to offer such a wide variety of high quality books. In addition, the series will be expanded and up-dated each year. No other publications in the area of special education can equal this. We stress high quality content, a superb advisory and consulting group, and special features that help in understanding the course of study. In addition we believe we must also publish in very small enrollment areas in order to establish the credibility and strength of our series. We realize the enrollments in courses of study such as Autism, Visually Handicapped Education, or Diagnosis and Placement are not large. Nevertheless, we believe there is a need for course books in these areas and books that are kept up-to-date on an annual basis! Special Learning Corporation's goal is to publish the highest quality materials for the college and university courses of study. With your comments and support we will continue to do so.

John P. Quirk

0-89568-111-0

©1980 by Special Learning Corporation, Guilford, Connecticut 06437

First Edition

2 3 4 5

SPECIAL EDUCATION SERIES

* ● Abnormal Psychology: The Problems of
    Disordered Emotional and Behavioral
    Development
  ● Administration of Special Education
  ● Autism
* ● Behavior Modification
    Biological Bases of Learning Disabilities
    Brain Impairments
  ● Career and Vocational Education for the
    Handicapped
  ● Child Abuse
* ● Child Psychology
  ● Classroom Teacher and the Special Child
* ● Counseling Parents of Exceptional Children
    Creative Arts
  ● Curriculum Development for the Gifted
    Curriculum and Materials
* ● Deaf Education
    Developmental Disabilities
* ● Diagnosis and Placement
  ● Down's Syndrome
  ● Dyslexia
* ● Early Childhood Education
  ● Educable Mentally Handicapped
* ● Emotional and Behavioral Disorders
    Exceptional Parents
  ● Foundations of Gifted Education
* ● Gifted Education
* ● Human Growth and Development of the
    Exceptional Individual

  ● Hyperactivity
* ● Individualized Education Programs
  ● Instructional Media and Special Education
  ● Language and Writing Disorders
  ● Law and the Exceptional Child: Due Process
* ● Learning Disabilities
  ● Learning Theory
* ● Mainstreaming
* ● Mental Retardation
  ● Motor Disorders
    Multiple Handicapped Education
    Occupational Therapy
  ● Perception and Memory Disorders
* ● Physically Handicapped Education
* ● Pre-School Education for the Handicapped
* ● Psychology of Exceptional Children
  ● Reading Disorders
    Reading Skill Development
    Research and Development
* ● Severely and Profoundly Handicapped
    Social Learning
* ● Special Education
  ● Special Olympics
* ● Speech and Hearing
    Testing and Diagnosis
  ● Three Models of Learning Disabilities
  ● Trainable Mentally Handicapped
  ● Visually Handicapped Education
  ● Vocational Training for the Mentally Retarded

  ●　Published Titles　*Major Course Areas

TOPIC MATRIX

Readings in Special Olympics is a comprehensive source book which will enable the reader to 1) initiate 2) develop and 3) guide a program of athletic events for the retarded child.

COURSE OUTLINE:

Readings in Special Olympics

I. What is Special Olympics?
II. Therapeutic Recreation
III. Special Education and Physical Education

I. Spirit of Special Olympics
II. Value of Special Olympics
III. Improved Functioning of the Participant

Related Special Learning Corporation Readers

I. Readings in Mental Retardation
II. Readings in Educable Mental Handicaps
III. Readings in Down's Syndrome
IV. Readings in Counseling Parents of Exceptional Children

CONTENTS

Glossary of terms   VIII

Topic matrix   IV

1. The Spirit of Special Olympics: Sports Contribution to Participants

Overview   3

1. **What is Mental Retardation?** *The Pres-*   4
    ident's Committee on Mental Retardation,
    Government Printing Office, Washington,
    D.C. 1977.
    A factual chart showing levels of retardation,
    educational programs, and rehabilitation
    services as compiled by the president's panel
    on mental retardation.

2. **Special Olympics, Fifth International**   16
    Special Olympics Games, Eunice Kennedy
    Shriver.
    A speech made by Eunice Kennedy Shriver
    at the Fifth International Special Olympics
    Games at Brockport, N.Y. on August 9, 1979.

3. **When the World Comes to Visit,** Original   17
    article by Peter N. Smits.
    An account of the Special Olympics in
    Brockport, N.Y. from preparations to com-
    pletion on August 9, 1979.

4. **State University and State Residential**   20
    Facility Co-Sponsor Special Olympics,
    Susan Meyers-Winton, School of Education,
    Department of Special Education, San Jose
    State University, San Jose, California, un-
    published article.
    This article describes the cooperation between
    a residential facility and a state university in
    preparing and implementing an invitational
    Special Olympics track and field event.

5. **Special Olympics,** Maryann Mitchell, King   25
    County Park Department, Seattle, Washington,
    Recreation's Role In the Rehabilitation of The
    Mentally Retarded, Larry Neal (Ed.), Rehabil-
    itation Research and Training Center in
    Mental Retardation, University of Oregon.
    This article indicates goals of the Special
    Olympics program and describes important
    things that transpired to a group of Special
    Olympians and their chaperones at the
    National Special Olympics.

6. **Always Where the Action Is,** Rafer Johnson,   27
    past head coach, Special Olympics, Inc.,
    Parks and Recreation, Vol. 10, No. 12,
    December 1975.
    This article describes the volunteer spirit
    among celebrities in the Special Olympics.

7. **One Person Makes a Difference,** Eunice   28
    Kennedy Shriver, Executive Vice-President
    of the Joseph P. Kennedy, Jr. Foundation
    and Presidents, Special Olympics, Inc. *Parks*
    and Recreation, Vol. 10, No. 12, December
    1975.
    This article describes the importance of
    volunteers in the Special Olympics. The
    author articulates the role of "huggers" in the
    Special Olympics, and indicates the differences
    a person can make in the lives of mentally
    handicapped persons.

8. **Special Olympics,** Richard Alfred Scarnati,   31
    Chief Physical Therapist for Southwest Cook
    County Cooperative Association for Special
    Education, Worth, Illinois, *Journal of Health*
    Physical Education and Recreation, Vol. 43,
    No. 2, February 1972.
    This article describes the author's success in
    developing a Special Olympics program. Also
    included is a compilation of specific respon-
    sibilities that will enable people to implement
    similar programs.

9. **Sometimes They Stumbled--,** The Special   34
    Olympics Committee. Original article by
    Frank J. Hayden.
    A detailed recollection of the Special Olympics
    held in Chicago's Soldier Field.

10. **And Nobody Tried to Win,** Jim Murray,   37
    Business and Finance, Friday, August 18,
    1972.
    This article describes what is "special" about
    the Special Olympics and cites a variety of
    achievements in the Games.

11. **The Special Olympics,** Robert M. Montague,   39
    Jr. Article reprinted by permission from the
    1976 Compton Yearbook, 1976 Encyclopedea
    Britannica, Inc.
    On August 7, 1975, in Perry Shorts Stadium,
    Mount Pleasant Mich, the Special Olympics
    was held.

2. Value of Special Olympics/Transfers Effects

Overview   51

12. **Special Olympics Volunteers: 250,000**   52
    "Someone Elses", Original article by
    Colman McCarthy.
    The affect the Special Olympics has on those
    who volunteer is related.

13. **Volunteering and the Handicapped,** *Pro-*   54
    grams for the Handicapped, Department of
    Handicapped, Department of Health, Educa-

tion and Welfare, Office for Handicapped Individuals, No. 2, March/April 1979.
This article describes the benefits that a cadre of volunteers can play in mainstreaming and advocacy activities for the handicapped.

14. **Convict Volunteers,** David Dewey, Director of Leisure Time Activities, Muskegon Correctional Facility, Muskegon, Michigan, *Therapeutic Recreational Journal,* Vol. X, No. 3, Third Quarter, 1976. 57
This article describes a program where mentally handicapped children were taught physical skills by a group of volunteer prisoners in order to prepare them for the Special Olympics.

15. **A Play Center for Developmentally Handicapped Infants,** Florence Diamond, Coordinator of Special Projects at Villa Esperanza School for the Developmentally Handicapped in Pasadena, California, and Founder-Director of the Edward Levy Infant Center, *Children,* Vol. 18, No. 5, September/October 1971. 60
This article describes the initiation of a playschool for developmentally handicapped infants. The author articulates the curriculum followed, the role of parents and indicates that play is essential in the total human growth and development of handicapped infants.

16. **Therapeutic Play Facilities for Handicapped Children,** Gene A. Hayes, Program Development in Recreation Service for the Deaf-Blind, John A. Nesbitt and Gordon K. Howard (Ed.) Recreation Education Program, College of Liberal Arts, University of Iowa, Iowa City, Iowa, 1974. 65
This article provides an historical perspective regarding play for the handicapped child. The author describes a variety of play facilities for the handicapped and also provides the reader with a classification of handicapped children.

17. **Improving Free Play Skills of Severely Retarded Children,** Paul Wehman, Assistant Professor, Department of Special Education, Virginia Commonwealth University, Richmond, Virginia, and Jo Ann Marchant, Teacher, Hickory School System, Richmond, Virginia, *The American Journal of Occupational Therapy,* Vol. 32, No. 2, February 1978. 77
This article examines the effects of a behavioral training program on the autistic, independent, and social types of play of four severely and profoundly retarded children.

18. **Play as Occupation: Implications for the Handicapped,** Scout Lee Gunn, Coordinator of Therapeutic Recreation Program, University of Illinois at Urbana-Champaign, *The American Journal Of Occupational Therapy,* Vol. 29, No. 4, April 1975. 82
That play is a need-fullfilling and appropriate occupation in the life of every person, and particularly in the life of the handicapped, is the basic assumption of this article. Play is defined, characterized, and discussed in relationship to its role in the treatment process.

19. **The Untapped Reservoir of Human Energy.** Original article by David M. Compton. This article contemplates the idea of integrating all people into one concept. 86

20. **A Community Research Program for the Mentally Retarded,** Mary Jo Mitchell, Recreation Director of the Mentally Retarded and Physically Handicapped, *Therapeutic Recreation Journal,* Vol. V, No. 1, 1971. 92
This article outlines recreation facilities set up in the Washington, D.C. area to serve retarded children.

21. **Special Olympics Athletes Face Special Medical Needs,** Original articles by Andrew V. Bedo, MD, Marilyn Demlow, RN, Patrick Moffit, BS, and Kenneth W. Kopke, ATC. This article discusses the medical needs of the retarded child in the Special Olympics. 97

Focus 104

3. Improved Functioning of the Participants

Overview

22. **Play and Mentally Retarded Children** Original article by Joe L. Frost and Barry L. Klein, *Children's Play and Playgrounds.* This article deals with the problems and needs of children to play. 108

23. **Sports and the Mentally Retarded Individual,** Mike Nychuk, Executive Director, Ontario Floor Hockey League, 40 St. Clair Avenue, W., Toronto, Ontario M4V 2M6. This article deals with Canada and their attempt to bring organized sports activities to retarded children. 112

24. **The Recreation Advocate: Your Leisure Insurance Agent,** Andrew Weiner, Crisis Intervention Teacher at the Georgia Mental Retardation Center, Athens Unit, Athens, Georgia, *Therapeutic Recreation Journal,* Vol. IX, No. 2, Second Quarter, 1975. 116
This article describes competencies needed along with responsibilities of therapeutic recreators advocating for the handicapped. The author indicates that the handicapped individual pays premiums for which he is entitled to receive leisure services.

25. **Recreation for the Retarded: One Institutions Approach,** Nicholas Rusiniak, Recreation Supervisor, Southbury Training School, Southbury, Connecticut, *Journal of Health, Physical Education and Recreation,* Vol. 45, No. 4, April 1974.
This article outlines the different and varried activities made available at the Southbury Training School.   120

26. **Weight Training for Severely Mentally Retarded Persons,** Richard A. Ness, Director of an S.R.S. Grant at Denton State School, Denton, Texas, *Journal of Health Physical Education and Recreation,* Vol. 45, No. 4, April 1974.
This article describes the benefits of a weight training program in increasing the strength of severely retarded people at a state institution.   122

27. **The Potential of Physical Activity for the Mentally Retarded Child,** Julian U. Stein, Chairman, AAHPER Task Force on Programs for the Mentally Retarded. *Journal of Health, Education and Recreation,* April 1966.
The needs for physical activity in the mentally retarded youngster is shown.   125

28. **APE, The Tip of the Iceburg,** Robert E. Cipriano, Ed.D., Associate Professor and Chairman of the Department of Recreation and Leisure Studies, Southern Connecticut State College, New Haven, Connecticut; Lisette Walter, Elementary Physical Education Teacher, Walpole School System Walpole, Massachusetts, *Journal,* The Massachusetts Association for Health Physical Education and Recreation, Vol. XXV, No. 3, Spring 1977.
This article describes an adapted physical education program for elementary school children. The authors present a state of the art regarding physical education for mentally handicapped individuals, and indicate the viability of physical education programming in enhancing the human growth and development of children.   129

29. **Sport, Myth, and the Handicapped Athlete,** Richard E. Orr, *Journal of Physical Education and Recreation,* Vol. 50, No. 3, March 1979.
This article deals with the difficulties in getting sport events organized for the handicapped person.   131

30. **Mainstreaming at Dae Valley Camp,** Betty H. Owen, Assistant Professor of Health, Physical Education and Recreation in the College of Education at Memphis State University, Memphis, Tennessee, *Journal of Physical Education and Recreation,* Vol. 49, No. 5, May 1978.
This article describes a day- camp where normal campers and handicapped children attend. Ability rather than class or label is used in grouping children for instruction.   134

31. **Hands Across the Border,** Judy Newman, Arizona Training Program at Tucson, 29th Street and Swam Road, Tucson, Arizona. *Challenge,* American Alliance for Health, Physical Education and Recreation, Vol. 10, No. 3, April/May 1975.
This article describes the success of an experimental 10 week swimming therapy and recreational swim program for children with various handicapping conditions.   137

32. **Aquatics for the Handicapped,** William T. Muhl, *Journal of Physical Education and Recreation,* Vol. 47, No. 2, February 1976.
The benefits of swimming for the handicapped is outlined.   139

33. **Cross Country Skiing for the Mentally Handicapped,** Nola Sinclair, Physical Education Instructor, Riverview School, Manitowoc, Wisconsin, *Challenge,* American Alliance for Health, Physical Education and Recreation, Vol. 10, No. 1, January 1975.
This article describes the benefits of cross country skiing to the increased functioning ability of mentally handicapped children and youth.   141

Special Focus - Texas Tech University   143

GLOSSARY
OF
TERMS

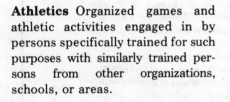

Athletics Organized games and athletic activities engaged in by persons specifically trained for such purposes with similarly trained persons from other organizations, schools, or areas.

Atypical Characteristic A characteristic of an individual in a given chronological age group which is markedly different from that of the mean.

assessment Comprehensive appraisal of strengths and weaknesses of a person's learning. Also, assessment refers to the present educational status of the child.

apprehensive child A child who approaches most learning tasks by being frightened of anything new, strange, or complex in nature, thus equating learning with anxiety which tends to further confuse and disorganize his thought processes.

autism A disorder in which the person does not respond normally to stimulation, acting upon internal demands in their place. He is thought to live in a world of his own. May be associated with prematurity, convulsions, and brain damage. Can be treated by drugs and attendance at day-care programs, depending on individual symptoms.

behavior modification A set of educational procedures designed to influence and develop the occurrence of a wide range of language, social, cognitive, motor, and perceptual behavior patterns.

brain damage A structural injury to the brain which may occur before, during, or after birth and which impedes the normal learning process.

central nervous system In humans, the brain and spinal cord to which sensory impulses are transmitted.

childhood schizophrenia A childhood disorder characterized by onset after age 5, consisting of unusual body movements, extreme emotional abnormalities, and perceptual distortions.

conceptualization The ability to formulate concepts by inferring from what is observed.

Competition The act of contending physically or mentally against one's self or an opponent.

Down's Syndrome Named for Dr. John Langdon-Down, who first identified it in 1886, this condition is caused by an extra number 21 chromosome in each cell of the body making a total of 47 chromosomes.

This disorder occurs in all degrees of retardation severity. Those affected have similar physical characteristics.

Educable Mentally Retarded Those individuals whose IQ range is approximately between 50 and 70. This population is able generally to learn elementary school skills.

electroencephalogram The record produced by an electroencephalogram, an instrument used to record changes in electric potential between different areas of the brain.

emotionally disturbed Characterized by inner tensions and anxiety, there is often a display of neurotic and psychotic behavior, which often interferes with the lives of others.

Figure-ground Perception The ability to attend to one part of a stimulus in relation to the rest of the field.

Gross Motor Most frequently relates to use of the large muscles of the body to perform acts of motion such as turning, jumping, running. Gross motor also involves the ability to coordinate large muscle movements.

hyperactivity Excessive and uncontrollable movement, such as is found in persons with central nervous system damage. Controllable with drugs or environmental changes.

individualized education plan (IEP) A formal written program developed by school personnel, a child's parents, and when appropriate the child him/herself, in order to delineate assessment, placement, goal setting, special services, and evaluation procedures.

Kinesthesis The sense whose end organs lie in the muscles, joints and tendons and are stimulated by bodily movements and tensions.

Laterality The preferential use of one side of the body, especially in tasks demanding the use of only one hand, one eye, or one foot.

mainstreaming The placement of handicapped students into educational programs with normal functioning children.

Mentally Retarded Exceptional persons with impairment in learning potential that adversely affects the performance of an individual.

Mild Retardation Those persons whose I.Q. falls approximately between 50 and 70. They are considered educable and can learn simple academic skills.

Moderate Retardation Those persons whose I.Q. falls approximately between 30 and 49. They can be taught simple speech and are considered trainable. Although they may require supervision all their lives, they can learn basic self-help skills.

Perception The process of organizing or interpreting stimuli received through the senses.

Perceptual Motor The interaction of the various aspects of perception with a motor activity, i.e. visual, auditory, tactile, kinesthetic.

perception The process of organizing or interpreting stimuli received through the senses.

perception of position The perception of the size and movement of an object in relation to the observer.

perception of spatial relationships The perception of the positions of two or more objects in relation to each other.

perceptual disorder A disturbance in the awareness of objects, relations, or qualities, involving the interpretation of sensory stimuli.

psychomotor Pertaining to the motor effects of psychological processes.

Sensori-Motor A term which relates to the combination of the input of sensations and the output of a motor activity indicates what is happening to the sensory organs such as sight, hearing, tactual and kinesthetic sensations.

sensory-motor (sensorimotor) Pertaining to the combined functioning of sense modalities and motor mechanisms.

Severe Retardation Those persons whose I.Q. falls approximately between 0 and 29. They require constant, lifelong care.

Special Olympics Program A program created and sponsored by the Kennedy Foundation to provide athletic training and competition for the mentally retarded.

Special Physical Education Refers to a physical education program that has as its chief purpose adapted, corrected, and developmental outcomes for the handicapped student.

shaping Modifying operant behavior by reinforcing only those variations in responding that deviate in a direction desired by the therapist.

social learning Increasing a child's competence in making relevant decisions and exhibiting appropriate behaviors.

soft neurological signs The behavioral symptoms that suggest possible minimal brain injury in the absence of hard neurological signs.

time-out from reinforcement A therapeutic intervention in which a reinforcing condition is removed or altered for a period of time immediately following the occurrence of an undesirable response.

Therapeutic Recreation A process that utilizes all or some aspect of recreation services and activities to intervene and bring about a desired change in the growth and development of ill, handicapped and infirmed people.

Trainable Retardation Those persons whose I.Q. falls approximately between 30 and 49. They can be taught simple speech and self-help skills.

Training A planned and systematic sequence of instructions under competent supervision designed to impart predetermined skills, knowledge, or abilities with respect to designed objectives.

vestibular Pertaining to the sensory mechanism for the perception of the organism's relation to gravity.

visual-motor The ability to coordinate visual stimuli with the movements of the body or its parts.

visual perception The ability to identify, organize, and interpret what is received by the eye.

FOREWORD

Eunice Kennedy Shriver
President
Special Olympics, Inc.

For more than two thousand years, to be an Olympian has been the noblest ambition of every athlete. And to take part in the Olympics is the crowning achievement of every athletic career.

Until 1968, mentally retarded individuals had little chance to develop athletic skills and essentially no chance of ever being an Olympian. Special Olympics, created in 1968 by the Joseph P. Kennedy, Jr. Foundation, now makes it possible for mentally retarded individuals to develop athletic skills and participate in Olympic-type competition internationally.

Striving to be an Olympian has never been easy. It takes intense personal commitment, endless hours of training, dedicated and capable coaches and support from one's parents and many friends and usually entire communities. To be a Special Olympian requires all of this and more. Special Olympians and their families are challenging the common wisdom that says only intellectual achievement is the measure of human life. They have proved that the common wisdom is wrong. Special Olympians and their families -- more than one million of them -- are proof that the value of human life should be measured in many ways. The world has seen, through Special Olympics, the enduring value of skill, sharing, joy and courage which Special Olympians exhibit so clearly at the 20,000 Special Olympics events which now take place every year.

I hope that everyone who uses this book will strive to promote the Spirit of Special Olympics - the skill, joy, sharing and courage which one million Special Olympians already demonstrate - so that many more mentally retarded individuals will have opportunities to become Olympians too.

Eunice Kennedy Shriver
President
Special Olympics, Inc.

THE SPIRIT OF SPECIAL OLYMPICS: SPORTS CONTRIBUTION TO PARTICIPANTS

It is clear that Special Olympics has an important impact on the participants. It is also evident that the Special Olympics has an equally important impetus in communities in which Special Olympians live. Community attitudes and knowledge about mental retardation have improved as a result of having a Special Olympics program in the community. People living in the community have had their attitudes regarding the capabilities of the mentally handicapped increased as a result of having a Special Olympics program in their community. This increased awareness of what mentally handicapped children can accomplish has created a more positive individual and community position toward mentally handicapped people.

The Special Olympics offers a unique opportunity for the mentally handicapped to integrate with society and fulfill their need to compete with peers. In addition, Special Olympics involves a broad cross-section of educational, recreational and community leaders in the planning and implementation of the program. The Special Olympics has enabled physical educators, special educators and recreators to provide a wide range of sports competition for the mentally handicapped; this participation was virtually non-existent prior to the start of the Special Olympics.

The Special Olympics transcends more than the win/lose concept. This is summed up in the Special Olympic Oath: "Let me win, but if I cannot win, let me be brave in the attempt." Every participant in the Special Olympics is treated like everyone else. A positive self-concept is enhanced when mentally handicapped people are provided with opportunities to safely and successfully engage in sports competition. Since 1968, Special Olympics has become the largest sports program for the mentally handicapped in the world. It is also one of the largest volunteer organizations and one of the most widely respected therapeutic activities for the mentally handicapped. The Special Olympics has served as a catalyst for thousands of community, school and institutional physical education and recreation programs. Special Olympics has provided a set of experiences for those participants predicated upon the feeling of success and accomplishment. It offers a year-round program of physical education, recreation, sports training and competition for mentally handicapped individuals.

The true spirit of the Special Olympics has focused upon the positive attributes each athlete possesses. The Special Olympian is viewed as a precious individual capable of being successful in a variety of activities. No longer does the "failure syndrome" prevail in all segments of the person's life. No longer is the person thought of as being less than adequate in our fast paced society. The Special Olympics has provided much more than merely an arena in which is staged a massive sporting event. Rather, the spirit of the Special Olympics reaches out and touches the lives of all who participate...parents, volunteers and the athletes themselves.

WHAT IS MENTAL RETARDATION?

"Mental Retardation: Past and Present ", from *What is Mental Retardation?*, The President's Committee on Mental Retardation, Government Printing Office, Washington, D.C. 1977.

Mental retardation presents itself in so many forms, degrees, and conditions, from so many known and unknown causes, with so many questions unanswered, that it is difficult to say clearly: these are the people who are retarded and this is what they can do, and this what we can do for them, and this is how we can eliminate the problem.

To reach into the problem we have to know what it is.

To reach the people who have the problem we have to know who they are, how to understand them and how to help them.

Who Are They?

Mental retardation refers to significantly subaverage general intellectual functioning existing concurrently with deficits in adaptive behavior, and manifested during the developmental period.

This is the formal definition published by the American Association on Mental Deficiency in 1973 and widely accepted today. It identifies mental retardation with subnormality in two behavioral dimensions—intelligence and social adaptation—occurring before age 18. The definition is a culmination of long debate and revision, and may well be modified in the future.

The severely retarded person has an obvious incapacity to exercise the expected controls of reason and of personal management necessary for normal living in any human culture. Left to himself, anyone so impaired cannot easily survive. The great majority of severely retarded individuals also have physicial characteristics which suggest a central nervous system defect as the basis of the developmentally retarded behavior.

In many cases no detectable physical pathology accompanies the deficiency of intelligence and adaptation. The limited ability to learn, to reason and to use "common sense" is often unexplainable. Can undetected physical pathology be assumed?

Further questions arise when we discover that milder degrees of intellectual and adaptive deficit are commonly associated with particular families who have serious social and economic problems. Do poor living conditions produce mental retardation, or is it the reverse? Or does each condition compound the other? Still further, members of certain minority groups tend to be highly represented among those identified as having intellectual and adaptive problems, especially in the school-age years. Is such overrepresentation of certain groups a product of racial inferiority or of racial and ethnic discrimination and disadvantage?

For a long time, mental retardation (or its earlier terms idiocy, feeblemindedness and the like), was thought to have much in common with insanity, epilepsy, pauperism and social depravity, all of which were lumped together. And so, a concept of mental deficiency in terms of social deviance developed.

Then, as knowledge advanced, retardation was identified with congenital brain defect or damage, and assigned to heredity. This approach led to redefining mental deficiency in medical terms as an organic defect producing inadequate behavior. Mild forms of intellectual "weakness" became associated with forms of immoral behavior and social disturbance (the "moral imbecile"), and ascribed to more subtle defects of inherited character. Legal definitions in terms of social behavior began to appear.

During the 19th and early 20th century what we now call "mild" retardation was not recognized except as associated with disturbed or delinquent behavior. There was no simple way of diagnosing the more mild or incipient forms of mental retardation until the development of psychometrics around 1910. Then the "IQ" rapidly became a universal means, not only of identifying mental deficiency, but also of measuring its severity.

Goddard, in 1910, in applying the new techniques of Binet and Simon in the public schools, discovered there were ten times as many feebleminded as anyone had suspected, and promptly coined the term "moron" to cover them! Thus a psychometric definition of retardation came into being.

The intelligence test actually measured behavioral performance on tasks assumed to be characteristic of the growth of children's ability at successive ages, but it was interpreted as a measure of capacity for intellectual growth and therefore as a predictor of future mental status. It was assumed to represent an inherent and usually inherited condition of the brain with a fixed developmental potential.

Persistent debate over the nature and composition of intelligence finally led to an operational definition that it is "whatever an intelligence test measures." Since intelligence measurements are scalar, and degrees on the scale were found to correlate rather well with other clinical and social evidences of mental proficiency, low IQ became virtually the sole basis for a diagnosis of mental retardation and for its classification at levels of severity from "borderline" to "idiot."

This measurement was especially important in schools for which, in fact, the first tests were devised by Binet and Simon. IQ tests became the standard means of determining school eligibility and classification. Intelligence tests also were used extensively as sole evidence for determining legal competency and institutional commitment, as well as the subclassifications of institutional populations. The leading authorities, Tredgold, Goddard, Porteus, Penrose, Doll, Clarke and Clarke, all rejected a strictly psychometric definition, but it nevertheless became standard practice in diagnosis and classification.

In the meantime, research in twins, siblings and unrelated children had shown that general intelligence (i.e., measured IQ) is strongly inherited as a polygenic characteristic, following a normal Gaussian curve of frequency distribution in the general population. A slight negative skew was attributable to brain damage or genetic mutation. This deviation led to a theory of mental retardation which divided it into two major groups on the basis of presumed causation. One group consisted of the more severely deficient type with brain damage or gross genetic anomaly characterized by various physical abnormalities and IQ generally of 55 or less. The other group consisted of the lower portion of the negative tail on the normal curve of distribution of polygenic intelligence with IQ between 50 or 55 and 70 or 80 and not otherwise abnormal (Kanner, 1957, Zigler, 1967). This theory could explain the association of milder forms of low intelligence with low socio-economic status and its concomitants. In other words, the less competent tend to sink to the bottom of the social scale in a competitive society. The issue of cultural bias was raised immediately, however, with respect to racial and ethnic groups who scored consistently lower on the standard tests.

Evidence began to accumulate which generated a variety of additional controversial issues. The "constancy of the IQ" was questioned on both statistical and experimental grounds. The pioneering work of Skeels, Skodak, Wellman, and others, in the 1930's (e.g., Skeels, et al., 1938) had indicated that measured intelligence as well as other observable behavior could be substantially modified by drastic changes in the social environment of young children. The quality of the infant's nurture was found to have enduring effects of intellectual functioning, especially in the absence of detectable brain pathology.

Follow-up studies of persons released from institutional care and of those who had been identified in school as retarded showed high rates of social adaptation, upward mobility and even substantial increases in measured intelligence in adult years (Cobb, 1972). Epidemiological studies have consistently shown a "disappearance" of mildly retarded persons in the adult years.

Explanations for these findings could be offered without abandoning previous assumptions: Improvement in low IQ scores over several repetitions simply exemplifies the statistical regression toward the mean, inherent in errors of measurement: those who improve with stimulation and environmental change were never "really" retarded, but exhibit "pseudo-retardation" which masks true capacity.

Eventually, evidence converged to show that measured intelligence is modifiable within limits, that it is not in any case a measure of fixed capacity, but of the continuity of a developing intellectual and social competence in which "nature" and "nurture" are inseparable components and individual "growth curves" may take a variety of forms and may be influenced by many factors.

A gradual trend developed toward the

definition of mental retardation in functional rather than in structural terms and not tied either to specific cause or to unchangeable status. There were those, however, who continued to find a dual view of retardation more credible than a single continuum.

The Stanford-Binet and similar measures of intelligence came to be recognized as primarily predictive of school performance of an academic or abstract nature requiring language skills, and less predictive of other non-verbal types of behavior. Consequently, the need developed to measure other dimensions of behavior. The Army "Beta" test of World War I anticipated this development. New tests, such as the Wechsler series, combined linguistic with non-linguistic performance or quantitative elements and yielded a "profile" of distinguishable mental traits. Factor analysis of measures of intellectual behavior had demonstrated that "intelligence" is not a single trait but a composite of many distinguishable functions.

The measurement of adaptive behavior presented even greater difficulty. Such measures as the Vineland Social Maturity Scale were extensively used but had only a limited validity. The Gesell Infant Development Scale, the Gunzburg Progress Assessment Chart, and subsequently, the AAMD Adaptive Behavior Scale all attempted to measure the non-intellectual dimensions of developmental adaptation but they lacked the precision and reliability of the intelligence measures. Consequently, there has been a continuing reliance, especially in the schools, on measures of IQ alone as the criterion for mental retardation. This practice is defended by some authorities as legitimate in the absence of better measures of adaptive behavior (Conley, 1973.)

In the meantime the issue of cultural bias became an increasingly serious problem. All measures of either intelligence or of adaptive behavior reflect social learning, hence tend to be culture-bound. Their validity, therefore, is dependent on the cultural population on which the norms have been standardized. No one has succeeded in developing a universally applicable "culture-free" test of behavior. Attempts to devise "culture-fair" tests which employ comparable but culturally different elements have as yet failed to yield valid bases of comparison.

Recent studies by Mercer (1973 and 1974) and others have shown the extent to which cultural bias affects the frequency with which members of minority cultures are labeled "retarded" and assigned to special education classes. This is especially true when only measures of IQ are used; representatives of lower socio-economic and of Black, Mexican-American, Puerto Rican, Indian and other ethnic groups are identified as retarded far out of proportion to their numbers in comparison with middle-class Anglo children. Social evaluations of such children show that a high proportion are not significantly impaired in their adaptation in non-school environments.

This discovery has led to a coining of the term "Six-Hour Retarded Child," meaning a child who is "retarded" during the hours in school, but otherwise functions adequately (PCMR: *The Six-Hour Retarded Child,* 1970).

Mercer has called such persons who are identified in one or two contexts but not in others the "situationally retarded," in contrast to the "comprehensively retarded," who are identified as such in all the contexts in which they are evaluated. "Situational retardation" occurs by far most frequently in school settings, and next most frequently in medical settings, and much less frequently in ratings by families or neighbors or in settings officially responsible for the comprehensively retarded. "We conclude," Mercer says, ". . . that the situational retardate is primarily the product of the labeling process in formal organizations in the community, especially the Public Schools" (Mercer, 1973).

The work of Mercer and others has led to litigation and legislative action, especially in California, limiting the use of IQ tests as the sole criterion for labeling and special class placement, on the ground that such practices systematically penalize minority groups and violate their rights to equal educational opportunity (Mercer, 1974).

The present tendency is to accept the 1973 AAMD formulation by Grossman which requires *both* an IQ of less than 70 *and* substantial failure on a measure of adaptive behavior. The requirement of age of onset prior to 18 is more open to question and not always regarded as critical. The Grossman formulation differed from the AAMD definition of Heber (1961) principally in requiring a criterion of more than two standard deviations below the mean, rather than more than one s.d., as Heber had proposed. This was an extremely important difference because it excluded the "borderline" category which accounted for about 13% of the school age population!

Mental retardation, by any of the proposed criteria, occurs with varying degrees of severity. Many attempts were made in the past to classify differences of severity, usually on the basis of social adaptation or academic learning criteria. Social adaptation criteria distinguished borderline feebleminded, moron, imbecile and idiot. Academic Criteria distinguished slow learner, educable, trainable (with no term suggesting learning capability for the still lower category). Heber (1958) proposed using neutral terms to indicate standard deviation units on the continuum of the IQ and any other scales employed. This is continued in the Grossman (1973) AAMD system to categorize levels of intellectual functioning, thus:

Level of Function	Upper S.D. Limit	Stanford Binet IQ/ (S.D.=16)	Wechsler IQ (S.D.=15)
Mild	−2.0	67–52	69–55
Moderate	−3.0	51–36	54–40
Severe	−4.0	35–20	39–25 (extrap.)
Profound	−5.0	19 and below	24 and below (extrap.)

Note that the borderline category (−1.0 to −2.0 s.d.) is not included under the definition.

Mercer has identified still another variable of a significant sociological nature. A majority of children who rated low on both IQ and adaptive measures by the Grossman criteria, and therefore technically "retarded," came from homes that did not conform to the prevailing cultural pattern of the community (socio-culturally nonmodal). This group appeared to be identified as retarded more because of cultural difference than because of inadequate developmental adaptation. Further evidence showed that members of this group who were identified as retarded children tended more than the socio-cultural modal group to "disappear" as identifiably retarded on leaving school.

Mental retardation, as an inclusive concept, is currently defined in *behavioral* terms involving these essential components: *intellectual functioning, adaptive behavior* and *age of onset.* The causes of retardation are irrelevant to the definition, whether they be organic, genetic, or environmental. What is indicated is that at a given time a person is unable to conform to the intellectual and adaptive expectations which society sets for an individual in relation to his peers. In this sense, mental retardation is a reflection of social perception aided by a variety of clinical and nonclinical techniques of identification.

Within this broad functional definition, the deficits indicated in a diagnosis of mental retardation may or may not be permanent and irreversible. They may or may not be responsive to intervention. They may persist only so long as the person remains in a culturally ambiguous situation, or at the other extreme, they may be of life-long duration. Or perhaps only their consequences may be ameliorated in greater or lesser degree, not the condition itself.

Consequently, it is difficult to estimate how frequently mental retardation occurs and how many retarded people there are.

How Big Is the Problem?

The *incidence* of a disorder refers to the frequency of occurrence within a given period of time. For example, the incidence of smallpox in the United States might be expressed as the number of cases in a specific year per 100,000 population; the incidence of Down's syndrome might be expressed as the average number of cases per year per 1,000 live births. The purpose of determining incidence is to yield information as to the magnitude of the problem with a view to its prevention and to measure the success of preventive programs.

The *prevalence* of a disorder refers to the number of cases existing at a specified time in a specified population and is usually expressed as a percentage of that population or as a whole number. Thus, the prevalence of *diabetes mellitus* in the United States might be expressed either as the percent or as a whole number of the total population known or estimated to have the disease in a designated year. The prevalence of people crippled from poliomyelitis can be expressed as a gradually decreasing figure as the result of the greatly reduced incidence of the disease following the discovery of the vaccines. This shows that prevalence is derived from incidence, but modified by the extent to which cases disappear by death, recovery or inaccessibility. The value of prevalence rates is in determining the magnitude of the need for care, treatment, protection or other services.

Incidence

By definition mental retardation can be diagnosed only after birth when appropriate behavioral indices have developed sufficiently for measurement. During gestation the identification of certain conditions usually or invariably associated with mental retardation may be detected and *potential* retardation inferred.

From the examination of spontaneously aborted fetuses, it is estimated that probably 30 to 50 percent are developmentally abnormal and that if they had survived many would have been mentally deficient; but this information gives us only an incidence of fetal mortality and morbidity, with an estimate of some types of developmental deviation, not an incidence of mental retardation itself.

The mortality rates of the potentially or actually retarded vary with severity of defect, which means that many developmentally impaired infants die before retardation has been, or even can be, determined. Anencephaly, for example, is complete failure of brain cortex to develop; the infant may be born living and exhibit a few responses typical of the neonate, but survival is brief. Is such a case to be counted as an instance of incipient mental retardation or only of anencephaly in particular or birth defect in general?

Since mental retardation manifests itself at different ages and under different conditions, there is no single time—e.g., at birth or at one year of age—when it can be determined of every child that he is or *ever will be* identified as mentally retarded.

Mildly mentally retarded persons are most frequently identified, if at all, during school years, and frequently disappear as recognizably retarded after leaving school.

The methods of identifying retardation are still highly varied; consequently, surveys of incidence or prevalence are frequently not comparable.

The degree of subnormality employed as criterion for identification as retarded greatly affects the count of incidence. For example, the 1961 AAMD definition used a criterion of standard deviation greater than one (S.B. IQ < 85). The 1973 version uses a more restricted criterion of more than two standard deviations (S.B. IQ < 68). This change in criterion reduces the incidence of mild mental retardation automatically by 80%!

A similar problem is created by the use of multiple dimensions rather than a single dimension. If only IQ is employed, say at two standard deviations (IQ < 68 or 70), a global incidence of about 3% of school-age population will be found (cf. Conley 1973). But if a second dimension of impaired adaptive behavior is also required, then some with IQ below 70 will not be classified mentally retarded, and some with low adaptive scores, but IQ above 70, will not be classified as retarded. This reduces the obtained prevalence rate to more nearly 1%. If, following Mercer, a still further determination is made on the basis of "socio-cultural modality" the rate may be still further reduced in some heterogeneous communities.

Taking many such considerations into account, Tarjan and others (1973) estimate that approximately 3 percent of annual births may be expected to "acquire" mental retardation at some time in their lives, of which 1.5% would be profoundly, 3.5% severely, 6.0% moderately and 89% mildly retarded. Currently, however, in view of the problems of arriving at truly meaningful estimates of the incidence of mental retardation on a global basis, emphasis for purposes of prevention is placed on the incidence from specific known causes. Unfortunately, these comprise only a small proportion of the total identified as retarded (Penrose, 1963; Holmes et al, 1965). The following are examples.

One of the earliest success stories in the reduction of the incidence of mental retardation was in the case of endemic cretinism. This condition occurred rather frequently in certain localities, notably some of the Swiss alpine valleys. The problem was attacked in the second half of the 19th century. The first step was to identify the condition with the occurrence of goiter, an enlargement of the thyroid gland. The next step was to relate this condition to the people's diet, and finally to the absence of trace iodine in the soil and water supply. Iodine was found to be necessary to the functioning of the thyroid gland in its production of the hormone thyroxin, the absence of which can cause cretinism.

The addition of iodine to table salt resulted in reducing mental retardation caused by endemic cretinism to near zero. It also led to the preventive and therapeutic use of extract of thyroxin in the treatment of myxoedema or hypothyroidism from other causes (Kanner, 1957).

The incidence of Down's syndrome is well-documented. It has been identified with a specific chromosomal abnormality which occurs most frequently as an unpredictable non-disjunction of autosome 21, but infrequently also as the Mendelian transmission of a translocated portion of autosome 21. The former type is definitely related to maternal age, occurring at about .33 per thousand live births to mothers under age 29 but rising sharply after age 35 to a rate of about 25 per thousand to women over age 45.

Overall, the incidence of Down's syndrome is 1 in 600 to 700 live births, with over half occurring to women over 35 (Begab, 1974). The overall incidence of gross chromosomal malformation of children born to women over 35 is 1 to 2 percent (Lubs and Ruddle, 1970; Begab, 1974). The existence of the condition is detectable by amniocentesis (analysis of a sample of amniotic fluid) during pregnancy.

This knowledge creates the possibility of reducing the incidence of Down's syndrome substantially by: a) limiting pregnancy after age 35; b) detecting the transmissable karyotype of translocation in either the male or female and limiting reproduction; c) identifying the condition early in gestation and terminating pregnancy.

A third example of incidence is more problematic, but nevertheless significant. From prevalence studies, it is known that mild retardation is more frequently found in families of low socio-economic status, especially in families in which the mother is mildly retarded. Heber and others have determined that the incidence of retardation in such families can be reduced by early intervention in providing stimulation to the child and home assistance to the mother.

These examples are sufficient to illustrate the values of pursuing the study of incidence to identifiable causes or correlative conditions as a means of identifying preventive measures (see Stein and Susser, 1974; Begab, 1974). Further discussion of currently known preventive measures appear in later chapters on prevention.

Prevalence

The principal problems of obtaining reliable prevalence estimates relate to definitions, criteria and administrative procedures on the one hand, and to the absence of uniform and centralized data collection, on the other. The former problems are gradually becoming resolved. The latter requires vigorous and sustained efforts by Federal and State governments to establish an effective data bank.

Prevalence is a product of cumulative incidence modified by loss. Loss may be the result of death or cure or unaccounted disappearance. Whereas measures of incidence are important to the problem of prevention, measures of prevalence are important to the provision of service resources. As prevention requires differential classification by identifiable cause, so service provision requires differential classification by types of need.

Overall estimates of prevalence of mental retardation have been made by two methods: by empirical surveys and by selection of a cut-off point on a Gaussian curve for the distribution of intelligence scores. The latter has led to a widely used estimate of 3%, ambiguously referring to either incidence or prevalence. This would correspond to an IQ level of approximately 70 and is, in fact, an average general prevalence found in some surveys of children (Conley, 1973; Birch et al, 1970).

However, it possible to select a 9% cut-off at about IQ 80 or 16% at IQ 85, the 1961 AAMD criterion. All surveys, however, show that mental retardation does not represent a simple portion of the lower tail on a general Gaussian curve. It is far from being normally distributed, varying widely by age, by socio-economic and ethnic factors. The use of an IQ cut-off alone also assumes a one-dimensional definition of mental retardation, contrary to the AAMD formula and other leading authorities (Tarjan, 1973; Mercer, 1973).

Tarjan (1973, p. 370) points out that the estimate of 3% prevalence, or 6 million persons in the United States, makes four dubious assumptions: "a) the diagnosis of mental retardation is based essentially on an IQ below 70; b) mental retardation is identified in infancy; c) the diagnosis does not change; and d) the mortality of retarded individuals is similar to that of the general population." The first assumption ignores the adaptive behavior component; the second holds only for a small portion, nearly always organically and severely impaired; the third holds only as a generality for those of IQ below 55, and the fourth holds only for the mildly retarded.

As a statement of potential incidence, Tarjan (1973) is probably quite conservative in estimating that 3% of all infants who survive birth will at some time in their lives be identified as mentally retarded in some context—most probably in the public schools.

Epidemiological surveys conducted in various parts of the United States and abroad show comparable prevalence rates for the more seriously retarded—i.e., moderate, severe and profound levels on the AAMD classifications or IQ below 50. Fifteen such studies converge on an average rate of approximately .46% or 4.6 cases per thousand population (Stein and Susser, 1974). These surveys generally covered ages roughly 10 to 20, obscuring the high mortality rate in early childhood. When the surveys are divided between general and rural populations, the three rural studies average at more than double the general rate, or 9.84 per thousand, while the remaining twelve cluster quite closely around 3.6.

Penrose (1963) suggests that prevalence of malformation predictive of profound retardation at birth might be as much as 1 percent, Conley (1973) suggests 1.5 to 1.7 percent, including severe and moderate levels. The rate among prematurely born infants is much higher than among full-term babies. The rate among lower-class nonwhites is higher than among middle-class whites, but the differences are not so striking as is the case in mild retardation levels. Higher rates of prematurity, higher health risk and inferior maternal and child health care could account for the difference at the more severe levels.

In any case, the presumption of actual prevalence of the severe forms of defect predictive of mental retardation would be highest at birth, declining rapidly by mortality to a relatively low rate of .2% in adult life.

Prevalence rates of the severely retarded have been affected by a number of tendencies in the past 20 years. On the one hand, modern medicine has made enormous strides in its ability to preserve life. Infant mortality rates have fallen markedly; survival of prematures at progressively younger ages has become possible, with correspondingly increased risk of developmental damage; recovery from infectious diseases by use of antibiotics has become commonplace. Consequently, along with other infants and young children, severely and profoundly retarded children now have a better chance of prolonged survival.

On the other hand, improved health care, especially for mothers at risk, immunization, protection from radiation exposure, improved obstetrics, control of Rh isoimmunization and other measures have prevented the occurrence of some abnormalities and reduced the complications which formerly added to the incidence and prevalence of retardation. New hazards appear, however, in environmental toxic substances, strains of microorganisms more resistant to antibiotics, new addictive and nonaddictive drugs, new sources of radiation, environmental stress, all of which are potential producers of biological damage and mental retardation (Begab, 1974).

On balance, it is possible that incidence of severe retardation is falling while prevalence is continuing to rise.

The high birth rate of the post World War II period produced a record number of severely retarded children who are surviving longer than ever before. The future, envisioning more control of the causes with a lower birth rate more limited to optimal conditions of reproduction may in time yield lower prevalence rates of the moderate, severely and profound retarded. Currently, a very conservative estimate of their number in the United States is approximately 500,000 (Tarjan, et al, 1973) but may actually be nearer a .3% level or 660,000 surviving beyond the first year of life.

The prevalence of mild retardation is quite a different matter. Where the severely retarded show a declining prevalence by age, based wholly on mortality, the mildly retarded show a sharply peaked prevalence in the school years (6–19) and a rapid falling off in the adult years. This phenomenon cannot be a product of mortality, because the mildly retarded have shown longevity very nearly that of the general population. There are two possible alternatives, both of which may be the case. Large numbers remain retarded but cease to be the objects of attention; or they in fact cease to be retarded. In any case, no survey has yet found prevalence rates of mild retardation remotely approaching a constant across ages, such as would be expected on the assumption of unchanged relative mental status. Tarjan suggests that the rate of 3% traditionally projected as a constant across all ages, actually holds only for the school-age, with rated prevalence in selected age groups of .25% in the 0–5 group, 3.0% from 9–16, .4% from 20 to 24, sinking to .2% in the population over 25; the overall prevalence being approximately 1% (Tarjan, et al, 1973, p. 370). This would yield a total of approximately 2.2 million retarded persons in the United States, as against 6.6 million if an overall 3% is assumed.

In studies of the Riverside, California, population, Mercer (1974) showed that the prevalence and social distribution of mild mental retardation differed markedly according to the definition and methods of identification employed. She compared the application of a "social system" definition ("mental retardate" is an achieved status, and mental retardation is the role associated with the status) with a "clinical" definition (mental retardation is an individual pathology with characteristic symptoms which can be identified by standard diagnostic procedures).

It was found that the use of a one-dimensional clinical definition (IQ less than 69) yielded an overall rate of 2.14% retarded, with Blacks showing a rate 10 times and Mexican-Americans 34 times the rate of Anglos. When a two-dimensional definition is used (IQ less than 69 *plus* deficient adaptive score) the overall rate shrank to .9% which is the "clinical" rate predicted by Tarjan. The distribution now showed Blacks approximately at the same rate as Anglos, but Mexican-Americans still 15 times greater. When pluralistic, culturally adjusted norms were used for both IQ and adaptive behavior, the overall rate reduced still further to .54% but the total shrinkage in this case was accounted for in the Mexican-American group where sociocultural nonmodality (a cultural pattern distinctly different from the predominant mode) and bilingual background were most prominent. Furthermore, when higher criteria for IQ and adaptive behavior were used, the disadvantage to both Blacks and Mexican-Americans, as compared with Anglos, was markedly increased.

The social distribution of mild mental retardation has been found by all investigators to be inversely related to socioeconomic status. It is, according to Conley (1973) 13 times more prevalent among poor than among middle and upper income groups and found most frequently among rural, isolated or ghetto populations. Controversy persists concerning the contribution of constitutional and social learning factors to this distribution, but it is a question of the relative wieght rather than an exclusive alternative. No one doubts the multiple effects of environmental deprivation on both physical and psychological development. Nor is there much doubt that social learning enables the great majority of those with mild intellectual limitations to assume normal social roles in adult life. It is evident that what might appear to be a manifestation of the normal distribution of polygenic general intelligence is really a complex product in which the genetic component is only one among many factors yielding varying degrees and rates of retarded behavior, among varying populations at varying ages.

There is little point, then, in arguing who is "really" retarded. There is great point in determining who is in need of developmental and supportive assistance in achieving a reasonably adequate adult life, in determining the relationships between identifiable characteristics and the kinds of services that will be profitable, and in employing terminology that will aid rather than obscure these relationships. A critical issue is the degree to which cultural pluralism is reflected in the educational process.

The classification suggested by Mercer (1973) involves a four-dimensional matrix in which potentially handicapping conditions, including mental retardation defined in either "clinical" or "social system" terms, may be identified:

a) The dimension of *intellectual functioning,* measurable on a continuous scale represented by IQ. On this scale, following the 1973 AAMD standard, an IQ of 69 or less is regarded as potentially handicapping and is one clinically defining characteristic of mental retardation. Mercer terms the person with *only* this dimension of disability as *quasi-retarded.* Ordinarily this will be reflected in learning difficulties in the school setting and justifies individually prescriptive educational assistance.

b) The dimension of *adaptive behavior,* measurable on a developmental scale of behavioral controls accommodating the person to his environment. On this dimension a person falling substantially below age norms (perhaps in the lowest 3% of a normative distribution) is regarded as potentially handicapped. This constitutes a second clinically defining characteristic of mental retardation of the 1973 AAMD standard. Mercer terms the person who

has *only* this dimension of disability as *behaviorally maladjusted,* but she identifies the person with disability in both a) and b) as *clinically mentally retarded,* requiring services in both school and non-school settings.

c) The dimension of *physical constitution,* describable in terms of the health or pathology of the various organ systems of the body. While not a defining characteristic of mental retardation, physical impairment may be in itself potentially handicapping and may be the cause of or magnify the handicapping limitations of a) and b). The probability of organic impairments being present increases with the severity of mental retardation, from 3% at mild retardation levels to 78% at moderate levels and 95% at severe and profound levels (Conley, 1973, pp. 46–7). Individuals characterized by only c) may be termed generically as *physically impaired,* and in combination with a) and b) as *organic mentally retarded.* The term "multiply handicapped" is commonly used, but this would apply equally to persons with more than one substantial physical impairment.

d) *Sociocultural modality* is a fourth dimension which is distinguishable from the other three. It refers to the extent to which sociocultural variables of family background conform or do not conform to the modal culture in which the individual is assessed. When the family background is substantially non-modal, in this sense, the individual may be potentially handicapped in relation to the prevailing cultural expectations because of lack of opportunity for the appropriate learning. Such a person may be termed *culturally disadvantaged.* Mercer found that non-modality yielded effects which, to the dominant culture, appeared as low IQ, low adaptive behavior, or both when measured by the norms of the dominant culture. Utilizing a pluralistic model of mental retardation, sensitive to socio-cultural differences, Mercer found a substantial reduction in the prevalence of mental retardation in the Mexican-American as compared to the Anglo population of Riverside. Throughout the investigation, the Anglo sample yielded a constant rate of 4.4 per thousand identified as mentally retarded (i.e. no Anglos in this sample were judged either quasi-retarded or non-modal culturally). The Mexican-

American population yielded the following succession of rates per 1,000:

a) One dimensional—only standard IQ norms, 149.0

b) Two dimensional—standard IQ + standard adaptive behavior norms, 60.0

c) Partial pluralistic two dimensional—standard IQ, pluralistic adaptive behavior norms, 30.4

d) Pluralistic two dimensional—pluralistic norms for both IQ and adaptive behavior, 15.3

(Mercer, 1973, pp. 235-254)

The residual differences between the rate of 4.4 for Anglos and the 15.3 rate for culturally adapted assessment of Mexican-Americans may be attributable to the pervasive effects of their bilingual status.

Granted that Mercer's research is based on a single local population sampling and is a first approach to a "social systems" definition of mental retardation, it suggests the need for much more highly refined procedures in the definition and epidemiology of mental retardation as a basis for the adequate and appropriate delivery of developmental and supportive services where they are needed.

There is complete agreement that it is impossible, at our present state of knowledge, to determine accurately either the incidence or the prevalence of mental retardation. There is far less agreement on what we can do to remedy this situation. Among the most urgent issues in classification:

1. **Definition.** The formulation adopted by the American Association on Mental Deficiency involving two-dimensional deficit in the level of behavioral performance unquestionably is responsive to many problems arising from older definitions. But a number of issues remain:

a) The two dimensions are not independent, but are, in fact, highly correlated, the degree of correlation being related to severity of deficit, suggesting the distinction of intellectual and adaptive measures has not been sufficiently refined. In practice, more reliance is frequently placed on IQ measures than on measures of adaptation or other bases of clinical judgment.

b) The cultural contamination of standardized tests as currently used makes their findings suspect. Mercer and others require a corrective for cultural insensitivity of the instruments employed.

c) The use of a global IQ measure which may be adequate for epidemiological purposes obscures the complexity of intellectual functioning and the variability of individual profiles which is the basis of service provision. Global IQ measures are rapidly losing favor among professional providers of service but are maintained for administrative convenience and ease of determination.

d) Differences in the conditions associated with mild retardation as compared to the more severe forms in terms of organicity, comprehensiveness of impairment, resistance to modification, relatedness to cultural norms, etc., suggest to some that the two types are sufficiently different as to require separate classification, probably based on organic (or presumed organic) versus psychosocial etiology.

2. **Services.** Since the instruments for the measurement of intelligence and adaptive behavior are scalar, with continuous variation on both sides of central norms, the relationship between a specific level of deficit and the need for specific types of service and treatment may be highly artificial. This appears to be the central question underlying the controversy over the criterion level in the AAMD definition which now excludes persons with IQs from 70 to 85 who formerly were included. The fact that relatively few scoring above 69 IQ manifest significant deficits in adaptive behavior may miss the point. Adaptive behavior may be quite specific and situational, especially where culture modality may also be in question. The real issue is to determine individual need, which cannot be derived from the IQ or adaptive behavior. This issue has been exacerbated by legislation which requires categorical classification as a condition of eligibility for service.

3. **Labeling.** Titles are necessary for any scientific system of classification, and may be useful for certain administrative purposes; but their use in human service systems is a different matter. The attachment of a label to a species of plant or a type of rock makes no difference to the plant or the rock. The label assigned to classify a human being does make a difference. To label a person mentally retarded has consequences of a psychological nature if the person is cognizant of it and can assign a meaning to it; it has consequences of a social nature insofar as other persons assign meaning and respond in terms of that meaning. This is especially the case with the label of "mentally retarded" because all terms associated with deficiency of intelligence are, in our culture, highly charged with negative values.

There have been many attempts to use systems of intellect classification as a means of adapting school and other programs to individual differences without making those differences appear invidious. These have not been entirely successful because value systems, even for children, tend to filter through the most subtle of euphemistic terminology.

This is a difficult issue to resolve. Success is possible only if: a) classification for epidemiological purposes is entirely separated from need-evaluation for purposes of social grouping and prescriptive treatment, b) all treatment is person-centered rather than system-centered, c) cultural value systems are recognized and respected, and d) eligibility for categorical assistance is based, not on global statistical criteria, but on the individual's need.

4. **Recording, Registering and Information Control** (corollary to labeling). Obviously, the best data base for the epidemiologist would be a computerized data bank including all information on every case. This has, in effect, been advocated since Samuel Howe's first attempt to catalogue the "idiotic" population of Massachusetts in 1848, long before modern systems of information storage and retrieval were dreamed of. However, rights of privacy and confidentiality have become a critical issue. The problem is one of reconciling the needs of the service delivery system and the individual recipient, so that he will neither be "lost" as an anonymous number nor stigmatized for having his needs recognized.

5. **"Negativism."** The nature of retardation lends itself to definition and assessment in the negative terms of deficit from desirable norms. The individual person, however, is not made up of deficits but of asset characteristics, however meager or distorted some of them may be. All treatment rests on the positive capacity of the person to respond, whether physiologically or psychologically. The issue of negatively versus positively defined traits and classifications is a basic one between the purposes of epidemiology and the purposes of service assistance.

Who are the people who are mentally retarded? They are individuals whose assets for effective living in their cultural and physical environments are insufficient without assistance. The screen by which they are brought into view to be identified and counted is composed of a mesh of intellectual and adaptive behavior norms. But the screen is a somewhat crude and abrasive instrument and requires to be refined and softened by concern for the individuals it exposes.

How many mentally retarded people are there? The loss of potential for normal development and even survival affects a high proportion of those who are conceived, and probably 3% of those who survive birth. In addition to those hundreds of thousands who are not well-born, there are millions who are not well-nurtured by the world in which they live. How we sort out these millions, how many will be called "mentally retarded" will depend on our definitions and our perceptions of need. The roots of these needs are not yet under control, nor have we sufficiently provided for their assuagement.

PLATE I

Sketch from the colored illustration of the simplest picture in the series, the demonstration picture, with the inserts which particularly relate to this picture. Of course only one is quite correct, but the others can be inserted with some show of reasonableness

SPECIAL OLYMPICS

FIFTH INTERNATIONAL SPECIAL OLYMPICS GAMES
BROCKPORT, N.Y. --AUGUST 9, 1979

This is a marvelous day for Special Olympians, and particularly for their parents. My only regret is that my parents are not here. For it was they who gave to my sister Rosemary the dignity, the love, the pride in accomplishment, that are at the very core of Special Olympics.

Every parent is called on to make sacrifices in the name of love, but the parents of Special Olympians have done more--they have challenged the spirit of the times that say only intellectual achievement is the measure of human life. I believe that is wrong. So do your parents. You are proof that their commitment has been to the values that count and will endure--courage, sharing, skill and joy.

Tonight we stand in the presence of 6 olympic gold medal winners. They are among the best athletes the world has known. But tonight they are here to salute *you* and to honor *you* as their equals.

For great world athletes like these who enter the olympic games, the contest may last only minutes. Then it is over and these men and women have won or lost. But for you Special Olympians the contest can last a lifetime. The challenge begins again each day. What you are winning by your courageous efforts is far greater than any game. You are winning life itself and and in doing so you give to others a most precious prize...faith in the unlimited possibilities of the human spirit.

I saw how that spirit works in a great athlete a few weeks ago. Let me tell you the story.

Johnny Jones, an olympic gold medal winner in the 400 meter relay came up to me at the Texas Olympic Games and handed me his medal. "Mrs. Shriver," he said, "I want to give my medal to Texas Special Olympics."

"Why your medal" I asked. And he answered, "right now I don't have a lot of money. But I have the medal. And by giving that I'm giving a part of myself."

That spirit shown by Johnny Jones isn't his alone. It is yours to give to your fellow athletes and to us all.

For this we honor you tonight, You are True Olympians.

Congratulations and Good Luck

Eunice Kennedy Shriver

WHEN THE WORLD COMES TO VISIT

Peter N. Smits

Vice President for Institutional Affairs
and Development
State University of New York
College at Brockport
International Games Director
Special Olympics

For Special Olympics, the world's largest program of athletic training and competition for the mentally retarded, Brockport, New York is as important a place as Chicago, Los Angeles, Boston and New York City. This tiny and rural village in Upstate New York hosted the largest, most exciting event in the eleven year history of the program - the 1979 International Summer Special Olympics Games. Nearly 3500 athletes, their 1000 chaperones and 3000 parents, friends and relatives traveled to Brockport from all fifty states, all United States Territories and twenty eight coutries to join together in this spectacular demonstration of the courage and determination of the mentally retarded.

No stranger to Special Olympics competition, the College at Brockport had served as the site for the 1975 and 1976 State Games. By the end of the 1976 Games,

Brockport's fascination with Special Olympics had turned into an all-out love affair, and the College and residents of the Village were challenged to expand that relationship into something on a more meaningful scale. In late 1976 officials from the College contacted Special Olympics Headquarters in Washington, D.C. Would Special Olympics be interested in entertaining a bid from the College to serve as hosts for the Fifth International Games? The answer was electrifying: Special Olympics was not only interested, it was excited. Now honored to have the opportunity to bid, Brockport turned to the most difficult task of preparing the document.

A steering committee of six people was formed to analyze the strengths and weaknesses of Brockport, its people and its facilities. Dr. Albert W. Brown, President of the College and perhaps the most enthusiastic supporter

1. SPIRIT

of the idea, recruited forty-five individuals to assist the steering committee in developing core areas of the bid, and to serve as chairmen of the necessary committees were the bid to be accepted. Professional sports teams, businesses and corporations, service clubs and civic groups, politicians and influential leaders in New York State were asked to submit letters of support for the Brockport bid, and no one refused.

Gradually, the document began to take shape. In all, it contained 275 pages of material, pictures, plans and letters of support. President Brown, several members of the steering committee and a representative of the State University of New York presented the bid to Eunice Kennedy Shriver, President of Special Olympics, in May of 1977. Since no institution had ever presented such an imposing bid before, its impact was enormous. Following a visit by the site selection committee in June, Mrs. Shriver weighed the evidence and in August 1977 announced that the State University of New York College at Brockport would serve as the site for the Fifth International Summer Special Olympics Games. At a press conference at the Plaza Hotel in New York City, Mrs. Shriver was joined by Hugh L. Carey, Governor of the State of New York, and made the annoucement to the world, Brockport began a journey that was to change the community forever.

With little delay reality, began to sink in. The bid spoke glowingly of the community's ability to carry out the biggest event Special Olympics would ever conduct, and now we had to get to it: the world was coming to visit in 24 months.

Founded in 1829, Brockport served for a time as the western terminus for "Clinton's Ditch", now known as the Old Erie Canal. With its tree-lined streets, shopping plazas, restaurants and movie houses, Brockport has grown to a village of approximately 7500 residents, and is located sixteen miles west of Rochester and nine miles from the shores of Lake Ontario. But above all, Brockport is a college town. Trees, grass, rolling ground and the canal blend with modern and older buildings on the campus of ten thousand students. The College's sixty buildings and athletic fields occupy approximately one-quarter of the 591-acre campus. Of particular interest to Special Olympics was the Ernest H. Tuttle Physical Education Complex, completed in 1974 and containing six gymnasiums, an indoor ice rink, an Olympic-sized fifty meter pool, gymnastic rooms, weight training facilities and handball courts. Physically, the site would serve Special Olympics well. The State of New York funded a rehabilitation of the running track that upgraded it to an eight-lane, all weather surface without equal in Upstate New York, and a private fund raising campaign made it possible to construct a 10,000 seat stadium.

The stage was now set for the human resources to plan and implement an ambitious program for the Games, which included a five day schedule of competition, teaching clinics, cultural and social events. The Competition committee

geared up to conduct competition in all twelve Special Olympics sports that included track and field, swimming and diving, gymnastics, bowling, wheelchair events, basketball, poly hockey, floor hockey, soccer, volleyball and frisbee-disc. Nearly 1600 athletes would compete in track and field, while the swimming committee planned for 500 and the bowling committee looked forward to nearly 300. Over fifty teaching clinics were planned to offer athletes the opportunity to participate in an activity that perhaps they had never experienced. Golf, inner tube water polo, racquetball and even ice skating were among the many developed.

Food service personnel prepared for the enormous task of cooking and serving nearly 70,000 meals in five days, many of which included special diets and served at strange hours. The Housing staff took steps to prepare to check in 4500 people in one day, and then to check them out again in just five shorts days. The transportation people had to plan to gather our guests from both the airport and the train station, which proved no easy feat since most arrived at staggered times. Of particular importance to the planners was the arrival of the Special Olympics Special, an AMTRAK train which brought in 600 delegates at 9:30 pm, and another 400 at 5:00 am. These courageous souls battled airline strikes, worldwide communication delays (Korea's travel plans arrived by telegram three hours after the delegates) and 9000 pieces of luggage.

The fund raising committee set about the task of raising nearly one million dollars to cover the costs of the Games, and ended up topping the million dollar mark. Dances, dinners, contests and a successful sponsor-an-athlete program made the difference. Two courageous souls even paddled a canoe across Lake Ontario to collect four thousand dollars in pledges, no simple feat since it had never been done before on the trecherous and unpredictable lake.

Ceremonies decorations, signs (nearly 1700 of them), special events and awards committees, joined by a total of seventy-one other committees, worked diligently and on a volunteer basis for two years to attend to the myriad of details. Planners for Adventure Day, a trip by all 4500 delegates to Niagara Falls, often thought that it would be easier to mvoe the Falls to Brockport than transport all those people 120 miles in 100 school buses. In the end, the most difficult obstacle was the acquisition of six thousand gallons of gasoline.

And the volunteers. Noted Washington Post columnist Colman McCarthy has said, "More than any movement in American sports in the past decade, Special Olympics has gone into communities, neighborhoods and families to spread a spirit of playfulness that is, or should be, the essential vibrancy of sports." McCarthy refers to Special Olympics volunteers as "250,000 Someone Else's ", and

5000 had to be recruited for the International Games. They came from everywhere: parents, high school students, Boy Scouts, students and faculty at the college, track and field officials, celebrities. The most popular job was that of the "hugger", one who stands at the finish line of any sport and hugs the finisher, whether he or she comes in first or last. Volunteers rallied to accomplish many of the unsung and not so glamorous tasks so vitally important in an event of such magnitude. Blowing up balloons, making beds, picking up litter, escorting athletes, driving buses, answering telephones, translating the twenty-one foreign languages. The tasks were so numerous that the entire volunteer assignment program had to be computerized.

Many of the volunteers are famous friends of Special Olympics. One of the first to arrive (nearly six days before the Games) was actress Susan St. James. She came early, she said, because she wanted to work, and that she did. Other celebrity friends were to arrive and add to the festive atmosphere: the great Muhammad Ali came to sign autographs and conduct a boxing clinic. Hank Aaron, Arnold Schwarzeneggar, Bobby Orr, Rafer Johnson, Dick Fosbury, Phil Esposito and other sports greats gave of their time to attend the Games and conduct several teaching clinics. Sally Struthers, Dick Sargent, Christopher Reeve, Marlo Thomas and other television and film greats joined in the celebration.

The spirit of Special Olympics spread as far as the Soviet Union, where Soviet artist Zurab Tsereteli designed a monumental sculpture dedicated to the International Games and the International Year of the Child, and his government donated the entire ten-ton assembly to the College at Brockport. Valued at $1.25 million, it was designed and fabricated at the artist's studio in Tbilisi, the capital city of the Soviet Republic of Georgia. The artistic conception consists of five bronze sculptures surrounding a fifty foot diameter pool, with a central fountain. Each of the pieces is the artist's stylized version of the Special Olympics logo, designed with figures in bas relief that depict various sports activities. It is the first gift of such proportions ever given to the United States by the Soviet Union, and was dedicated on the first day of the Games.

Also dedicated on opening day was the first postage stamp ever created to commemorate Special Olympics. Designed by Mr. Jeff Cornell of Connecticut, the stamp depicts the skill, sharing and joy of Special Olympics, and was presented to the public by Postmaster William Bolger during a "First Day of Issue" ceremony.

After three years and three months of planning, the sculpture and stamp dedication ceremonies completed, the time finally arrived for the largest opening ceremony ever held at any Special Olympics event. Twenty-two thousand spectators watched as the Royal Canadian Mounted Police Band led the delegates onto the field in a colorful and rich parade held in the true Olympic tradition. Governor Hugh Carey welcomed the delegates, Eunice Kennedy Shriver paid tribute to the athletes and their parents, and Senator Edward M. Kennedy, President of the Joseph P. Kennedy, Jr. Foundation, declared the Games open. Cadets from the U.S. Air Force Academy "Wings of Blue" parachute team descended with the Special Olympics torch, and Special Olympians brought the torch to the Flame of Hope, where they were joined in the lighting of the torch by five former Olympics Gold Medal winners.

Throughout the remaining days of the Games, athletes could compete in their sports, have their picture taken with a celebrity, attend a victory banquet and dance, and watch a variety show emceed by t.v.'s Phil Donohue. Prior to their departure for Niagara falls, the delegates participated in the closing ceremonies that featured a circle of friendship with representatives from each delegation. During the ceremony, athletes placed an item unique to their home state or nation in a time capsule that will be buried in Special Olympics Park, site of the Soviet sculptures. ABC's "Wide World of Sports" captured the five days of thrilling competition, clinics and special events, and aired the spirit of the Games on national television on September 1.

Brockport has returned to the job of education, farming and manufacturing, but the village and the college are remarkably different than they were before those five glorious days in August. A sense of pride in a job well done pervades conversations everywhere; citizens now more sensitive to both the needs and the accomplishments of the mentally retarded are joining together to continue the tradition of service to our special friends.

Eunice Kennedy Shriver has said, "In Special Olympics it is not the strongest body or the most dazzling mind that counts. It is the invincible spirit which overcomes all handicaps. For without this spirit winning medals is empty. But with it, there is no defeat." That spirit was remarkably evident in Brockport during the International Games. But because it is so often the case that the mentally retarded give more to us than we can give to them, that spirit, which these courageous athletes brought to Brockport, now remains. It has changed the lives of the thousands who attended the Games, altered our way of thinking, and continues as a spirit which encourages us to not only be thankful for that which we have, but for us to continue to be a part of those 250,000. "Someone Elses" who are behind the athletes of Special Olympics - coaching them, cheering them and loving them.

STATE UNIVERSITY AND STATE RESIDENTIAL FACILITY CO-SPONSOR SPECIAL OLYMPICS

Susan Meyers-Winton

San Jose State University

San Jose State University and Agnew State Hospital, a residential facility for developmentally disabled individuals, co-sponsored an invitational Special Olympics track and field event for four major Northern California State Hospitals on March 10, 1979. Everyone was a winner; the ninety San Jose State University students who organized and ran the event, the State Hospital staff who benefited from an Olympics designed to meet the special needs of their residents, and the athletes who enjoyed the enthusiasm and encouragement of the five hundred University students who acted as volunteers.

The Role of the University

The Special Education Department at San Jose State University offered a three unit course entitled *Special Olympics*. The class, which met three hours each week, was divided; ninety minutes for lecture and ninety minutes for committee and organizational work.

The course was designed to give students an academic background and an opportunity to apply their knowledge and skills.
Course content included:

1. History and purpose of the Special Olympics
2. Mental retardation, definitions, causes, educational and vocational opportunities for mentally retarded individuals
3. Psychological aspects of mental retardation
4. Physical training programs for mentally retarded individuals, how to create and implement these programs
5. Adaptations of physical skills and games for mentally retarded individuals
6. Leadership, communication, organization and evaluation skills

At the outset each of the forty students received a copy of the "Special Olympics Directors Guide", a packet published by the Jospeh P. Kennedy, Jr. Foundation. This packet contains sixteen working guides which describe the responsibilities and procedures for each committee involved in a Special Olympics event.

After reading this packet, students chose to participate in one of eight committees: awards, ceremonies, meals and snacks, public relations, registration and hospitality, sports and scheduling, special events, and volunteers. Each committee chose a representative and a ninth committee was formed of these eight representatives to ensure good communication between the committees.

The facililty and necessary security were arranged by the event director-course instructor with the co-operation of the Special Education Department Chairperson and the University Police.

Each committee was instructed to create a time line showing the steps they would be taking to complete their responsibilities and expected dates of completion for each task. These eight time lines were then compiled in a flow chart, thus students saw the relationship between committees and how each committee was dependent on the efficiency of the other seven committees.

The committees then made a list of the materials they would need. Various members of the class volunteered to procure donations of materials and monies. Communtiy businesses and organizations were assured recognition of their contribution in the news media and Special Olympics program to encourage their support.

As the semester progressed, each committee gave weekly reports of their progress and asked for assistance from other class members when needed. In this way each of the students had an opportunity to learn the various functions of all of the committees.

In order to provide an opportunity for more students to be involved in the Special Olympics, a one unit course was established. The course offered lectures concerning:

1. Mental retardation, definitions, causes, educational and vocational opportunities for mentally retarded individuals.
2. History and purpose of the Special Olympics
3. Physical training programs for mentally retarded individuals

Student Requirements

Each of the students in the one unit course was responsible for running an event the day of the Special Olympics. They were also required to write an evaluation report after the event.

The sports and scheduling committee met with the one unit students and described the rules for the events, as well as how each event was to be organized; i.e. heats, awards, measurements, timing, and recording. Students then chose a specific event.

Students in the three unit course were required to be an active participant in one of the eight committees,and to become involved in the training program at Agnew State Hospital. In addition, they were to keep a log with notes from class, committee meetings and their individual responsibilities on the committee. Students also wrote three evaluation reports; one describing their committee organization, leadership and communication, a second concerning their work in the training program at the State Hospital, and a third evaluating the overall organization of the Special Olympics and the fulfillment of their individual responsibilities on the day of the track and field event.

The Course Instructor

The course instructor acted as lecturer as well as advisor to the committees. The instructor met with each committee twice during the semester and with the committee of representatives bi-weekly. She co-ordianted efforts of the Residential Facility with the work done at the University, and was over-all director of the Special Olympics track and field event.

The Role of the State Residential Facility

An individual from the Residential Facility was appointed as liason between the Residential Facility and the University. This individual attended class meetings and acted as an advisor to the committees. She organized a tour of the facility, explained the philosophy and teaching methods as well as the roles of the various specialists; occupational therapists, physical therapists, speech therapists, teachers, nurses, and recreational therapitst. Several of these specialists delivered lectures at the weekly class meetings.

The recreational therapists supervised the students participating in the physical training program at the Residential Facility.

Equipment for special events such as ping-pong blow and bowling ball roll were provided by the Residential Facility. Financial assistance was also available as well as food and utensils for residents requiring special diets.

It was extremely important to clarify the responsibilities of the University and the State Residential Facility before the course began. Written communication was coupled with oral communication to avoid misunderstandings between the two large, complex institutions.

The Day of the Special Olympics

Students from the three unit class arrived at 7:00 A.M. to set up tables, chairs and banners for awards, registration, special events, clerks of course, volunteers, meals and information, as well as equipment for the various events.

Five hundred volunteers arrived between 7:30 and 8:00 A.M. and were instructed by the volunteer committee. Their role as either companion to an athlete or worker in an event was explained and written instructions concerning meals, toileting, and emergency procedures were distributed. Each volunteer received a Special Olympic shirt, making them easily distinguishable on the field.

Registration of the athletes took place between 8:00 and 9:00 A.M. Each athlete was assigned a volunteer companion for the day.

Opening ceremonies began with a parade complete with marching bands, a float, Disney Characters and the athletes with their companions. Community dignitaries spoke, the athletes sung, recited the Special Olympics Oath and lit the Olympic torch signaling the beginning of a day the students agree they will always remember with pride.

Special events including bands, dancing, face painting, farm animals, magicians, new games, movies, puppet shows and crafts, ran continuously throughout the day.

Meals were provided for all of the athletes, except those who needed a special diet. Food and drinks were available for the volunteers to purchase.

An emergency ambulance and first aid care was available, as well as a Doctor and members of the staffs from the four Residential Facilities.

Awards were given to every athlete upon completion of their heat in each event. First, second, third place and participation ribbons were pinned on the athletes by community celebrities.

Closing ceremonies began at 4:00. A tired, but elated crew of athletes, students, volunteers, and residential staff, doused the Olympic flame.

Clean-up was the responsibility of the combined one unit and three unit classes.

The week following the Special Olympics, certificates of appreciation were mailed to every individual, organization, and business, who had donated time, materials, or financial assistance.

Conclusion

What made this Special Olympics outstanding? The enthusiasm of ninety students generated throughout a semester. Comments from their written evaluation give testimony to their feelings of accomplishment.

"The class as a whole was a *total* learning experience. The field work and class discussions were helpful in that they allowed others to understand the work and effort it took to get the *ultimate* experience."

"It was a most beneficial experience. The participants really did materialize, the organization and preparations by the committees paid off, people co-operated and had a great time. It was a wonderful learning experience for all."

"Being given the chance to work with other people towards the goal of putting on the Special Olympics, and seeing it really happen successfully made the class important for me. This was my most inspiring and satisfying accomplishment of the year."

"This experience was possibly the best learning experience I could ever have. I not only learned about myself, but also I saw and learned about compassion that humans have for each other. I can't say enough, it was fantastic!"

The feelings of the staff at Agnew State Hospital and the professors at San Jose State University mirrored those of the students. Both institutions promised continued support...this was our first annual Special Olympics.

Special Olympics Class Required Reading:

Begab, M.J., & Richardson, S.A. (Eds.) *The Mentally Retarded and Society: A Social Science Perspective.* Baltimore, Maryland: University Park Press, 1975. (pages 468-510)

Hackett, L.C. *Movement Exploration and Games for the Mentally Retarded.* Palo Alto, California: Peek Publications, 1970.

1. SPIRIT

MacMillan, D.L. *Mental Retardation in School and Society.* Boston, Mass.: Little Brown and Company. 1977.

Mental Retardation Past and Present, President's Committee on Mental Retardation, January 1977.

A New Kind of Joy, Special Olympics, Inc. Joseph P. Kennedy, Jr. Foundation, Washington D.C.

Special Olympics Event Directors Guide, Special Olympics, Inc. Joseph P. Kennedy, Jr. Foundation. Washington D.C.

Special Olympics Instructional Manual, Special Olympics, Inc. Joseph P. Kennedy, Jr. Foundation. Washington D.C.

SPECIAL OLYMPICS

Maryann Mitchell

King County Park Dept.
Seattle, Washington

The ultimate goal of the Special Olympics program is to create opportunities for sports training and athletic competition for all retarded children.

Recent scientific research has shown that physical activities, sports and competitive athletics are a major means of reaching the retarded. Here is an area where he can succeed and start building a positive self-image, gaining confidence and self-mastery as well as psysical development. As a child improves his performance in the gymnasium and on the playing field, he also improves his performance in the classroom, at home and eventually on the job.

The Special Olympics program serves as a motivational framework within which physical education, recreation and sports activities can take place. Specifically we are striving to:

1) provide motivation for the initation of physical education and athletic programs where none exist.

2) provide supplementary materials which will aid those currently conducting such programs.

3) provide opportunities for athletic competition through local, state, regional, and international Special Olympics.

4) give each retarded child a "feeling of belonging" by offering him membership in a national athletic club with membership certificates, periodic news letters, etc.

5) instill in the retarded child a "sense of pride" by giving him a chance to win an award, be honored at a school assembly or have his picture in a newspaper . . . by giving him a chance to know success.

At the National Special Olympics (Chicago, Ill.), we had some things happen that we felt were very important. For instance, when we got on the plane with the children, they were happy, but then I looked back and saw the parents' faces. They were absolutely stricken; we were taking their children away from them. It gave me just a small inkling of the trust and confidence they

"Special Olympics." Maryann Mitchell. *Recreation's Role in the Rehabilitation of the Mentally Retarded.* 1970. Rehabilitation Research and Training Center in Mental Retardation. University of Oregon.

must have had in us to let us take these protected children so far away from them. I am sure that the experience was traumatic for the parents. It was not for the children.

After we crossed the Rocky Mountains and the earth became flat with the rivers winding, one of our boys looked out the window and said, "Hey look, a map!" I thought how beautiful if we could always teach geography in this way, if we could just take them up in a plane and let them see this.

On the bus, going from the airport into the hotel, one of the boys said to another boy, "Boy, their freeways are just as bad as ours." I think he felt right at home. The girls pretended that the hotel rooms were apartments and they did not like us to call them hotel rooms. We placed ourselves in rooms, not with the children, but between their rooms, so they could room together with their friends. They had the independence of being in their rooms alone and they felt as if they were really grown up, living in their own apartments.

The name of the important people there, such as Eunice Kennedy Shriver, did not mean very much to them, but something about being around these people made their faces change from being "so you are standing there," to "who are you?" And you could see that something was coming over them, a beginning of some kind of a feeling for these people that was important. We found they met other children very, very easily. They talked with them, they inquired about where they were from. We had some children ask our children, "What institution are you from?" Our girls did not know what the other child was talking about. They had quite a conversation, the institutional kids trying to find out, "Who takes care of you if you do not live in an institution? Where do you go at night?" They did not have an understanding of what it meant to "just live in a house." The questions they asked afterward were real eye openers to me. Our children grew in stature as we were there and by the time we came home on Sunday morning, they were checking all our baggage. They did not need help from us; they did not need anything extra from us at all. I am sure they stood taller.

During this last year, the directors have been keeping very careful watch on these children. They have progressed, some of them two divisions in their athletic ability. We have documented evidence that these children, after being exposed to this program on a year-round basis, are growing. Some have moved from the novice category, which is now called division four, to a goal category, which is really a tremendous jump in their physical ability.

One last incident from this trip illustrates the importance of the program. When we got back to the airport, and the parents came and there was much hugging, kissing, greeting, and so forth, one of the over-protective fathers said to his little girl, "Where is your suitcase?, Oh, it is over there." He said, "I will get it," and she said, "Dad, I can do it myself." And I thought this was a really beautiful ending to what we had put so much effort into, a very rewarding experience for us all.

Always Where the Action is

Rafer Johnson

Mr. Johnson is head coach, Special Olympics, Inc.

IT STARTED with a phone call back in 1968. I had met Eunice Kennedy Shriver once or twice very fleetingly. And each time she would fix me with those piercing blue eyes and say, "I'll be getting in touch with you."

Suddenly there was that unmistakable Kennedy voice on the wire. "Rafer, we are organizing a Special Olympics for mentally retarded children in Chicago. You have got to be there."

I was there. A request from Eunice Shriver is not given or taken lightly. It is never for something frivolous or wasteful. It is volunteer activity at its highest level—doing something for people who really need your help—like the retarded.

On a July day, I traveled out to Soldier Field in Chicago not knowing what to expect. I looked for Eunice on the reviewing platform, in the stands, in the club house, in the VIP room. She was not there.

Then I saw a big cluster of kids out on the field. They were doing strenuous exercises, and right in the midst of them was a lady in slacks and a blouse doing everything they did—running, jumping, falling to the ground, getting up again.

"Come on, Rafer," she called, when I got up close. "This is what you are going to be doing for the next two days."

She was right. Her celebrity volunteers did not stand around giving interviews or autographs. Every one of them spent long hours in the hot July sun with the kids—showing them how to do the things they had won their reputations in.

I remember Stan Mikita coaching floor hockey and Paul Hornung and Hopalong Cassidy teaching pass patterns. Wayne Embry was on the basketball court and a dozen Olympic track stars led by Jesse Owens were running wind sprints with the Special Olympians.

I thought the decathlon in Rome was tough. Being a volunteer for Eunice Shriver made me wish I was still in training and eight years younger. We never thought of taking a break that day because Eunice was right there with us every minute.

She was on the trampoline helping world champion Gary Erwin run his clinic. She organized a touch football game with 25 kids on each side and celebrities like astronaut Jim Lovell, Rosey Grier, Congressman Bob Mathias, and her sisters, Pat and Jean. She got all 1,000 athletes doing calesthenics to a record of "Chicken Fat" on the public address system and even had Mayor Daley exercising.

The kids loved every minute of it, and so did we. Celebrities became participants, and participants became celebrities. They were hugged and cheered and encouraged to do their best. And wherever there was a close race or an exciting team event, Eunice was there with a "Well done."

That first Special Olympics sold me on the volunteer spirit as it is practiced by Eunice Shriver. Get into the action. Don't hold back. Never ask anyone to do what you are unwilling to do yourself.

When I am asked about the Kennedy charisma, that is how I describe it—helping others through action, not talk, and getting others charged up with the desire to pitch in.

My first experience as a Special Olympics volunteer took place seven years ago. I have been right in the thick of things ever since.

If you go to a Special Olympics meet today, chances are that you will see a slender woman in slacks down on the field, calling out in that unmistakable Kennedy voice, "Nice work. Now, come on—let's do it better *this* time."

And because Eunice asks them to, they *do* it better. And so do we.

"Always Where the Action Is," Rafer Johnson, *Parks and Recreation,* Vol. 10, No. 12, December 1975. Parks and Recreation.

27

One Person Makes a Difference

Eunice Kennedy Shriver

Ms. Shriver is executive vice-president of the Joseph P. Kennedy, Jr., Foundation and president, Special Olympics, Inc.

FRANCIS BACON wrote, "In this theater of man's life, it is reserved only for God and for angels to be lookers-on."

This is still the best rationale for voluntarism I know. So much work remains to be done in this unfinished and imperfect world that none of us can justify standing on the sidelines. Especially in a society like ours, volunteering is an expression of democracy in its purest form. For the volunteer is a participant, not a looker-on, and participation *is* the democratic process.

In a world full of problems, it is tempting to ask, "What can one person do?"—and do nothing. But each of us can cure an ill, teach a child to play, to run, to read. Each of us can reveal to a child the beauty and wonder of nature. Each can reach out and touch another human being. Give something and receive something.

That is what volunteering is all about—you and another human being. It is about understanding another's needs. It is a commitment. It is acting—sometimes boldly, sometimes unconventionally, sometimes quietly—but acting.

For, as my brother Robert said, "In our country it is no longer enough to count the poor, to sympathize with the struggle for equality, to watch with sadness the decay of our urban life. We must *do* something to change the facts of our present life."

It is no accident that the sports and recreation programs sponsored by the Joseph P. Kennedy, Jr., Foundation are among the largest volunteer efforts of their kind in the world—over 150,000 in Special Olympics and 20,000 in the foundation's new Families Play to Grow program.

Without volunteer support, without willing hands and caring hearts, the mentally retarded would not be able to take part in those activities we have historically reserved for the "normal."

It requires volunteer participation almost on a one-to-one basis to organize and put on a Special Olympics meet. Volunteers must coach and train the young athletes, accompany them to the games, make certain they get to the starting line at the right time, cheer them on as they take part in their events, help organize and coach clinics and demonstrations,

serve as timers and judges, present medals and ribbons, serve and supervise meals, chaperone dances and other social events, and just be there with their athletes throughout the games to lend a hand and speak an encouraging word.

The Fourth International Special Olympics Games held August 7-11, 1975, in Mount Pleasant, Michigan, produced a new kind of volunteer who played a most significant role in the success of the games. These were the "huggers"—hundreds of boys and girls, men and women, who stood at the end of every lane at every race and gave each athlete a warm, enthusiastic hug as he or she crossed the finish line.

You will not find this position listed on any table of organization, but the hugger is essential to the spirit of the Special Olympics, which places effort above win-

Celebrity volunteer Sally Struthers salutes a Maryland Special Olympian.

a Difference

ning and caring above competition.

It used to be that the mentally retarded were shut away in huge, impersonal institutions where an overburdened staff herded them into barnlike dayrooms where they sat out their lives in empty isolation.

Now, thanks to volunteers, the mentally retarded are breaking out of this imprisonment. Thousands are returning to society, to halfway houses in their own communities where volunteers are helping them to get jobs, enjoy community facilities, take part in social and recreation activities.

Because of programs like Special Olympics, communities are opening their playgrounds, school yards, gymnasiums, and swimming pools to the physically handicapped and mentally retarded. And schools and institutions themselves are letting the world into their classrooms and back wards and bringing the retarded out into the world.

At Western Carolina Center, a marvelous state institution for the retarded in North Carolina, volunteers have organized horseback riding classes, camping, skiing, and outdoor recreation programs of all kinds for the retarded. There are even lovely cottages built in the pine woods surrounding the center, where parents, the most important volunteers of all, can spend weekends with their youngsters playing games with them and taking them on nature walks through the countryside.

At the Military Road School, a public school for the retarded in Washington, D.C., the absence of large playing fields has not been an obstacle to recreation for the children. Teachers, parents, and volunteers have taken advantage of nearby Rock Creek Park for horseback riding, nature walking, and outdoor games. They have used the Kennedy Foundation's Play to Grow program as the basis for these activities.

In Maine, Vermont, Utah, and many other states, winter Special Olympics are now held each year. Children who only got the chance to be outdoors on nice days, if at all, are now joyfully competing in snowball throwing contests, "flying saucer" slaloms, ice skating, and skiing. Volunteers make these opportunities possible.

Examples of volunteer activities in Special Olympics are legion.

Great athletes like George Foreman, Muhammad Ali, Chris Evert, Arthur Ashe, Bart Starr, and Franco Harris are just a few of the devoted celebrities who work with the Special Olympians to improve their skills and are there with a handshake and a "well-done" when they have run their race or played their game. All the team members and coaches of the National Basketball Association, the American Basketball Association, and the National Hockey League are involved in an international program which supports the basketball and floor hockey activities of the Special Olympics. Olympic medalists Rafer Johnson, Bill Toomey, Mark Spitz, Lillian Watson, and Diane Holum are volunteer members of one of the most impressive coaching staffs in the world. And they do not just talk voluntarism. They have put in thousands of hours and traveled thousands of miles to let Special Olympians everywhere know that they are admired and respected by the world's finest athletes.

On a different level, high school students all over America are taking part in the "Train-A-Champ" program through which Special Olympians are coached in sports events on a year-round basis. How many parents have heard their teenagers complain, "There

Huggers greet Special Olympics runners.

is nothing to do?" There is always something to do—a hundred outlets in every community for the energies and dedication of our youth.

Special Olympics provides a challenging opportunity for youngsters who have been blessed with gifts of normal intelligence and physical capacity to enrich the lives of boys and girls, much like themselves, who have been less fortunate than they. They will find almost immediately that the handicapped have great gifts to bestow on them in return—gifts of love and loyalty, gifts of improved skills and growing self-esteem.

As President Kennedy so often said, "Oh, the difference one person can make."

Although 400,000 mentally retarded youth are already taking part in the Special Olympics, more than 1 million are still standing on the sidelines. Volunteers everywhere, young and old, are needed to bring them onto the playing field, to give them a chance to expand their abilities and explore the unknown limits of their potential.

Eight years ago, there were no volunteers in Special Olympics and very few volunteers anywhere bringing sports and recreation to the retarded. Now, more than 150,000 are joined together in a great movement that started simply because, one by one, human beings cared for other human beings. And that is all it takes—especially to bring the blessings of the outdoors and the benefits of recreation to the handicapped. You do not have to leave your own block or your own community. You do not need to involve large groups of people or organize a complicated bureaucracy. All you have to do is *do* somethings.

And in the doing, you will have started a great movement—"harnessing for God," as the philosopher said, "the energies of love."

Programs for handicapped

Special Olympics

RICHARD ALFRED SCARNATI is chief physical therapist for Southwest Cook County Cooperative Association for Special Education, 6401 W. 111th Street, Worth, Illinois 60482.

On Saturday, May 15, 1971, a Special Olympics was held at the Tinley Park High School in Tinley Park, Illinois. This Olympics was developed by the author, a chief physical therapist for the Southwest Cook County Cooperative Association for Special Education. This special education cooperative serves over 25 school districts and has more than 800 handicapped children.

Most of the ideas for the development of our Olympics came from *A Guide for Local Programs* published by the Joseph P. Kennedy, Jr. Foundation Special Olympics which has been developed for retarded children. In the Kennedy Olympic Guide Book, the following statements were made: "There really shouldn't be a 'Special Olympics' just for the retarded. There should be a 'Youth Olympics' for all youngsters with competition divisions by age, sex and ability. However, there is no program of this nature for all children, and so, since our specific concern is for the retarded, we have made one available for them."

Since our Special Education Cooperative is composed of all exceptionalities, I wanted to develop an Olympics for all of the children, and since our program was so successful I would suggest that the Kennedy Olympics develop a program to include all exceptionalities since they have state, national, and international programs.

Our Olympics motto was "Win or Lose, Let Me Do My Best," and our Olympics symbol depicted a child jumping and reaching for recognition.

Training for Special Olympics not only increases all physical aspects such as strength, endurance, motor ability, and developmental skills, but also has inherent educational, cultural, social, and moral value not only for the handicapped but for all of us who help to make this dream a reality. Special Olympics have received support from government officials and others from all walks of life.

Initially, the following chairmanships were developed and responsibilities outlined so that an effective program could be assured:

1. Special Olympics Director, responsible for the total development of the program.
2. Special Olympics Coach Consultant, who developed a training program for all the children. A training guide was developed for each classroom teacher and suggestions made when specific problems arose. Many teachers coordinated their olympics training program with the school's physical education program.
3. Training Committee consisting of each classroom teacher.
4. Games Event Committee, consisting of a head coach (teacher) responsible for setting up each particular event, such as the 50-yard dash. There was also an official for each event to record names and scores.
5. Promotion and Publicity Chairman, who developed all media coverage, press conferences, and TV and promotional activities.
6. Printed Materials Chairman, whose responsibility included structure, layout, and reproduction of all printed materials for the program, including the printed program for the day of the Olympics.
7. Medical and Emergency Service Chairman, to obtain insurance, doctors, nurses, Red Cross accident station, and ambulance standby service.
8. Olympic Ceremony and Parade Chairman, responsible for the

"Special Olympics," Richard Alfred Scarnati, *Journal of Health, Physical Education and Recreation,* Vol. 43, No. 2, February 1972   American Alliance for Health, Physical Education and Recreation.

31

opening and closing ceremonies and parade.

9. Special Olympics Announcer for the day of the Olympics.

10. Olympic Village Chairman, responsible for the development of the Olympic Village (luncheon) for the contestants. This was developed by the Special Education PTA.

11. Safety Chairman who developed an overall safety program for the Olympics.

12. Budget and Fund Collection Chairman to obtain pledges, etc., from organizations, businesses, and individuals to cover the cash needs of the program.

13. Awards Chairman to secure medals and awards for the contestants.

14. Special Events Chairman to contact "personalities"—ballplayers, movie stars, public servants, etc.—and secure their services for the Olympics.

15. Transportation Chairman to coordinate private (parent) transportation with special education bus transportation. Parents were instructed to bus their own children if possible.

16. Parent Communications Chairman, who wrote to all parents regarding the Olympic program.

The events for the non-physically handicapped were 50-Yard Dash, 300-Yard Run, Softball Throw, Standing Broad Jump, and Swimming Meet. For

the physically handicapped the events were Indianapolis 500 (Krazy Kar race) for very young children, shot-put (ball throw), discus (ring toss) and wheelchair race. The children were divided into groups according to chronological age, ability, and sex.

Community response for the program was tremendous. The McDonalds Corporation supplied all the participants with a free Olympic tee-shirt and lunch, and made each child a member of the Ronald McDonald Fun Club. The Jolly Jesters Clown Club of Chicago supplied a clown for the younger children. Prizes were donated by various merchants for participants and raffle contest. Gold, silver, and bronze medals were made and donated so that each child received one. Every child was a winner.

Community service organizations such as the American Red Cross, Association of Parents of the Physically Handicapped, Jaycees, Lion's Clubs, Boy Scouts, American Legion, and Life Guard (Pool) Association gave outstanding assistance for the program. The Tinley Park Police Department served without pay and did a fine job of helping make this program a success. Dave Hale of the Chicago Bears was on hand for the occasion.

Over 70 special education classrooms were represented in the meet. Each classroom teacher had been instructed to have his class develop a classroom olympic flag or banner. This not only was an art project and motivating factor but also looked quite impressive in the Olympic Parade. The spirit of competition was keen as flags and banners unfurled, each participant hoping his classroom would be best. As the chief physical therapist, I trained most of the physically handicapped children for this event. In my years of experience, I have never found a more motivating factor in therapy than the desire to train for the Olympics. The children trained very hard. The hearts of Olympic champions would glow if they could have seen how hard these children worked in therapy.

Eunice Kennedy Shriver of the Kennedy Olympics said, "Special Olympics seems to do something for everyone it touches—not just the children, but also the parents, teachers, coaches, the officials, the volunteers—all of us. I know it will give you a lifetime of memories."

Before Saturday, May 15, 1971 I had never seen a special or any other type of olympics, let alone developed one. But on this day it happened, a happening, and the beautiful things that took place on this day will remain with me always. I am very happy to have had the privilege of developing this program and am extremely indebted to all of our people who made this day a day of winning for our children.

SOMETIMES

THEY
STUMBLED---

FRANK J. HAYDEN
EXECUTIVE DIRECTOR, SPECIAL OLYMPICS, INC.

UNDER A HOT JULY SUN, in Chicago's Soldier Field, 1.000 boys and girls ran and jumped and swam their way to victory in the First Special Olympics for the mentally retarded, an international event sponsored by the Joseph P. Kennedy Jr. Foundation and the Chicago Park District. Victory—not only for themselves but for retarded children everywhere.

From across the nation they came—New Hampshire. Virginia. Florida, New Mexico. California, Washington, Colorado, Kansas, Michigan — 85 groups from 25 states and Canada. And they put on a performance such as Chicago had never seen.

Every retarded child in the country was a winner that day. The outstanding efforts of the 1.000 Special Olympians has resulted in the creation of a national Special Olympic Training Program—a program which will enable millions of retarded youngsters to experience the thrills and rewards of athletic training and Special Olympic competition. The Chicago program will provide the prototype for local and regional Olympics in 1969 and the Second International Special Olympics in 1970. Mrs. Sargent Shriver has announced a pledge of $75.000 from the Joseph P. Kennedy Jr. Foundation to underwrite this program during the coming year.

In Chicago, competition categories were determined not only by age and sex but also by ability. Competitors were required to complete the AAHPER-Kennedy Foundation Special Fitness Test before coming to Chicago.

--AND SOMETIMES THEY FELL BUT THE WOMAN WITH THE KENNEDY VOICE HAD TOLD THEM TO DO THEIR BEST AND THEY DID.

BILL BRADEN, CHICAGO SUN-TIMES

"Sometimes They Stumbled," The Special Olympics Committee. Original article by Frank J. Hayden. Courtesy of Special Olympics, Inc.

The most impressive sport spectacle ever to occur in front of this author's bifocals.

—Dave Condon, Chicago Tribune

According to their scores they were assigned to the Novice, Silver, Gold, or Champ division—in one of four age groups. The events included the 50-yard dash, 300-yard run, standing broad jump, softball throw, high jump, 25-yard swim, and 100-yard swim. A total of 200 events were scheduled and performances recorded for the first three places in each.

The competition was most exciting, but it is only part of the story of the Chicago Games. Over 2,000 marched in the opening parade led by the Great Lakes Naval Training Center band. All of the Olympic pageantry was captured as 17-year-old Philip Weber carried the Special Olympic Flame into the stadium and lit a 40-foot-high John F. Kennedy Flame of Hope. As a flag bearing the newly-designed Special Olympic symbol reached the top of the flagpole, 2,000 yellow and blue balloons were released. Each carried a postcard bearing the name and address of one of the competitors, in the hope that the person finding the balloon would write to him.

Sports clinics were conducted throughout the day by a "Coaching Staff" of outstanding Olympic and professional athletes. When they were not competing, the Special Olympians could ice skate (on a special plastic surface) with Diane Holum, Barbara Ann Scott, or Michael Kirby; learn basketball skills from the Chicago Bulls, or how to jump rope from Joey Giardello; take swimming lessons from Adolph Kiefer, or a handoff from Paul Hornung. They could team up with Hornung, Johnny Lattner, Ziggy Czarobski, and Hopalong Cassady against a team of Notre Dame sophomores, or get coaching tips before their events from Rafer Johnson and Bob Mathias. World champion trampolinist Gary Erwin gave more than eight hours of individual instruction.

One of the most popular spots was the 80' x 40' x 4' pool installed in the stadium infield for the swimming events. Mrs. Shriver, who had spent 15 hours enroute from Paris for the Olympics, enlivened the activity there with a spirited water polo game. Then she and sister Pat Lawford joined in the fitness clinic conducted by the "Head Coach," Astronaut Jim Lovell, and the

Soldier Field has been the scene of many spectacular sporting events.

1. SPIRIT

But the fights, games, meets... would never match the Special Olympics.

—Jim Kernaghan, Toronto Star

President's Council on Physical Fitness, providing a real example of "how it should be done."

A major highlight of the day was an international floor hockey match between the Toronto Maple Leafs, a trainable group coached by regular Leaf Captain George Armstrong, and the Chicago Black Hawks. coached by Hawk star Stan Mikita. It was a tough, well-played contest, with the American youngsters coming from behind in the last minute of play to gain a 6-6 tie. Said Armstrong: "I've never seen any group of kids play with more heart than these guys."

Officials from the United States and Canada were so impressed in watching the performance of these young hockey players that they have approached the owners and Clarence Campbell, president of the National Hockey League, to establish an International Floor Hockey Tournament for the retarded. Entries would be sponsored by each of the N.H.L. teams. Plans call for the first tournament to be held in Toronto early in 1969.

Home for the athletes during their three days in Chicago was Special Olympic Village — Avery Brundage's La Salle Hotel. By Saturday night, when they were Mr. Brundage's guests for a victory dinner, they had won the heart of every waiter, elevator operator, and bellman in the hotel. Said one chaperone from Indiana: "Many of the staff showed affection to the children as though they were their own. Their first exposure to and awareness of retarded children was a memorable one. They couldn't have been nicer to our youngsters."

The La Salle's Grand Ballroom became the "training table." Dinner was followed each night by entertainment, music, and dancing. Some of the most outstanding performances were on the dance floor—even after a long day of Olympic competition.

It is interesting to note that among the 1.000 children there was not one serious medical problem all weekend. Although the First Aid Center at Sol-

dier Field was a beehive all day Saturday, the problems were no more serious than scrapes and bruises and too much sun.

The reactions of those who traveled with the athletes were unanimously enthusiastic. All have vowed to return in 1970 with a bigger and better team. In many communities children are training now for local and regional Special Olympics scheduled for next summer. Some groups have already arranged sponsorship for their team for "the big one" in 1970. There is no question that many records will fall at the Second Special Olympiad when more than 2,000 entries are expected.

It is impossible to describe the emotion that filled Soldier Field on July 20, 1968, as the Chicago Special Olympics drew to a close. One official said recently: "Thinking about it still puts a lump in my throat." Athletes, coaches, officials, and chaperones marching hand in hand — children wearing the medals they had won, beaming as they flashed their victory signs to the crowd—2.000 people link-

It was a beautiful thing. It was very nice.

ing hands to sing "Auld Lang Syne" as the flags were lowered. the Olympic Flame was carried from the stadium, and the athletes were asked to reassemble in two years—and, finally, three rousing cheers!

AND NOBODY TRIED TO WIN

Jim Murray

I guess if all of us could have one wish, it would be to remain forever age 7, a magical time when the world seemed good and we believed it was peopled by creatures like the tooth fairy, the Easter Bunny and Santa Claus, and happiness was an around-the-clock proposition.

We call people who remain in that wistful time zone "retarded." That is to say, they live in a world without malice or avarice. They have stopped well short of the urge to kill or covet. They have never come upon the low cunning which besets the unretarded majority.

Thay have never learned to lie, to cheat, to steal. They are more in harmony with nature than the brightest general who ever lived. I don't think one of them would consciously kill an insect. They have to be institutionalized, not because they are a threat to society but because society is a threat to them. Dale Evans, I believe, called them "Angels Unaware." They are at once our heartache and our boon. They make better persons out of those around them and how many of us can say that?

Some 3,000 of these special people were in our midst this week for the "Special Olympics." These are children who have learning impediments. Thus, they have not learned words like "hate," "compete," "victory," "revenge," "kill" or "cheat." Which, of course, makes them culturally deprived.

.To look with a child's eye on the world all your life would seem not such a burden. To be Peter Pan forever would be a gay adventure. To have comprehension disabilities would not seem a tragedy when you reflect on what there is to comprehend.

You very quickly learn what is "special" about the Special Olympics which was staged by the Joseph P. Kennedy, Jr. Foundation at UCLA this week. Nobody was trying to win.

There were no false starts. The races were run at a stately, dignified pace. Every athlete performed as if he were alone on the track. It was an achievement just to know direction. They ran with a kind of beatific joy. There were no tears from losers. In fact, there were no losers.

You take Angie, who ran in one of the lower divisions of the 300-yard-run. I used the word "ran" loosely. You can tell right away that Angie is no runner. Angie is one of those multiply-handicapped. An obvious glandular case, her torso is heavy with fat, and it took her several seconds just to clear the starting block. She peered down the track in dismay from behind her myopic spectacles. The field was in the home stretch before Angie was properly under way. She lost the race by 200 yards, you might say. On the other hand, she stopped several times in some bewilderment at finding herself alone, and at holding up the race behind her. But, from the stands, from her fellow competitors who had already finished, from her friends, came cheers, shouts of encouragement, handclapping. And Angie would start up again. About 20 yards from the finish, she got this expression of pure joy on her face as she strained and concentrated and actually SPRINTED across the finish line where she collapsed happily in the waiting arms of her friends with a wide smile of accomplishment.

That's what the Special Olympics are all about. There are stories of the time a winning runner knew a companion had tripped and fallen—and he circled back to help his pal to his feet, costing himself the gold medal. You hear that and your mind flashes back to an auto race where a driver sped past the burning car that had his brother in it. Ask your-

1. SPIRIT

A boy in Chicago ran on crutches, a girl long-jumped on an artificial leg and a blind boy followed the voice of his coach around the track.

self, who is retarded?

There was a boy from Chicago who ran on crutches. A girl who long-jumped on an artificial leg. There was the blind boy who followed the voice of his coach around the track. There was the basketball game without a single intentional foul. The score was incidental. There was the boy who finished the race and then kept running round and round the track because it felt so good.

There are over 2 million of these enchanted creatures among us. More civilized societies used to treat them with grave deference and respect. Ours used to chain them in one wing of the castle.

Never mind that Elree Bivens ran the mile in 4:48.2. Know the joy of the great ex-Dodger pitcher, Carl Erskine, who once struck out 15 Yankees in a World Series game, but who knew no thrill better than the day his little Jimmy first put his hands to his ears when the starter's gun went off but then finally took off and, though he finished last, he finished. Erskine wept but said, "There is no way describing the satisfaction of seeing Jimmy just finish the race."

As Eunice Kennedy Shriver, whose older sister has been special for nearly a half-century, told the lovely boys and girls: "The athletes we remember . . . are not the flawless, but the great human beings who have reached beyond themselves to achieve some glorious goal."

Matched on that yardstick, the athletes at Munich will be an inferior lot. It's no trick to win the long jump when you've got two legs and neither one is metal. It's no achievement to win the mile when you can see which way to go. And it's no honor to win the 440 when a fellow athlete stumbles and falls and you don't stop to help him up.

The Special Olympics

Robert M. Montague, Jr.

RAY CROWLEY

Robert M. Montague, Jr., brigadier general (ret.), U.S. Army, is executive director of the Joseph P. Kennedy, Jr. Foundation and Special Olympics, Inc. He was born in Hawaii, attended the U.S. Military Academy and the University of Virginia, served with the Vietnamese Pacification Program, and was deputy special assistant to the chief of staff of the Modern Volunteer Army (Washington, D.C.).

On Aug. 7, 1975, in Perry Shorts Stadium, Mount Pleasant, Mich., the Special Olympics program came of age. Seven years before, 1,000 mentally retarded youngsters had taken part in the first international sports event in which the retarded had ever been asked to compete. They had come from 24 states, the District of Columbia, Canada, and France. Olympic Village was the La Salle Hotel in Chicago. The mayor of Chicago and the governor of Illinois welcomed them. A 17-year-old mentally retarded boy carried the Special Olympics torch into Soldier Field and ignited a 40-foot-high Special Olympics Flame of Hope. The Special Olympics flag was raised as 1,000 balloons, each carrying the name of a Special Olympics athlete, soared into the bright July sky.

And then, these youngsters—age 8 to 16—forgot that many of them had come from state institutions and training schools, sheltered workshops, and halfway houses. They were athletes on that day, proving to every skeptic and doubter that the mentally retarded had courage and stamina to spare. They swam, ran the 50-yard and the 300-yard dashes, threw the baseball, and played floor hockey. They won joyfully, and they lost gracefully. Though few were in the stands to cheer them on, they competed in the true spirit of their Special Olympics oath, a motto adopted from the gladiators of ancient Rome, which Eunice Kennedy Shriver, founder of the Games, had recited to them: "Let me win, but if I cannot win, let me be brave in the attempt."

Two days later, joining hands in a giant circle of friendship, they sang 'Auld Lang Syne' in tribute to what they, their parents, teachers, and coaches agreed had been the most important event in their lives.

That was the first Special Olympics Games. It was the beginning of a movement that, since 1968, has become the largest sports program for the mentally retarded in the world; one of the world's largest volunteer organizations; one of the most widely respected therapeutic actvities for the mentally retarded; the catalyst for thousands of school, community, and institutional physi-

"The Special Olympics," by Robert Montague, Jr. Executive Director, Special Olympics, Inc. 1976. Compton Yearbook, 1976. *Encyclopedia Britannica Inc.* Encyclopedia Britannica.

1. SPIRIT

Since 1,000 youngsters participated in the first Special Olympics Games in 1968, Special Olympics has grown into a year-round, international athletic program for more than 400,000 mentally retarded children and adults. Not only has the program itself grown, but also the spirit of the Special Olympics has expanded to other athletic arenas. In 1975, for example, the arch-rival National Basketball Association and American Basketball Association joined together to sponsor the National Special Olympics basketball program, including the national run, dribble, and shoot competition, held in Louisville, Ky., at which the youngster below participated.

PAUL SCHUHMANN—COURIER-JOURNAL AND LOUISVILLE TIMES

cal training and recreation programs; the gateway to public acceptance and self-esteem for the more than a million children and young adults who have taken part in Special Olympics sports training and athletic competition; and a medium for public understanding that has played a major role in changing the image of mental retardation and in instilling an appreciation of the value of the retarded to our society.

At Perry Shorts Stadium in 1975, the progress achieved over eight years was self-evident. Instead of 1,000 youngsters who had been recruited with some difficulty, 3,200 athletes lined up to march onto the field. They had won the right to compete in the Fourth International Games by a process of selection in more than 20,000 local training programs and 3,000 local, area, and state meets and tournaments.

More than 400,000 mentally retarded youngsters and adults had taken part during the preceding months in these year-round Special Olympics activities, organized, helped, coached, and encouraged by 150,000 devoted volunteers. They came from every state, the District of Columbia, and a host of foreign countries including Belgium, Brazil, Canada, El Salvador, France, Mexico, the Philippines, and West Germany. In many of these foreign countries, Special Olympics was the first volunteer program ever organized to help the mentally retarded.

Not only the fastest and the strongest were chosen for the International Games; boys and girls and men and women who represented the complete spectrum of the mentally retarded came to participate in many varied activities. Some were blind, some crippled, some cerebral palsied; some were the products of poverty, lack of parental care, or poor early education. Others were brain damaged, mongoloid, epileptic, or emotionally disturbed as well as retarded. But all wore their state and national uniforms proudly, and each had developed within his or her own capabilities a proficiency in at least two individual events or one team sport. On the field they performed like champions: from 10-year-old Donna Brown of Texas, who ran the 50-yard dash and swam the 25-yard freestyle, to Corinne Scruggs of Florida, age 70, the oldest competitor in the International Special Olympics, who participated in the 25-yard wheelchair race and the baseball throw.

Unlike that first Special Olympics in Chicago, where the stands were empty, the stadium at Central Michigan University was filled with 20,000 cheering spectators. They had come to see an Olympics contest that was not an orgy of national pride or commercialism but a pure expression of what Baron de Coubertin, founder of the modern Olympics, had intended the Games to be: "The important thing in the Olympics is not winning," he had said, "but taking part. Not conquering, but fighting well."

Instead of competing in a handful of cautiously selected events —300 yards the longest foot race, 25 yards the longest swim— which had characterized the first Special Olympics in Chicago, these athletes were fully trained to compete in races up to a mile, swimming and diving, the pentathlon, the 440-yard relay, ice skating, floor hockey, basketball, volleyball, high jump, long jump, gymnastics, bowling, the softball throw, and special contests for the blind and the physically handicapped.

In 1968 the Joseph P. Kennedy, Jr., Foundation, which, together with the Chicago Park District, had sponsored the Games, had brought its own motion picture camera crew to record the Games and produce a training film. At Perry Shorts

Stadium, there were a dozen camera crews representing local television stations from all over. There was public radio to broadcast a continuous report of the Games to every community that had sent athletes. There were the television crew and famous sports announcers from CBS Sports Spectacular, which had commissioned a 30-minute special on the Games to be broadcast internationally.

Gov. William G. Milliken of Michigan was on the reviewing stand, as were the lieutenant governor of New York, the mayor of Mount Pleasant, and many other dignitaries. Head Coach Rafer Johnson, 1960 Olympic decathlon gold medalist, led the assembled athletes in the Special Olympics oath. Walter Kennedy, former commissioner of the National Basketball Association and chairman of the board of Special Olympics, declared the Games in session. Telegrams were read that had been sent by the four cochairpersons of the 1975 International Games: America's First Lady Betty Ford; Margaret Trudeau, wife of the prime minister of Canada; Anne-Aymore Giscard d'Estaing, wife of the French president; and Rose Kennedy, who had encouraged Special Olympics and attended many of the Games since the program's inception. And, of course, there was Eunice Shriver, sister of the late U.S. President John F. Kennedy, who had been convinced that the retarded would grow in mind, body, and spirit through participation in sports; who believed that experience in athletic competition would help them lead healthier, more fulfilled lives; and who had spearheaded the growth of this dynamic movement.

In the dust of that August day in Mount Pleasant, the 3,200 mentally retarded athletes were a testament to an amazing maturing process that our country has undergone in the past eight years. Their struggle for acceptance and for their civil and human rights had been a record of courage and perseverance not only on their part but on the part of parents, teachers, community leaders, and volunteers from all walks of life. Special Olympics had been a significant factor in their struggle, for in many ways it had forced the public to accept the retarded for what they are, to understand better both their limitations and their strengths, and to recognize their right to the same treatment, the same opportunities, the same respect accorded to any person of any level of intelligence or physical ability.

"What a fantastic night this is," Eunice Shriver said. "There is nothing like this anywhere else in the world.

"Running, leaping, swimming, throwing, gymnastics—all are a challenge. Most of us in the stands cannot do half as well as you do.

"In the world Olympics, nations compete against each other. But here we don't care where you come from. We don't care what color you are. The one reason we are here is to see you; to celebrate how well you do.

"It is not an athlete's bodily condition that counts here. It is the human spirit and determination. With these, there is no defeat."

In 1968, she had explained the need for the Special Olympics program in these words: "Colonel Red Blaik, coach of so many great Army football teams, devised a play featuring the 'lonesome end'. When the teams huddled, the lonesome end stood near the sidelines. As the teams lined up, he remained isolated and almost unnoticed—far from the rest of the formation. When the ball was snapped, he would be downfield and ready for a pass, frequently catching the opposition by surprise.

Wary organizers of the first Special Olympics Games in 1968 cautiously underestimated the participants' abilities, limiting the longest track event to the 300-yard foot race. Testimony to the public's growing awareness and acceptance of the mentally retarded as well as to the youngsters' improving physical skills—undoubtedly a result of their participation in year-round, nationwide Special Olympics athletic programs—the 1975 competition included, among a wide variety of track and field events, a mile run.

DAVE PETERSON—STATE JOURNAL, TOPEKA, KANSAS

1. SPIRIT

W. O'NEAL NORDLINGER

Founder and guiding force of the Special Olympics Games, Eunice Kennedy Shriver has witnessed in the past eight years the growth of Special Olympics into the largest sports program in the world for the mentally retarded. Prior to the founding of the Special Olympics and establishment of athletic training programs in all 50 states, the District of Columbia, and a host of foreign countries, 45% of all mentally retarded youth received no physical education at all.

"The mentally retarded are the lonesome ends of our society. At home, in school, in the community, they are always near the sidelines. Watching the action. Never allowed in the huddle.

"Sadly the ball is never thrown to them, even though, with great willingness, they are ready to do their best. Simply because society regards them as different, the mentally retarded have been traditionally kept out of the game.

"The Special Olympics program was developed to give these 'lonesome ends' a chance to belong and to make a contribution.

"First, it gives them a chance to develop and test their strength and coordination—to learn skills, to follow rules, to stretch the outside limits of their capabilities.

"Second, it provides an opportunity for individual competition and for team play. It offers vital experiences in winning and losing —but most of all in trying.

"Third, it develops confidence and self-esteem not only among the Special Olympics athletes but in parents, brothers and sisters, friends and neighbors.

"In the Special Olympics everybody wins. Not only the children but their parents, teachers, coaches, and volunteers. The Special Olympics is a shining example for all who believe that a just and good society is one which cares for those who may be less able, but who are in no sense less worthy."

The Dawn of Special Olympics

Until the first Special Olympics Games few retarded youth had ever experienced a regular program of recreation or sports competition. The shocking fact is that until Special Olympics was organized by the Kennedy Foundation, 45% of all mentally retarded children and youth received no physical education at all. Not so much as five minutes a week. Most of the retarded sat in the back wards and dayrooms of large forbidding institutions, where a harassed and undermanned staff watched over them as they spent their days in idleness.

For those parents and teachers who wanted to help their retarded youngsters develop physically, there were few facilities open. Many communities actually had ordinances forbidding the mentally retarded from using public gymnasiums, swimming pools, and playgrounds. They thought they had solid ground for such a policy. The retarded might hurt themselves. They required too much individual attention. They couldn't learn the rules of safety, much less the rules of sports. They would disturb the other "normal" children because they were so different. These were the myths and stereotypes that were prevalent as recently as 1968 and still persist today. Then, only 25% of the retarded were given as much as 60 minutes of organized recreation per week, most of that of little value in terms of producing physical fitness.

The Kennedy Foundation—in collaboration with the American Association for Health, Physical Education, and Recreation (AAHPER)—had previously sponsored an award program based on the President's Physical Fitness Awards, but, as relatively few children were involved, it had only minimal impact. The idea for Special Olympics grew out of the Kennedy family's belief in the value of sports training and athletic competition.

Visiting institutions for the mentally retarded all over America, Eunice Shriver was struck with the poor physical condition of the residents and the total lack of opportunity for play or recreation available to them. From the experience of her own family, she knew it did not have to be this way. Her older sister, Rosemary, had been born retarded and was not able to compete intellectually or socially with her energetic brothers and sisters, but she loved sports and was an excellent swimmer, which not only kept her fit but made her happier and more secure. "If Rosemary could do it," she said, "I knew any retarded child—within his own limitations—could benefit from regular physical training. Everywhere I went I saw pale faces and flabby bodies. Little laughter or sense of play which should be characteristic of all children. That's why Special Olympics was created. To give every special child the right to physical development, the opportunity for play."

Research conducted in the U.S. and in Europe had demonstrated conclusively that youngsters given the chance to exercise regularly not only develop physically but actually perform better in the classroom, adjust more quickly to life situations, and actually show marked improvement in problem solving and even in I.Q. Before that first Special Olympics could be held, however, there were many misapprehensions that had to be corrected. Even before a single athlete had set foot on Soldier Field in 1968, there were those—even some who qualified as experts in mental retardation—who maintained that the youngsters would be totally disoriented by a long journey and overwhelmed by the complexity of staying in a modern urban hotel.

Most of the contestants had never been away from home, never traveled in an airplane, never competed in an athletic event, never attended a banquet or a dance, never won a medal, ribbon, or commendation of any kind. Some experts said the excitement would be too much for the retarded. Others said the experience of losing would be a trauma from which they would not soon recover. Some insisted that the mentally retarded lacked the coordination and stamina to run as much as 300 yards. Others said that team sports could not be included because most mentally retarded youth could not obey the rules, could not understand the meaning of team play, and did not have the attention span to persist over an extended period.

Since most of the athletes had little experience in swimming, it was felt that 25 yards was too far to negotiate without resting. So the rules for the first Games incorporated a provision that swimmers could stand and rest halfway down the pool. At the first Games, however, every one of these myths and misapprehensions was proven wrong, and from 1968 to the present the perceptions of what the retarded can do have been continuously expanded. Thanks to Special Olympics, the public is now far more aware of the facts of retardation. It is *not* a mental illness. It is *not* accompanied by violent or antisocial behavior. It is *not* a total inability to comprehend the meanings of ideas or to understand the customs and regulations of society.

More than 80% of the 7 million retarded children and adults in the U.S. are simply slower in learning than most people. They score significantly lower than the intellectual and physical norms for their calendar age. Some live in a perpetual childhood, but if they are given the chance, most can learn to become independent, contributing members of society. Even among those who are severely retarded, who can never be independent, there is a far broader range of potential than had once been thought possible.

As for character and disposition, the public is becoming increasingly aware that the retarded possess rare virtues of loyalty, fidelity, courage, affection, and persistence. In many ways they

JAMES O LEARY – CHICAGO TRIBUNE. APRIL 1974

When the Third International Special Olympics Games were held in 1972, the competition had been expanded to include several new events, among them gymnastics, which has since become one of the most popular Special Olympics sports.

1. SPIRIT

"The word impossible just isn't in these kids' dictionary, and they've taken it out of my dictionary, too."

— Bill Toomey

GRAND RAPIDS PRESS

Special Olympics players compete in June 1974 in the third annual International Floor Hockey Tournament, held in Winnipeg, Man., and cosponsored by the National Hockey League.

have demonstrated that so-called normal society has much to learn from the retarded. The spirit of generosity and self-effacement that characterizes these athletes has done much to restore the noblest meaning to the word *Olympics*.

Growing in Body and in Spirit

The most significant activity following the first International Games was the formation in December 1969 of Special Olympics, Inc., a nonprofit corporation sponsored by the Kennedy Foundation, designed specifically to create opportunities for sports training and athletic competition for all retarded children everywhere. With Dr. Frank J. Hayden, a noted Canadian physical educator, as its first executive director, Special Olympics, Inc., began to recruit volunteer organizations in every state. Within one month of Senator Edward M. Kennedy's formal announcement of the formation of Special Olympics, Inc., requests for permission to organize local Special Olympics chapters were received from every state and 132 individual communities representing more than 50,000 children.

By the spring of 1969, 8 regional games representing all sections of the U.S. were held in addition to 18 state games and more than 400 local meets. Special Olympics was on its way. During that same year, professional athletics gave its first major recognition of Special Olympics when the 12 professional ice hockey teams then comprising the National Hockey League (NHL) each agreed to sponsor a team in the First International Special Olympics Floor Hockey Tournament, which was held in Toronto, Ont.

In 1970, the Second International Games took place, once again in Chicago. This time, every state was represented and 2,000 young athletes took part. Outstanding sports figures and national celebrities such as astronauts John Glenn and James Lovell; football greats Rosie Grier, Paul Hornung, and Bart Starr; hockey pros Stan Mikita and Bobby Orr; basketball stars Wayne Embry and John Havlicek; and many others from every field of sports attended the games to coach teams, direct clinics, award medals, and play in exhibitions. In fact the participation of professional teams and individual athletes has been a key to the success of Special Olympics. More than most children, the retarded need role models they can look up to and emulate. Neglected and put down for so long, their egos bruised by constant failure, they need the reassurance that comes from knowing that those who are famous and respected care about them.

The national coaching staff and the roster of athletes, sportswriters, and sportscasters for the Special Olympics Committee form an honor roll of most of the great names in sports. Athletes who compete professionally have an affinity for the Special Olympians who compete out of love. They have great empathy for athletes who must overcome so many obstacles simply to be able to get onto the playing field. As Bill Toomey, Olympic decathlon gold medalist, said, "The word *impossible* just isn't in these kids' dictionary, and they've taken it out of my dictionary, too. These boys and girls run, jump, and swim out of the sheer joy of competitive exercise. They love the crowds, the cheers, and the medals, but more than anything else, they love the chance to play." It is this love of sports for its own sake that prompted the U.S. Olympic Committee to give Special Olympics official sanction to use the name—one of only two sports organizations in America to which this privilege has been accorded.

W O NEAL NORDLINGER

One important element of the 1970 Games was the flowering of the clinics, which have become an integral part of every Special Olympics meet. Conducted by outstanding local and national athletes, the clinics give Special Olympians the chance to learn and practice the techniques of other sports. Gary Irwin, world's champion trampolinist, is a fixture at the International Games. Arthur Ashe has conducted tennis clinics. Jan Stenerud and Tommy Nobis have traveled great distances to teach football. Artis Gilmore and Julius Erving have coached Special Olympics basketball, Donna De Verona and Mark Spitz have spent hours at poolside with Special Olympics swimmers.

A Teflon ice skating rink was set up under the stands of Soldier Field where Olympic skating champions Diane Holum and Barbara Ann Scott King first taught Special Olympians to skate. Now ice skating is an official Special Oympics sport, and public as well as many private commercial rinks all over the continent open their facilities to Special Olympians.

The Special Olympics Comes of Age

Between 1970 and 1972 the program experienced phenomenal growth. Almost 100,000 Special Olympians were added each year, as the Kennedy Foundation's emphasis shifted from a single track and field meet in the spring to a year-round program of sports training and athletic competition.

Ongoing Special Olympics organizations were established in every state. Even though 90% or more of the administration was conducted by volunteers, the various chapters quickly became sophisticated in their ability to obtain state, local, and even national grants to supplement the seed money provided each year by the Kennedy Foundation. By 1975, 40% of the chapters received some financial support from these sources. State Games grew until participation in even the average state meet exceeded the number who took part in the first International Games.

About 2,500 Special Olympians converged on Los Angeles in August 1972 for the Third International Games. Because of the proximity to Hollywood, Calif., stars of motion pictures and television such as Carroll O'Connor, Cary Grant, Arte Johnson, Lorne Greene, and dozens of others gave the Special Olympians a generous gift of their time and affection. New events such as gymnastics had been added. Those who had felt that retarded youngsters did not have the necessary coordination or grace for gymnastics were again proved wrong by the likes of Eric Swanson, 23-year-old blind and retarded gymnast from Washington, and 10-year-old Toni Marie Chillemi, a mongoloid child from Florida, who were dazzling in their medal-winning routines.

Sportswriters used to the "winning is everything" philosophy of professional athletics were stirred by what they witnessed. Jim Murray, syndicated sportswriter for the *Los Angeles Times*, wrote of "a basketball game without a single personal foul" and of acts of selflessness he had seen on the track as many athletes preferred to help their friends who stumbled rather than go all out for their own victory.

In her opening remarks to the athletes, Eunice Shriver summed up the essence of what Special Olympics had become: "Special Olympics teaches us all that athletics is more than mere physical ability in running, jumping, swimming, and throwing a ball. Most animals can excel man in speed and stamina. Machines can lift greater weights or throw objects much further. In sports, the real

W O NEAL NORDLINGER

Rafer Johnson (in striped shirt), 1960 Olympic decathlon champion and now head coach of Special Olympics, added his name to the growing list of celebrities and professional sports figures who have lent their enthusiastic support to Special Olympics. Corinne Scruggs, of Florida (right), who at 70 was the oldest participant in the Fourth International Games, held in Mount Pleasant, Mich., in August 1975, took the bronze medal in the 25-yard wheelchair event.

value of the achievement lies in overcoming the odds against success. We are pleased when we read of a record being broken, but we are even more thrilled when some athlete has made a gallant attempt even when he fails. The athletes we remember most fondly are not the flawless mechanical performers but the great human beings who have reached beyond themselves to achieve some glorious goal. You, boys and girls, have proved to us all what the human spirit can do when it is encouraged and given the chance. You, as much as any athletes in history, prove what Baron de Coubertin said—that the Olympics brings together 'in radiant union all the qualities which guide mankind to perfection'." These words as well as a 19-minute segment of the 1972 International Games were broadcast nationally on ABC's Wide World of Sports, the first major telecast of the International Special Olympics Games and a significant breakthrough for all the mentally retarded.

It was decided then that in the future International Games would be held every four years, beginning in 1975. This would put the emphasis where it belongs—on local programming and year-round activities. Many states were holding winter Special Olympics for their athletes—with skating, skiing, sledding, and throwing events adapted to the abilities of the participants. Regional team tournaments in basketball, bowling, floor hockey, and volleyball were being held in their appropriate seasons. In 1974 the NHL again sponsored an International Floor Hockey tournament in Winnipeg, Man., in which all the league teams participated.

Wayne Embry, general manager of the Milwaukee Bucks, had long looked for professional sponsors for the Special Olympics basketball program. In 1975 his dream became a reality as Special Olympics basketball, with more than 110,000 participants, became perhaps the largest amateur basketball league in America. In 1975 two national programs were sponsored—an elimination basketball tournament, held in Washington, D.C., and a national run, dribble, and shoot contest, held in Louisville, Ky. What is remarkable about these programs is the fact that in sponsoring Special Olympics basketball the arch-rival American Basketball Association (ABA) and National Basketball Association (NBA) joined together for the first time. Cooperating on a regional basis, NBA and ABA teams supplied coaches, uniformed the regional winners, and donated trophies.

Fourth International Games

As 1975 progressed, interest and excitement in the Fourth International Games mounted throughout the world. The American Broadcasting Co. and Columbia Pictures teamed up to sponsor a benefit in Washington, D.C., featuring the world premiere of Barbra Streisand's 'Funny Lady', and Streisand herself performing, along with two Special Olympians, before a live audience that included U.S. President Gerald R. Ford. The Noncommissioned Officers Association of the U.S.A. put more than 3,100 of its members on the road, each running a mile across the entire U.S. to raise money for Special Olympics. Dozens of corporations and the sponsors of sports events donated funds so that no young athlete would be unable to attend. The three major television networks provided more than $1 million in television time during 1975 for Special Olympics spots.

When Central Michigan University was awarded the 1975 In-

THE BERGEN EVENING RECORD CORPORATION, HACKENSACK, NEW JERSEY

Recently designated as an official Special Olympics sport, ice skating is rapidly gaining popularity among Special Olympians, who had as their first skating coaches U.S. Olympic skating champions Diane Holum and Barbara Ann Scott King.

COURTESY. CENTRAL MICHIGAN UNIVERSITY

In keeping with the modest goals of the original games, the longest swimming event was the 25-yard freestyle race, with rest periods allowed. Today swimming events include a 50-yard freestyle, 100-yard relay, and 25-yard backstroke (above, left), breaststroke, and butterfly competition as well as one-meter diving. Displaying his technique on the balance beam, 14-year-old Michigan gymnast Michael Baker, born with one leg, exemplifies the determination of Special Olympians in his gold-medal performance at the 1975 Fourth International Games.

ternational Special Olympics, there was some question as to whether the Games could be held successfully in a small college community of 15,000 people. The answer came as the crowds began to gather in the stadium that August evening. There were 20,000 in the stands for opening ceremonies, more than the entire population of Mount Pleasant, and every event during the next few days was packed to capacity.

The university and the community combined in an unforgettable tribute to the Special Olympics athletes. If spectators came out of compassion, they stayed out of sheer delight. The Special Olympians put on individual and team performances worthy of the most polished athletes:

JAN PARSON

"When you watch these kids compete, there's no doubt on their faces—only the joy of competition."

—Rafer Johnson

There was Mike Baker of Michigan, retarded and born with only one leg, who thrilled the crowd with his gold-medal performance in tumbling.

There was the Team Canada *vs.* Team U.S.A. floor hockey game—as exciting a contest as any in the audience had seen. It was won by Team Canada, 1–0, but by the time of the final whistle, the score had become secondary, for the play—as it should be in sports—was truly the thing.

There was the International Games Mile won by Ronald Requilman in 5 minutes 10.4 seconds, an eminently respectable race in any league. The all-time Special Olympics record is an amazing 4 minutes, 42 seconds.

There was James Scott of Massachusetts, who has spent 33 of his 38 years in a state institution and set records in the two track events he entered.

And there were the hundreds of athletes who won no medals at all but who gloried in "the attempt."

As Marjorie Gray of California wrote to Eunice Shriver after the Games, "I think the International meet was fantastic. In the girls' relay we got a fourth. At first I thought it was unfair because two other girls from another school weren't very good. But then I realized how selfish I was because they tried their best. That's what the Special Olympics are for."

Now that Special Olympics is in its eighth year, the program is proud of its successes but well aware of its limitations. However, the enrollment of more than 400,000 mentally retarded youth represents only around 15% to 20% of those who meet the qualifications for participation—having an I.Q. of 75 or under or being two years or more behind their schoolmates in intellectual performance and in athletic ability. Goals for this Bicentennial year call for 500,000 Special Olympians, 200,000 volunteers, and programs in 20 countries. The foreign interest has been most gratifying, with new chapters scheduled for Australia, Nigeria, Hong Kong, the Bahamas, and several other countries.

As has been true since the beginning, the emphasis is not on a contest between the most skilled performers but on the opportunity for those of every range of skills to compete with their peers. While the experience of competition is important, there is a constant striving to reduce the emphasis on winning and to provide training so consistent that even the most handicapped and the least skilled are able to take part.

To evaluate the physical, mental, and social impact of Special Olympics on its participants, the Kennedy Foundation is sponsoring a major three-year research project that is being conducted by Texas Tech University. As Eunice Shriver said following the 1975 International Games, "We must not congratulate ourselves or boast that next year will be bigger and better. The numbers game is meaningless if it only signifies that we are giving more children a chance to run a 50-second race. The mentally retarded need much more than this, and Special Olympics will be successful only if it helps to transform the lives of the retarded and reshape the image others hold of them."

For
Special Olympians

the courage to try
is the
greatest victory of all

VALUE OF SPECIAL OLYMPICS/ TRANSFER EFFECTS

That physical education and recreation has a place in the total human growth and development of mentally retarded persons is fact. Special Olympics has provided a forum not only to assist the physical development of the mentally retarded person, but the psychological, social, behavioral and cognitive development as well. The mentally retarded, through positive experiences in recreation and physical education activities, gain confidence and self mastery and begin to build a self image associated with success. Each of the experiences may be transferred to situations during the daily life of the person. The success on the playing field has carry-over value into the home, the school and the community. There is strong evidence that physical training and athletic competition for retarded individuals not only enhances their physical, emotional and intellectual development, but, equally important, strengthens their confidence and self-esteem.

The mentally retarded, for many years, were protected and sheltered from many facets of our complex society, athletic competition being no exception. The Special Olympics has enabled mentally retarded individuals (including adults) to participate in a variety of experiences that heretofore they were excluded from. A concommitant value inherent in the Special Olympics concept is the improvement in physical education programs in the school and recreation programs in the community. In addition, many colleges and universities offer baccalaureate, master's and doctor's degrees in Therapeutic Recreation and Adapted Physical Education. This recent trend can be directly attributed to the popularity and demonstrated viability of the Sepcial Olympics.

Parents have indicated that participation in Special Olympic competition has provided their children with the following:

> (1) pride in competition, (2) improved socialization with peers, (3) improved attitudes toward school work, and (4) heightened interest in physical activities.

Mentally retarded people have significantly more leisure than their "normal" peers. This enforced leisure can become a problem for those who have not acquired the necessary attitudes, skills and knowledge to engage in activities during their leisure. Athletes who develop qualifications for good sports performance also develop their physical fitness, mental fitness, athletic skill, and sportsmanship.

Special Olympics has become a medium for public awareness and understanding in changing the image of mental retardation and in instilling an appreciation of the value of the mentally retarded as a contributing member of society. The value of the Special Olympics to those who work with the program has been expressed as most rewarding and enlightening.

Special Olympics Volunteers: 250,000

"Someone Elses"

by Colman McCarthy
Washington Post

AS with most other males who were conditioned early to believe that success in sports meant playing for big money in big arenas, I learned only slowly that that was false. My teachers in the lessons of true athletics have been some

mentally retarded youngsters, children who are part of the Special Olympics program.

More than any other movement in American sports in the past decade, Special Olympics has gone into communities, neighborhoods and families to

spread a spirit of playfulness that is, or should be, the essential vibrancy of sports.

If the poet Wallace Stevens is right, that "we are all hot with the imperfect," then what has been happening through the Special Olympics is unique: The mentally retarded are helping the intellectually retarded.

The latter are those of us whose minds build shelves for the handicapped and then stash them away like undusted bric-a-brac to be forgotten. Or those who hire zoning lawyers to defend the purity of the neighborhood when the retarded dare move into a half-way house. Or those who read the latest newspaper expose about the filthy conditions in the state home for the retarded

and murmur that "something should be done." By someone else.

One of the beauties of the Special Olympics is that it has attracted the someone elses in amazingly large numbers—the quarter of a million volunteers. Few national programs are receiving the unsalaried energies of more groups, from amateurs like the American Legion and the Road Runners Club of America to the National Basketball Association and the North American Soccer League.

As for those volunteers who do more for the retarded than any outsider can imagine—the fathers and mothers of the children—they report that Special Olympics can enhance family life in the

"Special Olympics Volunteers: 250,000 "Someone Elses," Original article by Colman McCarthy. Washington Post.

most uplifting of ways.

I have seen this in my own neighborhood, in Angela Mann, a 15-year-old who has Down's syndrome and who won two medals in the District of Columbia Special Olympics earlier this month. Her father, Dr. Jesse Mann, a professor of philosophy at Georgetown University and the only person I know who can discuss Heidegger while mowing his lawn, tells of Angela's new sense of her abilities. Now that she has seen herself excel in the 50-yard dash, she has become open to finding more occasions to excel.

Other families around the country report the same. Special Olympics, through its teaching clinics and the Let's Play to Grow Program, is helping parents gain knowledge and confidence in working with their retarded children.

Not every retarded child is in Special Olympics and not all parents are blessed with the spiritual strength to keep nurturing their child despite the seemingly slow progress. But in only a decade, Special Olympics has become a world-class example of what can be done if a few people put their minds — and their bodies — to it.

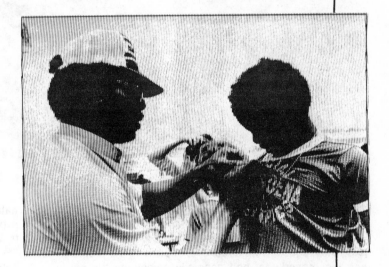

ROLAND REESE WORLDWIDE NEWS

Volunteering and the Handicapped

Throughout the White House Conference on Handicapped Individuals (WHCHI) in May 1977, volunteers were everywhere, registering and escorting people, carrying messages, giving directions, explaining the program and the procedures, and generally smoothing the way. The enthusiasm, energy, and expertise exhibited by these volunteers were graphic demonstrations of the valuable contributions volunteers, both able-bodied and disabled, can make to the handicapped movement.

A true American tradition, volunteering has doubled in this country since 1965 in response to the urgency of today's problems. Modern volunteers have improved skills and a deeper commitment, and are no longer relegated to merely mundane tasks of charity balls. Today's volunteer is an effective advocate, planner, evaluator, promoter, facilitator, and representative of human service programs.

Freedom from paid staff interests, professional status needs, or clinical perspectives gives volunteers a unique ability to cut through red tape and influence important people and decisions. Their fresh perspective and imagi-

nation can enrich program development. And since they represent a network of community connections to families, groups and organizations, volunteers are one of the most effective means of mobilizing public support for handicapped causes.

But despite the creation of a number of new advocacy groups for the handicapped and a variety of new programs for less common, previously unrepresented disabilities, organizations serving handicapped people have not taken full advantage of the volunteer potential. A 1971 study conducted by the Goodwill Auxiliary showed only 55 percent of community services had volunteers, and rehabilitation was not even mentioned as a field of volunteer activity in the 1974 ACTION/Census Bureau study of American Volunteering.

It was clear, however, that the many recommendations generated by the White House Conference will require accelerated citizen involvement, and participants emphasized that great opportunity exists to facilitate direct services and extend efforts in mainstreaming and advocacy through voluntary action.

Direct Services

Reflecting a practical concern for economics, WHCHI participants cited the cost effectiveness of volunteers. In this day of rising expectations and shrinking budgets, it was agreed that staff simply cannot do the job alone. Professionals, such as counselors, occupational therapists, physical therapists, recreation and social workers, to mention a few, can all extend the impact of their services by delegating less technical and oftentime consuming activities to volunteers.

Yet the laws for vocational rehabilitation programs have not encouraged nonprofessional citizens in direct service. To date, most direct service volunteers have been concentrated in working for the blind, and in recent years, serving the mentally ill and developmentally retarded. In these areas volunteers were used effectively and most frequently in recreation activities and in assisting staff members in duties related to counseling, testing, and education. Volunteers have also been effective in vocational skill training and in career exploration as role models.

The success of volunteers in these roles can serve as a model for a variety of other rehabilitative areas, and the variety of volunteer skills available is practically unlimited.

A study by Fancine Sobey for the National Institute of Mental Health identifies a taxonomy of volunteer functions to supplement staffing in mental health hospitals which reflects the changing role of today's volunteers. She breaks down the role of volunteers as follows:

- caretaking, such as feeding and escorting patients, not only in hospital settings but in the community and at the volunteer's own home. This reflects a shift from our traditional concern about volunteers getting too involved with clients to an active encouragement to get more involved. The caring and individualized attention offered by volunteers is a strong motivating force toward rehabilitation.

- social sustenance: personal, continuing relationships between friends or surrogate relationships such as a foster grandparent who encourages efforts toward self-help, independence, and competence.

- professional assistants who serve within a discipline as an extension of a professional time and effort by volunteers, such as a case aide under a caseworker, or a medical aide.

- bridging volunteers use and develop community resources and offer developmental experiences outside the institutions which give patients courage to enter the mainstream of community life. They represent the final link or connective tissue between the old service and new rehabilitative patterns of care. This prevents the client from being fragmented by the differences in the nature of the services he's getting.

Volunteer functions along these lines have been initiated or proposed in many private and some state vocational rehabilitation agencies. They include screening of applicants, diagnosis and evaluation, physical restoration, training, placement, counseling, supportive relationships for client and family, and environmental adjustment.

Volunteers have proven they can provide service at many levels of organization while also serving to bring the community into the rehabilitation process in a way that no other method has yet been able to do. But the effectiveness of volunteer participation is directly related to the effectiveness of volunteer management. Programs seeking to involve volunteers in their operations must give their volunteers good training, specific job descriptions, meaningful assignments, proper utilization of skills, support and recognition.

Mainstreaming

The most consistent recommendations of the White House Conference were for mainstreaming: providing equality of opportunity for handicapped persons, and eroding barriers to handicapped persons by raising the public consciousness.

For clients themselves, traditional volunteering can be an important step in the rehabilitation process. In the familiar setting of the home agency, and under the supervision of empathetic staff, the handicapped person can develop self-confidence and resume or begin work habits and skills.

Many handicapped people are currently volunteering their services in self-help groups or through team volunteering. People who have submitted to a great deal of service to correct a disabling condition or solve their own problems are in a unique position to help others similarly afflicted. They frequently serve as an inspiration to others and provide vital support through difficult times in the community, after a hospital stay, or in preventing institutionalization. There is nothing to match the special zeal of one who has "been through the fire."

In a team volunteering situation, each volunteer has an enabler role with the other. Although both may be somewhat limited, their skills and abilities are greatly enhanced in combination.

The insight the volunteer client has into the agency's service program can provide valuable feedback for the agency's decision-making authority and program design.

Handicapped persons also represent a valuable resource for traditional volunteer programs. Where they have been utilized, handicapped volunteers have proved to be reliable, often highly motivated workers in a wide range of programs and activities.

The first obvious place to improve the mainstreaming of volunteers is with the integration of handicapped youngsters into national membership groups such as the Girl and Boy Scouts, 4-H, and Y's. Relationships evolving in scout troops or recreation programs break down stereotypes about handicapped people and teach consideration of special needs. With access to the mainstream and early childhood education of the general populace, individual special education provisions will be less necessary and less attractive, since they are essentially divisive rather than integrative.

2. VALUE

Real mainstreaming will depend on educating and sensitizing the public to the special needs of each handicapped person. The need for more public support and education turned up in each work group at the White House Conference regardless of the disability or subject area. And in view of the vast link to the community volunteering can provide, it is obvious that voluntary organizations can play a much larger role in this process.

The concept of improving the quality of life for handicapped people is a powerful and very appealing one, and one that can be easily picked up as a theme for gaining more volunteer involvement. Most people would like to think of themselves as freeing someone from unnecessary restraints. With training and experience, volunteers—able or disabled—could be used increasingly in supportive roles such as in responding to public inquiries and on information hotlines, public speaking, distributing literature, updating libraries, validating current information, and in a number of related activities.

Voluntary groups can also play an influential role in reducing media overdramatization of handicaps by becoming more involved in programing and by making media advertisers aware that improving program content, or demythologizing, would improve their own images as sponsors. Public broadcasting is likely to be even more responsive since volunteers determine their policies.

Preventive themes, such as immunizations, nutrition, hygiene, parenting courses, marriage and child guidance counseling, could all be transmitted through voluntary membership organizations, and some have. Local women's clubs, PTAs, and United Cerebral Palsy chapters have all successfully initiated immunization programs through their national headquarters. UCP dramatically lowered the incidence of cerebral palsy through public education programs encouraging prenatal care and counseling. And the American Lung Association transformed former envelope stuffers into public health educators and activists against smoking.

Advocacy

"The possibilities for strengthening programs by volunteer advocacy are growing out of experience in community action programs and governmental services as well as more traditional voluntary agencies," says Harriet Naylor, Director of HEW's Office of Volunteer Development. "Acting as advocates, volunteers serve clients directly, help people find appropriate services, or mobilize resources in their behalf."

Volunteer advocacy spans the entire spectrum of services to the handicapped or promotion of their rights. A volunteer advocate, or ombudsman, may be one who attends to a handicapped individual through the various phases of rehabilitation, or refers and transports the handicapped individual to community resources, or pleads the cause of a handicapped individual or group of handicapped people, to decision-makers and program-planners, or one of a new breed of program or legislative "watchdogs" or lobbyists who ensure continuous attention to the problems of the disabled. It may also be someone who sits on a policy review board or on the board of directors of a foundation or corporation. The one thing all have in common is a true concern and commitment to improving services and rights of handicapped people.

The advocacy role that has gained the most attention in recent years is the demand by handicapped consumers to have a greater voice in the decision-making processes which affect both private and government programs and services for handicapped people. And, taking their cue from the Civil Rights Movement of the 1960's, handicapped consumers, with a significant assist from volunteer advocates, demanded that their government and institutions acknowledge and guarantee their rights to the same expectations and freedoms as any other American citizen.

Beginning with increased activity by specific disability groups to gain better services and greater protection of their rights, consumer groups started to band together in a coalition to mutually press their demands. As a result, local anti-discrimination legislation was enacted in several areas, and a movement was started in other localities for similar legislative initiatives.

As this voluntary advocacy movement became a national crusade, handicapped consumers and their many supporters mounted mass demonstrations and effective lobbying campaigns which eventually contributed to the passage of landmark legislation: the Rehabilitation Act of 1973 (P.L. 93–112), the Developmental Disabilities Services and Facilities Construction Act of 1970 (P.L. 91–517 and P.L. 94–103), and the Education for All Handicapped Children Act of 1975 (P.L. 94–142). The concerted voluntary action of consumer groups also led to the signing of the Section 504 Regulations for the Rehabilitation Act in 1977.

The new legislation not only guaranteed the rights of handicapped people and required their involvement in policy development, it recognized advocacy as a legitimate function of both government and social systems, and gave impetus to the advocacy movement by providing funds for the White House Conference on Handicapped Individuals, which for the first time, provided handicapped people a real voice in determining national policy. The more than 100,000 participants in the local, state, and national conferences were witness to the effectiveness of grassroots voluntary advocacy.

CONVICT VOLUNTEERS

David Dewey, M.A., R.R.T.

Mr. Dewey is Director of Leisure Time Activities, Muskegon Correctional Facility, Muskegon, Michigan.

Isolated from the community, and often forgotten by society, a group of Michigan convicts and about 25 mentally retarded children are giving each other a sense of worth and a measure of trust.

The children, all residents of the Muskegon Developmental Center, are being taught basic physical skills by a group of 15 volunteer prisoners from the Muskegon Correctional Facility, in a special therapeutic recreation program sponsored jointly by both institutions.

The prisoners, under the guidance of recreational therapists, helped the children from February to May, 1975, prepare for a very special event in their lives—the Special Olympics.

The Special Olympics is a program sponsored by the Kennedy Foundation, designed to allow mentally deterred individuals to participate in various olympic games. The games range from bowling and swimming to track and field events, and are held in the Spring of every year.

The Muskegon Correctional Facility is the newest prison operated by the Michigan Department of Corrections. The Facility houses residents who are felony offenders and are not considered severe risks to the community, nor are they likely to try to escape. As residents near their release dates, they are eligible for minimum security status which allows them to venture into the community for various recreation programs. It is from this group of residents that the first Developmental Center volunteers were selected.

The Correctional Facility is unique in that it resembles a college campus nestled in the woods, rather than a prison, and program emphasis is placed on education and community involvement, with residents venturing into the community on a daily basis to attend the Muskegon Community College and South County Vocational Training Center. In addition, the majority of the leisure time activities are carried out in such places as local high school gymnasiums, various City of Muskegon parks, the campus of the Muskegon Community College, and the Muskegon Developmental Center.

Residents of the Facility come from all over the State of Michigan, however, the majority are from the Detroit Metropolitan area. The men range in age from 17 to 30 years and are serving sentences varying from 1 to 15 years, for various felony offenses. Currently, the average age is 24.

Traditionally, corrections clients have been programmed in such a way that social involvement in the community has been restricted to work and education programs. The Michigan Department of Corrections recognizes the need for social growth experiences

"Convict Volunteers," David Dewey, *Therapeutic Recreation Journal,* Vol. X No. 3, Third Quarter 1976. Therapeutic Recreation Journal.

2. VALUE

and is attempting, through experimental programming at the Muskegon Facility, to create and demonstrate the feasibility of such programs.

The Muskegon Developmental Center is a 420-bed residential Facility for mentally impaired. The Center serves an eight-county area of Western Michigan and houses children with severe to moderate mental impairments. The fundamental obligation of the Center is to protect and nurture the dignity, health, learning opportunities, and development of these residents. One of the active programs at the Center is involvement in the Special Olympics program.

The Muskegon Developmental Center had a need for volunteers to assist the recreational staff in teaching basic skills to its clients in preparation for involvement in the Special Olympics program. Gross motor movements, such as running, jumping, and throwing, received emphasis in the training program.

With the assistance of Mr. William Reid, Activities Director at the Developmental Center, a program was established in which residents of the Muskegon Correctional Facility would assist, on a volunteer basis, in meeting this need.

The program was implemented in January of 1975 by conducting an open meeting at the Correctional Facility, featuring an inspirational movie, "Born to Win." Following the film, Mr. Reid explained the Special Olympics program in detail as it related to the clients of the Developmental Center, and the role the volunteers of the Correctional Facility could play in assisting and helping Developmental Center clients.

The initial response from the Correctional Facility residents was gratifying with over 60 men, or 25% of the total population, indicating they were interested in becoming involved in such a program. The initial screening process was begun to select the 15 men who would make up the first group of Muskegon Correctional Center volunteers.

Some of the men who volunteered for the program could not participate because they lacked the necessary clearance which would allow them to participate in off-grounds activities. Others were ineligible because the program conflicted with their academic or vo-

cational programming. Of the 60 men who originally applied, 36 had the necessary security classifications and were eligible for further screening. Of these, 15 who were serving sentences for non-violent type crimes and who had less than three years of their sentences yet to serve, were selected.

Following an orientation program, the big night finally arrived. Fifteen convicts met approximately 25 retarded children! The first meeting was one of excitement and apprehension for both groups. The Developmental Center clients were told only that a group of volunteers was to begin working with them, to help them prepare for the Special Olympics. The Correctional Facility volunteers, although being well-oriented, knew very little about actually working with mentally impaired children. To assist in developing relationships between the two groups, the staff organized a game of tug-of-war, and several other group games. After a short period of time both groups began to feel more comfortable with one another and the real work of training for the Special Olympics began.

Initially the program was conducted in a gymnasium; however, as the weather began to improve, the group went outside for further training sessions with emphasis on running and throwing skills. The first few minutes of the training sessions began with vigorous calisthenics led by staff of both institutions, or by the volunteers themselves. During the drills, volunteers participated with the group or assisted Developmental Center clients on an individual basis. Often one of the volunteers would take a client aside and assist him in developing specific techniques such as the proper way to do a jumping-jack, or push-up.

After the warm-up period, the group divided into four learning stations, each station working on developing a specific Special Olympic skill. Each of these stations was led by four or five volunteers working individually with the children in areas such as the soft ball toss or standing broad jump. In addition to teaching form and technique in the activity, the volunteers also spent time helping the children to read tape measures, stop watches, elementary signs, to count, and to develop basic survival skills. At 15-minute intervals each group of clients rotated to a different work station. When all of the clients finished all four work stations, the groups were further divided. Each volunteer selected one or two clients and worked with them individually. This individual help was within the area of Special Olympic training, or another area in which the client needed improvement.

Over-all supervision of the program is provided jointly by recreational therapists from the Muskegon Correctional Facility and the Muskegon Developmental Center. During the program, staff offers suggestions to volunteers as to how to best handle individual clients and various methods of presenting techniques so they can be better understood by the clients. At the end of each session, the volunteers are critiqued by supervisory staff as to their performance.

The Special Olympics is not all work. Often groups replaced a practice session with a game of soccer, kick ball, or other group activities. The group also participated in picnics, swimming, fishing, and hot dog roasts at local parks.

In May of 1975, the big day for the District Special Olympics program finally arrived, to find the volunteers still assisting by serving the noon meal to over 300 Special Olympic participants. The volunteers also had the opportunity to observe the clients with whom they had been working throughout the year compete in the Special Olympics games held at Orchard View High School, in Muskegon, Michigan. The meeting immediately following the District Special Olympics was one of pride for both groups. The Developmental Center clients knew that they had done their best and the Correctional Facility volunteers knew that they had helped bring pride and a

feeling of self-worth and accomplishment to other human beings.

The volunteer enthusiasm about the program can be seen in statements such as "the Program gives me a feeling of doing something really worthwhile. It sort of makes me appreciate being healthy and wanting to help that much more." "When you notice progress in a kid you're working with, it makes you feel kind of proud that you contributed to it."

The staff at the Developmental Center has indicated that the clients have found the program very rewarding. "The kids really look forward to you fellows coming down on Thursday nights."

The children themselves demonstrate their enthusiasm as can be seen by the happy smiles, handshakes, and much commotion when the volunteer bus arrives at the Developmental Center.

During the summer of 1975, the Special Olympics Program was not in operation as the Developmental Center clients were attending summer camp. The program was reestablished in the Fall of 1975, and all are again preparing for the 1976 Spring games. Because of the success of the volunteer program, involvement at the Muskegon Developmental Center has been expanded. A request was received from the Adult Basic Education Program at the Center for volunteers to assist in tutoring students at the Center. In January of 1976, two volunteers from the original group of volunteers began working as tutors with the educational staff. It is anticipated that this education program will soon accommodate up to 10 volunteers, thus bringing the total number of Muskegon Correctional Facility volunteers at the Developmental Center to approximately 25.

A PLAY CENTER FOR DEVELOPMENTALLY HANDICAPPED INFANTS

FLORENCE DIAMOND

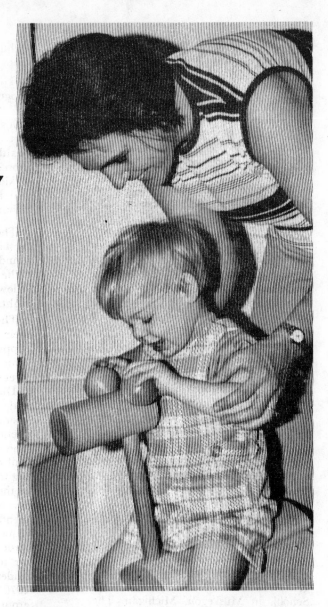

The time to intervene in developmental retardation is in infancy. Of this there is no longer any question. But how? One way has been initiated at Villa Esperanza, a nonprofit voluntary school in Pasadena, Calif. Here a tiny cottage—known as the Edward Levy Infant Center (Elic) in honor of a much loved "granduncle" volunteer—has been converted into a playschool for developmentally handicapped infants from 3 months to 2½ years of age.

The Elic program, now in its fourth year, is making converts of pediatricians who at first were skeptical. The goals of the Elic program are (1) to make possible a full and meaningful life for developmentally retarded children and (2) to help establish as early as possible normal living patterns for both the children and their parents.

Infants are considered developmentally retarded when they are functioning sufficiently below age expectations to cause professional concern about their delayed emotional, social, or cognitive progress. Major causes of retardation among our infants are birth injury, encephalitis, infantile autism, blindness, deprivation, and congenital factors such as rubella and Down's syndrome.

The retarded infant is twice disadvantaged. First, although he needs more assistance in progressing through the stages of development than the non-handicapped infant, he receives less and that less too late. Second, like all babies, his emotional health depends upon the good emotional health of his parents, but because he is a handicapped child, his parents suffer fear, anguish, bewilderment, and too often shame. Parents who have just realized that they have a handicapped child need emotional support not only from their families (and too often that is denied them) but also from the community.

In 1968 as chairman of Villa Esperanza's education committee, I undertook the task of developing an infant program that would serve the developmentally retarded. Perhaps because of my long association with nursery schools, I was propelled toward designing an ideal nursery school with a curriculum appropriate for children in the creeping and crawling stages. There was no model for us to follow. There was only the conviction on the part of the staff and Villa's director, Elene Chaffee, that we would find a way.

We started with five fundamental principles:

1. All infants, handicapped and nonhandicapped, are more alike than different.

2. The retarded are not equally handicapped in all areas of their development. They may even be advanced in some areas.

3. Each individual, whether parent, baby, or other, has a life that is to be respected. The preciousness of life is not to be measured in IQ points.

4. While all children are more alike than different, each is also different with his own patterns of development, satisfactions, and needs.

5. Teachers and parents must avoid the twin evils of overstimulation and inaction.

A successful infant program can take many forms. We like the one we are evolving. Elic is an infant play-school where planned programs are thoroughly mixed with love and laughter.

The setting

Our cottage has two adjoining playrooms, an observation room, a diaper and potty room, and a minuscule reception room. In deciding that babies do not need cribs, playpens, or much other furniture, we have taken a lesson from the Japanese. We and the babies live on the floor.

All adults doff their shoes upon entering the building. Instead of tatami on the floors, we have put in heavily padded wall-to-wall golden yellow carpeting throughout the building, except in the second playroom. Here we have vinyl—better for wheeltoys, wiping up food spills, and of course, for early toddling.

We opened with six babies—all we want at one time in our small cottage. My feelings on that first day (as I drove to the infant center) were a mixture of hope and anxiety. It was raining heavily, and I wondered if the parents would even come out. They did. They tenderly placed their little ones on our carpeted floor and stood back. We turned on soft music. The babies looked one another over, and the miracle happened. They smiled. We knew that Elic, the infant play-school, was born. Since then we have served 42 families.

In all of these cases we have been able to make a significant contribution. However, there is also an element of failure in about 10 percent of them. For example, there is the mother who never gave up her search for a complete magical cure of her son, severely handicapped by congenital rubella. Another "martyred" mother abruptly withdrew her neurologically handicapped daughter at the first dramatic signs of emotional improvement.

With a few exceptions, the parents have expressed great enthusiasm for the program. We have not rejected any applicants because of inability to meet our fees, thanks to our liberal scholarship program.

At first the children came three times a week from 9 to 11:30 a.m. But it is very hard to turn away babies and parents in need of help. So, in order to expand our services, we are now open 5 days a week. This schedule provides a total of 30 child-days each week for our infants. By assigning the 30 child-days in a variety of individual schedules, we attempt to get optimal grouping of infants according to their needs and interactions.

Agency cooperation

New parents learn of Elic through the Child Development Clinic, the Department of Public Social Services, the Regional Center for the Mentally Handicapped, Field Service for the Blind, our own parents, and increasingly from pediatricians who have seen the benefits to infants and parents.

The majority of the infants are evaluated by the Child Development Clinic in Pasadena, either before or immediately after they enter Elic. Others have been diagnosed at Children's Hospital of Los Angeles, USC Medical Center, the Neuropsychiatric Institute of UCLA, or by their own pediatricians. We participate in these evaluations and also make our own diagnostic studies.

We see to it that every child has the benefit of available services of agencies in the city and county. Our school nurse and our social worker help parents follow through on all recommendations. Excellent working relationships exist between our staff and the staffs of the agencies. For example, when physiotherapy is provided by the Crippled Children's Services, the head teacher is invited to observe the methods so that she can incorporate them into the child's program; when fieldworkers from other agencies want to get a fuller understanding of children they are also serving, they come to Elic.

The teaching staff consists of a head teacher, an assistant teacher, and a speech consultant who spends an hour each morning with the infants. In addition, the school nurse visits the cottage daily and the social worker and I are often present. Thus we are prepared to move swiftly to protect the infants if it should be necessary to evacuate the building or call upon an extra adult for a special service.

An infant teacher needs to be a warm, imaginative,

Every child needs to love and be loved . . . to achieve . . . to play and be played with

stable, tranquil person with a zest for life. We are fortunate in our staff. Elic's head teacher is a well trained and experienced nursery school teacher with a solid foundation in infant and child development. Her assistant is enrolled in career training.

Curriculum

The child's needs determine the curriculum. We start from the premise that every child has the need to love and be loved; to transmit and receive communications, to build, to explore, to achieve, and to play and be played with. Parents and teachers of nonhandicapped children usually have little difficulty in recognizing these needs. They have only to listen and watch.

But often the handicapped child cannot give the appropriate signals. Further, there tends to be an imbalance among his abilities.

For example, Harold reads facial expressions remarkably well. He is fascinated by pictures and shapes, but his legs are weak and he is limited in his explorations. He is also lagging behind his age group in his ability to communicate. These conditions are very frustrating to him.

If we and his parents followed the public school system of waiting until he was 6 or even 8 years old before providing him with learning experiences, the satisfactions he now has in fitting shapes and forms together, reading picture books, and building with blocks would have been denied him. He would have had no experiences of success, no joy in achievement. He would be withdrawn and apathetic. His abilities would have atrophied from lack of use.

It is our task to see that we do not allow our children to be reduced to the level of their most retarded function, but to help them to achieve in each area of their development whatever level they are comfortably able to reach. It is just as important that we do not force Harold to walk upon legs that are not ready, thereby subjecting him to unfortunate experiences of failure and frustration, as it is that we give him opportunities to enjoy the triumphs of building towers and bridges.

Handicaps are not necessarily physical. We have one baby, now in a foster home, whom we diagnosed as suffering from hospitalism. We are teaching this child to smile. We discovered that he likes sudden strong motion. We cuddle him, jiggle him, toss him in the air, and he crows. He is making progress. Now his formerly stiff body curves into the contour

of his teacher's. His cheeks are getting rosy, his eyes less empty, hair is growing on the back of his head, and the bed sores are disappearing.

Our first blind child came to Elic when he was 1 year old. We wondered, as he started to walk, if all the toys had to be removed from the floor so that he would not fall. Would all the furniture have to remain in exactly the same spot so that he could navigate better? We tried to clear his path, but somehow other babies were always getting in the way and somehow toys were strewn across the floor. We knew that our floor was cushioned and that nothing had sharp corners, so we relaxed and watched. He learned to walk, learned to avoid hazards and was very proud of himself. Visitors watching him move around could not believe that he was totally blind. When he came to us, he was retarded beyond the expected level of a blind child—content to sit and do nothing. Now he is no longer retarded.

Play is essential

As I have already mentioned, we incorporate into each child's program techniques and methods proposed by physiotherapists. We also use planned programing on occasion. But we include such techniques as part of fun time, for we belive that play is essential to a young child. Play is the way a kitten, a puppy, a baby chimp, or a human baby gains mastery and avoids anxiety. Anxiety comes with pressure and standards to be met. Whether or not pressured learning has a value for the child of school age may be debated by others. For the infant and toddler, it is assuredly detrimental.

We devote much of our program to developing speech. Our speech therapist reinforces speech patterns; stimulates, sings to, and rocks the babies; plays games with them and delights them by whispering secrets into their ears. Sometimes she lies flat on her stomach in front of a long horizontal mirror and talks to them through the mirror. They watch her lips and try to imitate her. It was a great day when Harold stopped babbling and started to use jargon. We knew that soon he would be talking.

Serendipity has played a big role in our selection of toys and equipment. The mirror hung on the wall near the floor is an example. It was installed for the usual reasons: to promote individuation and to assist in the teaching of speech. The mirror delights the children. They pat themselves and kiss themselves

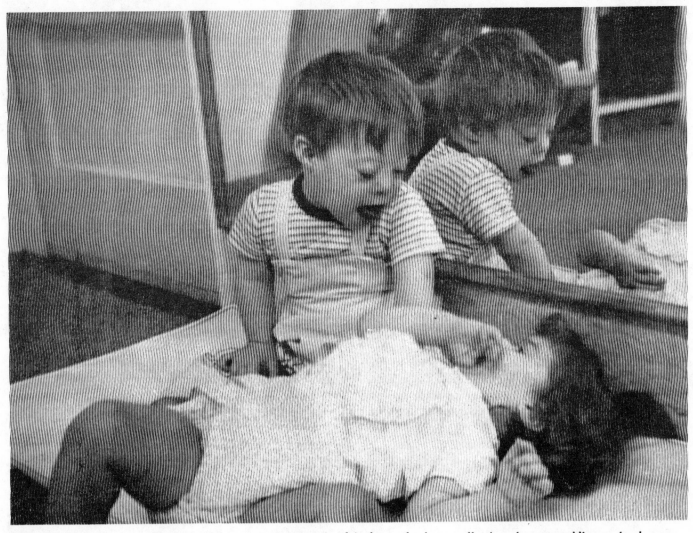

These developmentally handicapped infants are getting acquainted in front of a large wall mirror hung at toddler-eye level.

on it while they learn about themselves. The mirror has also proven to be a valuable method of communicating with disturbed children. A new face may be threatening to any young infant; eye contact may be even more threatening, especially to an autistic child.

The mirror allows the child to gain visual distance from the teacher while she has the advantage of still being in close physical contact with him.

We consider the rocking chair a "must" in our activities. We have also found beach and swimming pool items useful. Our babies have fun exercising on a partially inflated balloon, about 2 feet in diameter.

Tumble tubs, intended for swimming pools, work very well on a soft carpet—provided with a pillow, they serve as cradles in which an infant may be rocked. They are also round-bottom boats in which four may sit and socialize as they play rub-a-dub-dub.

Or, as Larry, a 2-year-old microcephalic, has shown us, they can be a most challenging saucer in which

an acrobat can stand and successfully maintain balance.

Rocking horses, kiddie cars, a set of shallow steps, a gentle slide, a sturdy walker, feeding tables, and cube-table-chairs are among the larger items we use. A good record player and a drum are other musts, because music and rhythm are meaningful to infants and toddlers. Then there are the many small items for the infants to feel, manipulate, mouth, rattle, ring, and build with. We select simple picture books. Toys are on open shelves, accessible to the infants.

We have a relaxed attitude about toilet training and we also help parents take a casual attitude. Modern disposable diapers and plastic bags have simplified the problems of sanitation and changes. When the child can sit with ease and can toddle, we introduce him to the potty chair, but we make no issue of it. We measure the success of this approach by what happens when the toddler graduates from the infant center and enters the nursery group. There he learns toilet training quickly and proudly.

2. VALUE

Parents

We are as much concerned about the parents as about their infants. What do parents need? They need to know that they are important as people—not because they are Harold's or Tillie's parents. They need to be able to let their children go forth. They need to know that they are not their child's only resource, that others care and are willing to help. They need to lead normal lives.

In the beginning we planned a didactic program, with scheduled parent participation, parent observations, and group meetings centered about the infant's needs or the parents' own feelings. As we watched the parents and gained greater security in our philosophy—the need to lead normal lives—we have developed a different, less structured approach to the program for parents. We do hold scheduled evening meetings, however, so that fathers can attend.

When an infant first enters the center, we ask the mother to stay with her child. She gradually moves from the playroom to the observation room with its one-way-vision mirror. When the infant feels secure in the center, the mother is free to leave his world for the morning. She may get her hair set, take a class (parents help one another arrange time), or play hookey in any way she likes. Of course, she may observe her infant whenever she wishes.

Friendships develop among parents. From concern about their own infants, they share concerns with other parents, and they delight in the progress of all the children.

The staff members are the catalysts for, not the organizers of, parent involvement. When the parents have special problems, the staff is always willing to find time for an informal conference. Often a mother will discuss a problem with me when I am in the observation room. Sometimes the informal conference will last only 5 minutes, sometimes an hour. If we realize that a parent is troubled, we initiate a discussion.

At Elic we serve as a resource by providing a learning situation. But we do not teach. When freed of anxieties, most parents do a good job in helping their handicapped child develop. Our greatest satisfaction is watching the lines of anxiety disappear from parents' faces, and the tight muscles in their necks and shoulders relax.

Soon, we hope, there will be other play centers for developmentally handicapped infants in Southern California. Consultants from three schools have been studying our program with the intention of establishing similar programs.

THERAPEUTIC PLAY FACILITIES FOR HANDICAPPED CHILDREN

Gene A. Hayes

Introduction

Play next to love, is the most important aspect in the formative stages of the child. Play is a serious and essential occupation, and to say that a child is only playing is to misunderstand the therapeutic and developmental elements in human growth. An infant who has not played enough will suffer from a deficiency disease just as surely as one who lacks enough milk to drink.

Normal children learn about the world through play. They begin by exploring the feel, taste and smell of different objects and gradually they being to use toys to represent real things. Play is generally assumed to be important to an infant's cognitive development.

Piaget (6, p. 173) believes that play permits the child to substitute an intellectual response through fantasy when he cannot make the response in reality. This allows the child to experiment with ways of coping with the world without risking defeat or jeopardizing his feelings of independence. He also believes that play helps a child to organize and retain information he has acquired in other situations.

According to Asher B. Etkes (3, p. 2) learning through play is one of life's most beneficial experiences for children, normal or handicapped. It inspires feelings of self reliance which strengthens the child for the part he will play one day in the real world. Only when the child can initiate games and follow his play visions to a satisfying conclusion will he begin to acquire spontaneity.

The function of play in childhood has been essentially misunderstood in the past. Surprising numbers of people still maintain that the primary function of play is to "let off steam" so that the child can return to the more important business of study and learning. Countless studies of how intelligence develops in children show that precisely the reverse is true - that play is the way in which children develop intelligence. To put it simply, play is a child's way of learning. (2, p. 23)

For many years children's play was thought to be little more than an expression of excess energy and good spirits, an activity that adults should indulge so that children would be better able to do serious work at home and at school. Their activities were not considered important, except as they impinged on the adult world; children, the saying went, should be seen and not heard. (2, p. 17)

"Therapeutic Play Facilities for Handicapped Children," Gene A. Hayes, *Program Development in Recreation Service for the Deaf-Blind*, John A. Nesbitt and Gordon K. Howard, 1974. College of Liberal Arts, University of Iowa.

2. VALUE

The Traditional Play Facility

A most common justification given for the existence of play
equipment like swings and slides is that they have always been used
and they are popular items. This traditional rationale has generally
been based, as Gramza (4, p. 1) points out, on a system of "hunch,
intuition and scattered field observations."

Another fault of the typical playground is its total lack of
anything to inspire the interest, curiosity or creativity of children. After a little swinging, sliding and seesawing, the ready-made
opportunities for play are exhausted and more likely than not so is
the child's patience. (2, p. 37) According to Dattner (2, p. 37) even
a poorly designed playground is a learning experience for children,
and what they learn becomes a part of the way they see the world a-
round them and the persons who inhabit this world.

Anyone who has watched children in a variety of situations knows
that they have a remarkable ability to initiate play around most any
object, even those not normally considered as play objects.

Dattner (2, p. 33), in his book Design For Play says

> These little clients are, obviously, the most intimately
> affected by every aspect of the design - it is their in-
> terest, excitement, and curiosity that must be sustained
> and their personal safety that must be considered. But
> although they are the most deeply affected group of users,
> they are presently the least able to influence the design
> of their environment. Not only are children seldom con-
> sulted about these matters, but their needs are often
> completely forgotten when facilities are being designed.
> The important decisions are made by another group at the
> other end of our spectrum of users. It is as if children
> were supplied with shoes with absolute disregard for the
> size of their feet -- the size of the shoes having been
> determined by persons who would never have to wear them
> on the basis of what sizes were available.

Since it is known that play is actually a child's way of learning
about himself, others and his environment, planners and administrators
should not think in terms of athletic facilities when they think of
playgrounds. The play facility possesses important learning potential
and should be given as much consideration and priority as the school
or academic facility.

The Therapeutic Play Facility

Handicapped children possess more similarities than dis-similari-
ties to their non-handicapped peers. This is especially true in the
realm of play. This does not imply that the handicapped or disabled
youngster will not encounter difficulties or obstacles in his attempt

to utilize a play facility. The handicapped may encounter various difficulties in perception, motion, etc., as well as architectural barriers, depending upon the nature of their disability. Many children are so severely limited as a result of their handicaps that most ordinary activities and experiences are not available to them within the typical play facility. However, the fact remains that to the extent of their individual abilities their patterns of play follow that of normal children. The expected outcome is the same for the handicapped as for the non-handicapped: individual growth and understanding of themselves and their environment and the potential for enjoyment and expression.

Richard Dattner (2, p. 109) "indicates that children with special problems need specially designed playground, but -- it cannot be repeated too often -- their essential requirements are the same as those of normal children. The environment in which they play must repond to that part of them which is healthy and capable, with help, of growth and development." As the children play, success should be built upon success resulting in greater confidence and self-esteem. The child should be helped to grow in pride, understanding, skill and learning which will better prepare him for adult life.

The Playground Corporation of America (5, p. 2) has found "that standard playground equipment like swings, slides, whirls and seesaws fail to provide the type of play mobility needed by the handicapped child. Not only is the child inhibited by the nature of conventional equipment in the formulation of creative play schemes, but their repetitious pendulum and cycling movements tend to be lulling and hypnotic." The type of activity fostered by the traditional apparatus mentioned above is regressive in nature and would be good if the objective is to enhance passivity and deny progressive development in the areas of motor, sensory and cognitive development and creativity. In addition to the regressive nature of the apparatus there is generally no coordinated or related pattern of placement of the objects within the play facility to allow a progression of graduated movement of the child from one area to another and from one piece of equipment to another, hence, the child is easily confused which may lead to failure and withdrawal.

Elements of a Therapeutic Play Facility

To be considered therapeutic a recreation or play facility should possess the following elements as discussed by Dattner (2, p. 47)

> A playground therefore should present a series of challenges, ranging from simple things that toddlers can master to ones that challenge older and more experienced children. There should be continuity, so that each always has the dual experience of having mastered some aspect of his environment while knowing that there are other aspects that he may still aspire to master.

2. VALUE

In addition to the above mentioned considerations the play facility should provide as many of the real world experiences as possible for the participants. There should be potential experiences to enhance all of the senses and abilities. The sense of touch can be exercised by the appropriate use of various objects and surfaces, i.e. rough-smooth, light-heavy, soft-hard, wet-dry. Other senses and abilities such as smell, sight and sensory-motor and perceptual abilities can be stimulated in similar fashion. The environment can be altered to include a greater or lesser variety of potential experiences depending upon the needs of the children.

The growing awareness that objects have many properties -- that they can be classified in a variety of ways -- is a product of the child's activity with them. Through manipulation (touching, lifting, holding, arranging, sorting, etc.) the child begins to take note of similarities among the objects that are alike in some respects and different in others. (1, p. 356) Piaget (1, p. 362) sees the origins of conceptual thinking in these activities. Also, this construction of logical thinking, according to Piaget (1, p. 363), depends not only on the child's activity with natural things, but also his social interaction with other children. Children must then be provided an appropriate social atmosphere in which to experience strong and sound relationships.

There are two other very important considerations that must prevail for a play facility to provide therapeutic value. First, the objects within the play facility must be visually attractive and possess a continuum of intellectual challenges enough to provide its own motivation. Second, a child should receive sufficient reward and reinforcement through participating within the confines of the play facility to make external reward superfluous.

A word of caution must be mentioned before a therapeutic play facility is designed for handicapped children. Consultation should be held with medical staff and/or those who work with the children to assist in determing what activities would be most therapeutic and which might constitute potential danger. Doctors, nurses, physical, recreation and occupational therapist and special education teachers can furnish specific information relative to the children with whom they work that will aide in designing an appropriate therapeutic play or recreation facility.

Children Who Need A Therapeutic Play Facility

Centuries ago Michel de Montaigne said, "The games of children... are their most serious business." We know that play is the serious business of children. We know that the handicapped child, like other children, needs the opportunities for healthy growth promoting play. Children learn through play, yet little attention has been given this fact of childhood as a means of aiding the handicapped to develop. The child's vital need for successful social interaction and recreational experiences is frequently intensified by isolation resulting from parental over-protection, the numerous failure experiences and by his exclusion by normal groups of children from their everyday play, group and social activities.

In discussing playgrounds for exceptional children Dattner (2, p. 51) says

> For a trained person a well designed playground can be an efficient tool for helping children with special problems. Play can be used both to diagnose a child's difficulties and to help him with them. We can hardly expect most playgrounds to have either the facilities or the expert staff necessary to evaluate how a child reflects his unconscious feelings, but these are very important considerations in designing playgrounds for children with exceptional problems, whether emotional, physical or mental (or as is really the case, a combination of all of these).

It must be remembered that physical, emotional or mental problems seldom exist in isolation - often times there is overlapping. For instance, a physically handicapped child may well have some accompanying emotional difficulties; and a mentally retarded child may also suffer some impaired perceptual or motor ability or a degree of physical disability. The majority of handicapped children, especially those who are institutionalized, are confronted with more than one disabling problem. It is difficult, if not impossible, to isolate these problems and to treat them separately; the child as a total being must be considered and all problems worked with simultaneously.

A most important fact that must be kept in mind is that the child usually possesses some strengths or abilities. These abilities must be reinforced and developed. It is ability and not disability that counts and the major efforts whould be directed toward encouraging these qualities.

Classification of Handicapped Children

Broadly speaking the children who need the experience that can be attained through involvement in a therapeutic play or recreation facility can be classified into three groups: emotionally disturbed, physically handicapped and mentally retarded. There are literally hundreds of thousands of children of all ages who, because of some emotional, physical or mental impairment, are isolated form the mainstream of society; who are confined to public and private treatment, training or custodial facilities or institutions; who attend special schools for "exception" children; who attend special classes for "exceptional" children within the public shcool systems; who are confined to their homes under the watchful eyes of either over-protective parents or extremely guilt ridden parents who do not want society to know that "their" child is "crazy," "an Idiot" or "deformed." There are also many children who are functioning on a high borderline level

2. VALUE

or who, as of yet, have not been identified as having an emotional, behavioral, mental or physical problem for which they may need special consideration. All of these children need to become involved in the appropriate and adequate experiences that can be gained through formal and informal, structured and spontaneous involvement and interaction programmed through a therapeutic play facility.

It may be of some help to very briefly define some of the types of illnesses or disabilities many children suffer and for whom special consideration may need to be given in the development of a therapeutic play facility.

I. Emotionally Disturbed Children

The emotionally disturbed or emotionally unstable is a nonspecific descriptive term which is sometimes used to describe a group of disorders which are more serious than transient situational disturbances and less serious than psychoses, neuroses and personality disorders. Emotional instability may be a feature of any type of personality, including the relatively normal.

One difference between the emotionally disturbed child and the physically handicapped (as well as some retarded) is that these children have full use of their bodies, with few exceptions. Their greatest problems are in the areas of judgment and perception. They may misjudge their abilities and limitations and mistake wishes and fantasies for reality; they may have a distorted image of time, space and their own bodies. Since these children most often seem to exaggerate reality the objects within the play facility and the types of activities generated should be reality oriented and extremes of all kinds be avoided as much as possible. For the emotionally disturbed child Dattner (2, p. 115) says, "Like all children, the emotionally disturbed need play facilities where they can learn about the physical world and themselves safely by means of graduated challenges and the opportunities to master new experiences. However, it is particularly important that the environment be reassuring and unambiguous." It can be safely assumed that any piece of equipment or object that presents a problem to a normal child this problem will be greatly enlarged to the emotionally disturbed child. There are many forms of emotional disturbance just as there are many forms of physical disability and mental retardation.

II. The Physically Handicapped Child

A. Blindness and Partial Sightedness

Individuals are classified as blind if they have a vision of 20/200 or less in the better eye with the best possible correction. This means that blind children will have varying degrees of vision - from total blindness to being able to travel without assistance.

While learning to go about independently is of prime importance to the blind child, he nevertheless needs time to feel his way. Helping too quickly or doing for him may rob him of the chance to become independent and the opportunity for self-expression.

B. Cardiac Conditions

Most heart diseases are the result of defects and malfunctions of other organs or systems which indirectly affect the structure and function of the heart tissue. There are many causes of heart disease and those which are most prevalent in youth include: congential heart defects and rheumatic heart disease resulting from Rheumatic Fever.

In working with children with cardiac conditions we should remember that it is desirable to have them lead as normal a life as possible and that youthful hearts have considerable reserve power. When a cardiac child is involved in the play facility a clear understanding must be obtained from the doctor regarding the amount of activity permissible, precautions and restrictions. Cardiac children should be protected against over-excitement, and should rest when fatigued.

C. Cerebral Palsy

Cerebral means related to the brain and the word palsy implies a lack of muscle control. Cerebral palsy, then, is a complex disability resulting from damage to the human brain before, during or after birth. There are many subclassifications of cerebral palsy and various etiological factors. Many cerebral palsy children are of normal or above normal intelligence and are capable of leading useful and relatively independent lives.

For the cerebral palsy children the activities of daily living, those activities which most people perform daily without thought, such as the mechanics of dressing, eating, walking, turning on a light switch, are important parts of the child's rehabilitation program. Activities which emphasize similar mechanics and motions as those mentioned in connection with the activities of daily living should be part of the therapeutic play facility. Also, it is important to remember that a relaxed child will be able to perform much better than a child who is tense, trying to hard or too excited.

2. VALUE

D. Deafness and Hearing Loss

The deaf cannot hear sufficiently for ordinary purposes of daily life. The hard-of-hearing, with difficulty, can hear. With suitable precautions and adjustments, both can participate in most activities.

Because of the fact that deafness, cardiac conditions and epilepsy are "non-visible" handicapping conditions, these children often require special tact and patience from those working with them.

E. Epilepsy

The word epilepsy is derived from the Greek word meaning seizure. The seizures themselves are not a disease, but are symptoms of other disorders. They may result from any of a variety of disorders affecting the body or the brain. The most common types of epilepsy are Petit Mal, Grand Mal, Psychomotor Attacks, and Jacksonian Seizures. Most individuals who have epilepsy have their seizures under control with medication.

F. Legg-Perthes Disease

This is a condition characterized by deformity and fragmentation of the end of the bone. In Legg-Perthes Disease this deformity affects the head of the femur (thigh bone). It is a hip condition which is self-limiting, occuring in children between the ages of five and ten years. The disease process is one to five years and occurs more frequently in boys than girls.

G. Muscular Dystrophy

This is a chronic, noncontagious, progressive disease manifested by weakness and wasting of the voluntary muscles with eventual involvement of the entire muscle system. Its cause is unknown and there is no known cure. Muscle deterioration progresses until the individual is completely helpless.

Depending on the pregress and stage of the disease the child may be ambulatory or confined to a wheelchair. The ambulatory child may have difficulty in walking, climbing stairs, and getting up from a fall or from a sitting position. A peculiar side-to-side waddling gait may be noticed and there is an increase in the size of the affected muscles.

H. Spina Bifida

This is a congential defect in the development of the spine which may occur in any part of the spine but more frequently the site of involvement is the lumbrosacral region (lowest bone of the spine).

All motor and sensory neurons below the level of the defect are involved and there may be complete or partial paralysis of the lower extremities and loss of sensation. Loss of bowel and bladder control may also be associated with this condition. With the loss of pain sensation children with spina bifida do not feel friction of braces, chafing, trophic ulcers, so careful inspection should be given to note any redness in possible friction areas.

From the partial listing of types of illness, diseases and disabilities that children may suffer it can easily be seen that children suffering the various conditions will have needs which will necessitate goals and objectives of a specific nature. For example, a child who is blind will require certain kinds of considerations which will differ from those required by a child who had muscular dystrophy. It is, therefore, difficult to list specific goals and objectives of a therapeutic play facility which will be generic to all handicapped children.

Suffice it to say, at this point, that the goals of rehabilitation for the physically handicapped would include stabilization of existing abilities, developing and strengthening abilities that are not fully developed or that have suffered some deterioration or atrophy and providing opportunities to develop alternate skills or abilities to replace those that have been irreparably damaged or lost.

III. The Mentally Retarded Child

The retarded child can be described in terms of his subaverage intellectual development which occured during his developmental period and is accompanied by his inability to adapt appropriately to his environment. It must be remembered that the retarded child has a mental age lower that than of his real or chronological age.

Because a child is mentally retarded this does not necessarily mean that he is also motorically retarded. There is a general rule of thumb, however, that states the lower the intellectual functioning level of the child the higher the probability of more severely limiting physical or neurological disability the child will suffer.

Both the mental age and the chronological age must be considered in planning play facilities for the mentally retarded. It is important not to design, plan or program facilities or activities that are inappropriate for the chronological age of the individual on the other hand opportunities must be provided for graduated success in activities.

Because there are many different levels of retardation based upon more than one hundred known and countless other unknown etiologies there will be varying goals and objectives for the retarded of various ages and those individuals classified at different intellectual and adaptive behavioral levels. The characteristics of mentally retarded children and the goals and objectives for specific groups of retarded children must be discovered and considered carefully when planning a therapeutic play facility for this group.

2. VALUE

Considerations In Planning A Therapeutic Play Facility

In considering the values and benefits of a therapeutic play facility for handicapped children the following skill and learning abilitites will serve as an example of what should be planned for in the design and development of such a facility:

1. Gross Motor Development
   A. Definition: The development and awareness of large muscle activity.
   B. Suggested Goals: Rolling, crawling, walking, throwing, skipping and self-awareness abilities should be stressed.

2. Physical Fitness
   A. Definition: Improvement of general physical condition both physiologically and psychologically.
   B. Suggested Goals: Increase the degree of strength, flexibility, balance, endurance, speed and coordination.

3. Sensory Motor Integration
   A. Definition: The psychophysical integration of fine and gross motor activity.
   B. Suggested Goals: Balance and rhythm involving gross and fine motor movements, time orientation, develop sensory-motor contact with the environment, directionality.

4. Perceptual Motor Skills
   A. Definition: The functional utilization of primary auditory, visual, and visual-motor skills.
   B. Suggested Goals: Develop abilities to: receive auditory stimuli, understand spoken words, retain and recall information, observe and accurately identify objects, coordinate fine movements in eye-hand tasks.

5. Social Interaction Skills
   A. Definition: The skills involved in social interaction and social problems.
   B. Suggested Goals: Ability to get along with peers, increase range of social interactions, social maturity, decision making abilities.

6. Conceptual Skills
   A. Definition: The functional level of concept attainment and general reasoning ability.
   B. Suggested Goals: Develop number concepts, arithmetic concept (add, subtract, etc.), ability to utilize general information, ability to identify and classify objects in the environment.

7. Emotional Responsiveness
   A. Definition: Freedom to express any affective feeling or emotion without fear of retribution.
   B. Suggested Goals: Develop feeling of freedom of being happy, angry, sad, to laugh, cry, or express friendliness either verbally or non-verbally.

8. Language Development
   A. Definition: The current functional stage of total psycho-linguistic development.
   B. Suggested Goals: Develop ability to understand words, ability to express oneself verbally, develop comprehension.

Some of the general purposes of play for the handicapped child are the release of energy and tension in a constructive way, providing opportunities for the development of skills which bring about a sense of accomplishment, creating interest in new activities and endeavors and providing opportunities for strengthening and developing the child physically, mentally and emotionally.

Integration of Handicapped and Non-Handicapped Children in the Play Facility

Mr. Oscar Schisgall (7, p. 120) concluded, with the following paragraph, an article entitled "Parents' Guide to Child's Play" which he wrote for the magazine section of the New York Times

> For a child the art of play is really the art of living. Play fills about 3500 of the 8760 hours in a year. To deny him the right of play leaves almost his life in a vacuum. It must never be forgotten that children must be encouraged to learn as they experiment, as they question, as they imitate. Play is the area in which children practice life's skills.

Handicapped children will have more than the 3500 hours referred to by Mr. Schisgall for play because they have a great deal of enforced free time thrust upon them. However, they are denied the right to participate in a adequate amount of "play" hours, and they are denied the right to encouragement and instruction in the procedures of play. Most handicapped children are further isolated and handicapped by negative or limited social developmental experiences which leads to social retardation.

It is believed that through the types of experiences the handicapped child could encounter during an integrated play or recreational experience the gap created by the lack of adequate play and social developmental experiences could be narrowed. The integrated play facility would expose the handicapped children to realistic social goals, expectations and behaviors and they would be expected to function accordingly. Also, the non-handicapped children would be exposed

2. VALUE

to their handicapped peers which would help in achieving community and individual understanding that the handicapped are more similar than dis-similar to the "normal" individuals of society. This would hopefully increase everyones awareness that the handicapped child is first of all an individual and secondly, an individual with a particular handicap or limitation.

In conclusion, one thing must be remembered: PLAY IS PERFECT - IT IS NOT PERFECTION!

FOOTNOTES

1. Millie Almy, "Spontaneous Play: An Avenue For Intellectual Development." Early Childhood Education Rediscovered: Readings. Joe L. Frost, Editor. Holt, Rinehart and Winston, Inc.; New York, 1968.

2. Richard Dattner. Design For Play. Van Nostrand Reinhold Company. New York, 1969.

3. Asher B. Etkes, "Planning Playgrounds For the Handicapped." Mental Health Services. Reprint. November-December, 1968. 1968.

4. A. F. Gramza, "A Behavioral Researcher Looks at the Design of Children's Play Equipment." Internal Report. Motor Performance and Play Research Laboratory. Children's Research Center. University of Illinois, 1969.

5. Playground Corporation of America. The Handicapped Child, The Playscape...and The Instructor. Playground Corporation of America. Long Island City, New York, 1969.

6. Brian Sutton-Smith. Child Psychology. Appleton-Century-Crofts. New York, 1973.

7. Oscar Schisgall, "Parents' Guide to Child's Play." New York Times Magazine, New York, September 10, 1967.

Improving Free Play Skills of Severely Retarded Children

Severely and profoundly retarded children are usually deficient in play skills. Since play facilitates socialization, language, and motor development, it is a vitally important skill to acquire. This pilot study examined the effects of a behavioral training program on the autistic, independent, and social types of play of four severely and profoundly retarded children. The training program involved the use of instructions, modeling, physical guidance, and verbal reinforcement. Results indicated that a marked increase in independent and social play occurred with the introduction of the training program with all four children. Occupational therapists can play an increasingly important role in helping educators formulate relevant educational programs for severely retarded children, particularly in the areas of play and motor skill development.

Paul Wehman
Jo Ann Marchant

Paul Wehman, Ph.D., Assistant Professor, Department of Special Education, Virginia Commonwealth University, Richmond, Virginia.

Jo Ann Marchant, Teacher, Hickory Hill School, Richmond Public School System, Richmond, Virginia.

With the recent influx of over one half million severely and profoundly retarded children into the public school classrooms (1), there is an increased need for occupational and physical therapists to participate with teachers in program planning, implementation, and evaluation. Most severely and profoundly retarded children exhibit extremely limited social skills as well as delays in fine and gross motor development (2). Inasmuch as play is a critical part of the socialization of most children (3), the development of free play skills of retarded students would appear to be an important instructional area in which occupational therapists could provide valuable program assistance.

Although mentally retarded persons with severe behavioral deficits have been trained in ball-rolling skills (4-6), simple table games (2, 7), independent free play (8), and social

"Improving Free Play Skills of Severely Retarded Children," *The American Journal of Occupational Therapy.* Vol. 32, No. 2, February 1978.   American Occupational Therapy Association.

77

play (8-10), little research is available that specifically assesses the development of different levels of free play skills in severely and profoundly retarded children. Parten (11) and also Barnes (12) reported observational data that shows that normal children typically proceed through a developmental sequence of play from autistic, independent, to social play. Unfortunately, severely and profoundly retarded children usually display low levels of free play with little development toward more advanced types of play (2).

The purpose of this pilot study was to report observational data gathered on the free play behavior of four severely and profoundly retarded children; and to examine the relationship between different levels of free play and an instructional program involving behavioral training techniques. It was also an important goal of this study to evaluate whether or not the play skills of these children

would become more advanced through instruction.

Method

Subjects and Setting. Two boys and two girls participated in this study. Their IQ scores ranged from 15 to 24 and each child was 6 years old with no more than a 7-month age difference between them. All the children were nonverbal and received daily instruction in self-help, language, and motor skills. During free play periods, little social play was observed. Most of the children either played alone or engaged in self-stimulatory actions such as body rocking or finger flicking.

The study took place in a public school setting during the second year special education for severely and profoundly retarded students was provided. The classroom staff consisted of a teacher, aide, and student teacher, all of whom were female. Support staff involved in the develop-

ment of the study included an occupational and a physical therapist. Play sessions were given each morning in 15-minute periods, four days (sessions) each week, for a total of 42 sessions.

Toys. Most of the play materials listed below were chosen for the study because they are reactive, that is, they "act back" when played with. Reactive toys usually facilitate free play in the developmentally young (13, 14).

Tus busy boxes, Stacking blocks, Slinky, Dowel rods, Jack in the box, Spinning top, Music box, T-V music box, Plastic keys on chain, Rattle with mirror, Ball with movable parts inside, See-through ball with gravel inside, Plastic squeeze duck.

Response Measures and Behavior Observation. For the purpose of this study, free play is defined as any action or combination of actions with objects the child engages in for the apparent purpose of fun. Definitions of the three categories of free play were adapted from Barnes (12), and Paloutzian and others (9). Autistic play was defined as any destructive physical action with toys or as no physical action with any toys. Independent play was considered as physical action with any of the toys but performed by the child alone and with no interaction with other children or adults. Social play was defined as initiation or receiving social interaction between two children or a child and teacher (15). Typical social play behaviors included sharing a toy or playing together with play materials.

The three categories or levels of free play were selected in order to facilitate assessment of progress. Each category is sufficiently different so that independent observers could reliably discriminate between the different levels of play.

A partial-interval time-sampling method was used to assess behavior for every session (16). An observer watched the children play the first 20 seconds of each minute in the 15-minute session; for the next 40 seconds the data were recorded. This observation cycle then began again. A minus was recorded for autistic play, a plus for independent play, and two pluses for social play. Percentages for the levels of play were computed by dividing the number of minuses, single pluses, or double pluses by the total number of observation cells and multiplying by 100.

Once a week a second independent observer also collected data in order to assess reliability of agreement. Reliability was computed by dividing the total number of agreements and disagreements and multiplying by 100. The mean reliability score for the entire study was 95 percent. Observers were trained in behavior observation methods and frequently included other aides within the school.

Experimental Design. A reversal design was used to evaluate results (17). In a reversal design, the baseline level of the target behavior (5) is assessed and then followed by a treatment program. Once the target behavior shows a substantial change from the baseline level, the treatment program is temporarily withdrawn. This is done to verify a direct relationship between the independent variable(s) and response measure. The treatment program is then reinstated.

In the present study, baseline data were collected for each child on the percentage of time in which they exhibited autistic, independent, and social play. An instructional program designed to improve the free play skills of the children was implemented once a stable response level was attained for each child. A return to the baseline period was then begun in order to establish the relationship between instruction and the different levels of play. After a brief assessment of the children's play behavior, the instructional program was then repeated.

Procedure. Through each phase of the program the children were placed on a 9.5 x 11.5-m (8 x 10 ft) rug with toys placed within a 1.5-m (2-ft) radius of each child. This area was open with no enclosed parts. In the baseline phases, the teacher and other classroom staff moved to a different part of the room. No commands or instruction to play were given. Only the baseline data were collected.

During the instructional periods, two staff members were seated in the play area with all four children. Four components were involved in the overall instructional program. The first component consisted of specific verbal instructions to play with different toys. Second, if this was not effective, the child was then shown how to use the toy through modeling and demonstration. The third component involved the use of manual guidance with the children who did not respond to the instructions and/or the modeling. Instruction was usually given 1:1 between a staff member and a child; however, whenever possible a staff member would work with a pair of children. The fourth component included verbal praise and physical affection.

This was used as immediate reinforcement when independent play and also social play were exhibited. The order in which toys were selected for use by each child was not controlled.

The two staff members involved in the training program each day were rotated so that all three staff spent an equivalent amount of instructional time with the children. The two staff assigned to the play program usually worked in such a way that they each worked directly with the same two children during a session. In this way, positive reinforcement could be given more frequently and instruction was more individualized.

The sequence in which the 42-session play program was conducted was as follows: 1. baseline, 9 sessions; 2. instructional program, 21 sessions; 3. return to baseline, 4 sessions; and 4. instructional program/response maintenance. In the final phase, the total amount of staff instruction time, which was 30 minutes (two staff for 15 minutes each), was gradually reduced by 5-minute increments over an extended period of time. That is, one staff member spent 15 minutes and the second adult was involved for only 10 minutes. This was done to program for maintenance of the improved play skills the children exhibited. Gradual removal of staff contingencies is one method of maintaining results in behavior modification programs (18).

Results

Tables 1 through 4 display the mean percent of time each child was observed to exhibit autistic, independent, and social play. Each table allows for an analysis of the mean percent of play that occurred in the different conditions of the study.

Each child showed a marked change in the type of free play exhibited with the introduction and removal of instructional periods. While this does not allow for a specific analysis of the effectiveness of different instructional components (19), it does suggest a direct relationship between the overall instructional

2. VALUE

Table 1

Mean Percent of Play—Risa

	Baseline (9)*	Treatment (21)*	Baseline (4)*	Treatment (8)*
Autistic	34.0	7.7	53.3	10.0
Independent	39.0	45.2	38.0	63.0
Social	27.0	47.1	8.7	27.0

*Numbers in parentheses indicate the number of sessions carried out for each phase, and apply in Tables 2-4 as well.

Table 2

Mean Percent of Play—Larry

	Baseline	Treatment	Baseline	Treatment
Autistic	40.0	20.7	20.0	18.0
Independent	60.0	32.3	80.0	62.0
Social	0	47.0	0	20.0

Table 3

Mean Percent of Play—Mack

	Baseline	Treatment	Baseline	Treatment
Autistic	83.0	42.6	64.0	45.0
Independent	17.0	24.0	36.0	43.0
Social	0	33.4	0	12.0

Table 4

Mean Percent of Play—Rosemary

	Baseline	Treatment	Baseline	Treatment
Autistic	7.0	13.3	5.0	32.0
Independent	93.0	46.3	95.0	42.0
Social	0	40.4	0	26.0

approach and the three types of play. Although, with instruction, the amount of autistic play decreased in all four children, the substantial increases observed in social play was a most significant result, an effect noted in each child.

The impact of the instructional approach is more pronounced if independent and social play percentages are consolidated into one category or level. Both of these types of play are more socially appropriate than autistic play; when combined, the range is from 55 to 90 percent across all four children.

Discussion

The results of this pilot study indicate that with these four children a behavioral training approach of instructions, modeling, physical guidance, and verbal reinforcement was used successfully to improve free play skills. The implications are that severely and profoundly retarded children require a structured instructional program in order to develop independent and, eventually, social play skills. As noted in a discussion of play problems encountered by mentally retarded persons:

Severely and profoundly retarded persons rarely act on play materials in a constructive or spontaneous manner without some form of external cue, supervision, or instruction. This may be due to not having previously experienced the reinforcing or pleasurable aspects of play, or it may be a failure to attend to the play materials presented, i.e., lack of sensory awareness. Also, free play behavior may not occur simply because of inappropriate teaching methodology utilized by the teacher or activity therapist. (2, p 11)

Occupational therapists are a key part of the interdisciplinary team for severely and profoundly retarded children, particularly in the development of self-help, motor, and play programs. Most educators faced with writing instructional programs for children with severe behavior handicaps require consultative services from specialists who are directly trained in these areas. This research can provide direction to those faced with developing play programs as well as a data-based model for planning, implementing, and monitoring a play program for severely retarded children.

The importance of developing play skills in severely retarded children is underlined by the role that play can have in facilitating social, language, and motor skills (2, 12). Reduction of autistic play and increases in independent and social play are more consistent with a normal developmental sequence of social behavior. Research is needed that involves a larger sample of children and that attempts to examine the differential effectiveness of instructional components in play programs.

Summary

This study reported the use of behavioral training techniques with children who displayed very limited play skills. Through the use of instructions, modeling, manual guidance, and verbal reinforcement, four severely retarded children increased independent and social play skills. In this study, occupational and physical therapists served a consultative role in advising teaching staff about the motor capacities of each child participating in the study. It was concluded that the occupational therapist will play an increasingly important role in developing appropriate individual instructional programs for severely retarded children.

Acknowledgments

The authors thank the Head Teacher, Mrs. Geraldine Brandon, for her support in carrying out this program as well as for the support of the Richmond School System, Department of Special Education.

Note: Requests for reprints should be sent directly to Paul Wehman, Ph.D., Assistant Professor, Department of Special Education, Virginia Commonwealth University, Richmond, Virginia 23280.

REFERENCES

1. Gilhool T: Changing public policies in the individualization of instruction: Roots and force. *Educ Training Retarded* 11: 180-188, 1976

2. Wehman P: *Helping the Mentally Retarded Acquire Play Skills: A Behavioral Approach*, Springfield, IL: Charles C Thomas, Publishers, 1977

3. Piers MW: *Play and Development*, New York: W.W. Norton, 1972

4. Kazdin AE, Erickson B: Developing responsiveness to instructions in severely and profoundly retarded residents. *J Behav Ther Exp Psychiatry* 6: 17-21, 1975

5. Morris RJ, Dolker M: Developing cooperative play in socially withdrawn retarded children. *Ment Retard* 12: 24-27, 1974

6. Whitman TL, Mercurio JR, Caponigri V: Development of social responses in two severely retarded children. *J Appl Behav Anal* 3: 133-138, 1970

7. Wehman P, Renzaglia A, Schutz R, Karan O: Training leisure time skills in the severely and profoundly handicapped. In *Habilitation Practices with the Severely Developmentally Disabled*, OC Karan, P Wehman, A Renzaglia, and R Schultz, Editors. Madison, WI: University of Wisconsin Rehabilitation Research and Training Center, 1976

8. Wehman P: Research on leisure time with the severely developmentally disabled. *Rehab Lit* 38 (4): 1977

9. Paloutzian RF, Hasazi J, Streifel R, Edgar C: Promotion of positive social interaction in severely retarded young children. *Am J Ment Defic* 75: 519-524, 1971

10. Strain P: Increasing social play of severely retarded preschoolers through socio-dramatic activities. *Ment Retard* 13: 7-9, 1975

11. Parten MB: Social play among school children. *J Abnormal Psychol* 28: 136-147, 1932

12. Barnes K: Preschool play norms: a replication. *Dev Psychol* 5: 99-102, 1971

13. Wehman P: Selection of play materials for the severely handicapped: a continued dilemma. *Educ Training Ment Retarded* 11(1): 46-51, 1976

14. Favell J, Cannon P: Evaluation of entertainment materials with severely retarded persons. *Am J Ment Defic* 81: 357-362, 1977

15. Williams WW, Hamre-Nietupski S: Teaching selected social skills to severely handicapped students. *School Appl Learning Theory* 8: 1-19, 1976

16. Powell M, Martindate A, Kulp S: An evaluation of time-sample measures of behavior. *J Appl Behav Anal* 8: 463-470, 1975

17. Hersen M, Barlow D: *Single Case Experimental Designs*, New York: Pergamon, 1976

18. Wehman P, Abramson M, Norman C: Transfer of training in behavior modification programs: an evaluative review. *J Spec Educ* 11 (3): 217-231, 1977

19. Wehman P: Effects of different environmental conditions on leisure time activity of the severely and profoundly handicapped. *J Spec Educ*, in press

PLAY

Play as Occupation:

Implications for the Handicapped

Scout Lee Gunn

That play is a need-fulfilling and appropriate occupation in the life of every person, and particularly in the life of the handicapped, is the basic assumption of this paper. Play is defined, characterized, and discussed in relationship to its role in the treatment process. Various classical and modern theories of play are presented, with the optimum arousal theory of play presented as most significant in the rehabilitation process of the handicapped individual. The approach to this assumption is basically theoretical, and concludes with pragmatic suggestions for optimizing the meaningful involvement of patients in play.

Traditionally, the term "occupation" engenders a mental image of the adult workaday world. Work often bears the connotation of basically adult behaviors instrumental in the process of sustenance and does indeed "occupy" a large block of most adults' time. However, to assume that occupation and work are synonymous is to forget that for many people "making a living" does not always occupy the major part of their time. In this paper, the meaning of the word occupation is extended to apply to those activities that occupy or engage one's time, meets the needs of the individual, and is appropriate to the individual's role in society. Since an individual generally occupies more than one major role in society at any one time, it will be assumed that he has more than one occupation. The basic assumption of this paper is that play is a need-fulfilling and appropriate occupation in the life of every person, and most particularly in the life of the handi-

Scout Lee Gunn, Ed.D., is coordinator of the therapeutic recreation program, University of Illinois at Urbana-Champaign.

capped individual.

The Occurrence of Play

Consideration has been given to the play behavior of people as being an important and necessary occupation of one's time. Ellis[1] broadly defines play as those activities that are not immediately critical for either the survival or the sustenance of any person, young or old. Most often play bears the connotation of "trivial" behavior, especially in cultures characterized by a strong puritanical element. At the 1970 *White House Conference on Children*,[2] it was recognized that play behavior could not occur until the primary existence needs such as food, health, warmth, and security had been met.

Neumann[3] identified criteria that, when satisfied, would set play apart from nonplay—these are locus of control of the player, the nature of the motive for the behavior, and the necessary constraints of reality. The locus of control implies that play behavior is intrinsically motivated by the individual. In play, the element of external obligation is absent. Play is seen then as self-regulating. Neumann

 "Play as Occupation: Implications for the Handicapped," Scout Lee Gunn, *The American Journal of Occupational Therapy*, April 1975, Vol. 29, No. 4. ©American Occupational Therapy Association.

Team competition in Olympic wheelchair games.

added the further criterion that no immediate rewards imposed from the outside existed in play behavior. Play is a behavior rewarded by the very act itself. Finally, play behavior should transcend the constraints of reality to include imaginative or cognitive extensions of previous experiences, such as daydreams, fantasies, or epistemic behaviors.

Play can be characterized as behavior in which the player is freed, as far as possible, from any imposed constraints or expectations to elicit specific responses. Play allows for optimum exploration of the unknown and is unpredictable to the extent that each player is free to respond in his own way. Play encourages creativity and develops the capacity to generate new and unexpected responses to new situations. In order to maximize play, individual freedom and self-regulation must be present.

In the case of the patient who receives a form of treatment through activity, the activity may, at first, seem obligatory, prescriptive, designed to produce specific responses, and extrinsically rewarded by the desired results of rehabilitation. However, as the activity is repeated

in the training and practice stages, it may become a challenging, enjoyable skill in which the individual may choose to participate for the sake of the intrinsic reward of the activity.

Simple woodworking activities may be used to improve a patient's manual dexterity, but as he becomes more skilled, the activity may become a creative hobby. Involvement in the activity may then cease to be therapy and becomes play or recreation. Similarly, the person employed in a setting where he is allowed a great deal of freedom to be creative and to function in a self-regulated manner may proclaim, "My work is my play."

Often play activities differ from work activities in that work implies profit and a specific set of behaviors that produce a product. To this extent work is obligatory and places constraints on behavioral responses. Work behavior is more predictable than play behavior and usually deals in knowns rather than unknowns.

Since life is not a set of "knowns," proper development demands that one learn to deal with the unknown and unexpected. Flexibility and spontaneity are essential to meet the va-

A honed play skill becomes intrinsically rewarding.

garies of everyday life. Occupation in play epitomizes opportunities to learn effective ways of coping with the unknown.

Theories of Play

One's explanation of why play occurs may be contingent upon one's theory, for example, to expend excess energy, to prepare for new ways of responding in later life, or to allow for recuperation from work.

There are many identifiable theories purporting to explain why people play. The best known are the classical theories of surplus energy, instinct, recapitulation, preparation, and relaxation. All are concerned with elements in the nature of man that lead him to occupy time playing. The surplus energy theory purports that play is caused by excess energy that must be expended.[4] The instinctual theory assumes that play behavior is inherited in the same way as genetic characteristics.[5] The recapitulation theory states that critical behavior occurring during the evolution of man is somehow encoded for inheritance and that through play the player recapitulates the history of the development of his own species.[6] In the preparation theory the player is preparing for new ways of responding in later life.[7] He is practicing such things as motherhood, authority, and perhaps even defeat. The relaxation theory describes play as the diversional activity necessary to allow one to recuperate for work.[8]

The more recent play theories of generalization, compensation, catharsis, psychoanalytic, development, and learning are concerned with the content of play behavior, but still fall short of explaining why people play. The generalization theory states that play is caused by the player's need to re-enact experiences that have been rewarding at work. According to the compensation theory play arises out of a need to satisfy needs not met in work. The catharsis theory attributes play behavior to the need to express primitive, aggressive emotions in a harmless way by transferring them to socially acceptable activities.[9] The psychoanalytic theory assumes that the player has a need to repeat unpleasant experiences in a playful way, thereby reducing their seriousness and allowing for their acceptance.[10]

Piaget was the best known representative of the school of developmentalism and learning theory, who assumed that play was caused by the growth of the child's intellect and occurred when the child imposed his concepts on reality. According to learning theory, play is the normal process that produces learning.[11]

The Optimum Arousal Theory of Play

Michael Ellis set forth the most modern

theory of play as being arousal-seeking behavior. Ellis states, "The need to maintain optimal arousal has achieved the status of a new drive, and much of the surplus or playful behavior that is enigmatic can now be explained in terms of this drive."[1] Rather than quiescence being the normal state of the human organism, the assumption is that man needs to be constantly receiving sensory input. Rather than seek restoration to a quiet state of homeostasis, man seeks to be constantly aroused—a state that is interrupted only by basic needs such as eating, sleeping, and evacuating. Arousing types of stimuli are those that are novel, complex, or dissonant. When the primary needs are satisfied, the human organism is driven to interact with his environment in an increasingly complex way. Ellis indicates that the natural state of man requires arousing interactions of a novel, complex, or dissonant nature, and to the extent that these are not met by work, they need to be met by play.

Implication of the Occupation of Play for the Handicapped

Rather than play being seen as a supportive or adjunctive activity to work, education, growth, and development, play is a necessary and vital part of need-fulfilling behavior. Play is motivated only by a need for stimulation or optimal arousal. The more novel, challenging, daring, complex, and dissonant the activity, the more arousing and thus need-fulfilling it becomes. The need to play is as great as the need for work satisfaction, intellectual satisfaction, and satisfaction in the areas of physical development, social development, emotional stability, sexual identity, and spiritual growth. To be lacking in any of these areas affects the total person.

A deficiency in a person's ability to play greatly impairs his ability to cope with novel, complex, and dissonant situations. It is therefore imperative that persons with apparent deficiencies in the area of physical well-being be allowed the opportunity to meet their needs for optimal arousal through play.

During the crisis period of an illness or disability, it is important to remember that play cannot take place until basic needs are met. When necessary, the activity therapist should assist in seeing that the patient's basic needs for comfort, security, sleep, and food are met. Immediately following the crisis, the novelty of adjusting to a new state of existence and learning to cope with the disability or illness may be more than enough to meet the patient's need for optimal arousal. Within a short time, the novelty will wear off and the patient will be ready for more challenging and complex activities that should be afforded through play.

In order for the patient to meet his needs for optimal arousal, the play activity must allow for self-regulation, increasingly complex skill acquisition, intrinsic rewards, creative and imaginative responses, and must be free of as many external constraints as possible.

During the introductory, training, and perhaps even practice phase of skill acquisition, structure of the activity may be important. However, structuring the majority of activity programs for patients robs them of the opportunity play can offer to be self-regulated and creative.

Activities that do not offer increasingly complex skill acquisition are also of little value to the patient. Making pot holders, for example, leads only to making more pot holders. Such activities may alleviate boredom momentarily, but they will not give the patients the opportunity to meet their needs for optimal arousal. Quiet games, passive activities, and simple crafts are of little value to the patient in the total rehabilitation process. It is important to remember that the normal state of the human organism is not quiescence, but rather constant arousal, and activities should offer opportunities for optimal stimulation.

Hunger is a drive that requires eating. The ability to choose the kinds and amounts of food that adequately meet the need to eat is behavior that is learned. The ability to play in such a way as to meet the need for optimal arousal is also learned behavior, and can only be taught by an individual who himself has learned to play.

Summary

This paper argues that play is an important occupation in that it offers optimum opportunities for expression of arousal-seeking behavior. It is particularly important for the handicapped patient to play, since the ability to cope satisfactorily with his handicap may be affected by his ability to play. Perhaps more than most people, the handicapped individual needs to occupy much of his time learning to play because play elicits responses to the unknown, offers an opportunity to learn confidence, and to be creative in facing novel and difficult situations—situations that are personified in the life of the handicapped individual.

THE UNTAPPED RESERVOIR OF HUMAN ENERGY

DAVID M. COMPTON

In the past several years, our countries have been faced with innumerable crises relative to obtainable goods and services. If it isn't a crisis, then it's a shortage, a production cutback or an escalated price that prohibits many consumers from purchasing necessary goods. Physical resources have been so squandered and misused by man in the past that we may arrive at the year 2000 with just a pittance of our necessary energy resources. Nobile and Deedy comment that man's relationship with the earth is a long one — and quite one sided. Further they state:

> Man has used the earth, exploited it, despoiled it. Now he is on the verge of overcrowding, exhausting, and rendering it unliveable, if not uninhabitable . . . a jungle of waste, a sea of pollution; they have dirtied the air and denuded the forests; they have exterminated animal and plant species by the score . . . America has been used as if its resources were a bottomless lode. (1972, xiix-xiv)

Although man has waded through physical resources, (i.e. minerals, oil, gas, etc.), at an appalling rate, the problem of human energy resources appears quite different. Human energy remains a relatively untapped reservoir which may yield results yet unknown to mankind.

Under Utilization

Imagine for a minute the minuscule amount of human energy we unleash and utilize today. It is clearly illustrated in the fact that: (1) man sleeps away approximately one-third of his life with no biological, physiological, or psychological precedent for the "eight hours of sleep theory"; (2) man uses only a minuscule amount of his total intellectual capacity; (3) the unemployment rate is approaching ten percent; (4) institutionalized individuals by the hundreds of thousands are confined by law or other means, and rarely return as viable, contributing members of society; and (5) only one percent of man's physical work is done by man himself — the rest is done by machines (Fabun, 1970). Unleashing the vast reservoirs of human energy to solve human, political, physical, or scientific problems may be directly related to our ability to convert free time into productive, self-actualizing time. Middle and upper class Americans and Canadians can readily convert free time into productive or inwardly satisfying time. This appears to be possible because of many individuals' socio-economic status, mobility, and experiences, etc. which allows them to concentrate or diversify their free time pursuits. Two key factors (1) economic status and (2) degree of freedom, appear to be central to the issue of whether or not an individual will attain the highest levels of Maslow's "hierarchy of needs."

For members of special populations including the poor, the aged, visually and auditorily impaired, retarded, criminal offenders, or those with physical or mental dysfunctions, free time is a constant problem. Socially and vocationally rejected, these individuals find the abundant commodity of free time a nagging cancer which erodes their ability to rise to their highest level of human potential. Time is rarely tapped as an energy resource by, or for special populations, and, as a result, many fall prey to the "malignancy of idleness."

Time utilization should be considered a "social" problem, not a scientific or economic one. It is not the shortage of time, but the abundance of time which is at the base of many significant problems facing us today. Unless we become capable of dealing efficiently with time and time-related problems we will almost certainly face an in-

"The Untapped Reservoir of Human Energy," Original article by David M. Compton. Leisurability.

numerable number of social problems in the near future. The challenge and potential solution is to tap existing reservoirs of human energy and provide ample opportunity for that energy resource to be converted into social, cultural, intellectual, self-actualizing power and action.

Participant Power: Human Energy Transformed into Action

Much has been written on the scientific conversion of physical energy resources into power. Recent physical energy shortages and near crises have scientists worldwide seeking ways of converting newly discovered energy sources such as oil shale, gas, solar energy, trade winds, etc. into functional power. On the other hand little has been written on converting human energy resources into power. It is interesting to note that quantitatively we are not faced with a human energy shortage or crisis, but are faced with the perplexing problem of overpopulation (overabundance) and stockpiles of human energy. This is pointed out by Dr. Paul Ehrlich, author of *The Population Bomb*:

> Our population now is doubling roughly every 35 years. A lot of people ask, "Why can't population grow forever?" The old statistics are still valid for a reply. At the current rate, in 900 years there will be a billion people on the face of the earth, or 1700 for every square mile. Projecting this farther into the future, in about 2000 or 3000 years people would weigh more than the earth; in 3000 to 4000 years, the mass of humans would equal the size of a sphere with the same diameter as the earth's orbit around the sun; in 5000 years everything in the visible universe would be converted into people, and their expansion would be at the speed of light. (Helfrich, 1970, p. 49)

It is only recently that social scientists, psychologists, recreators and the like have recognized that members of special populations indeed constitute a viable human energy resource. But in spite of this there seems to be some sort of institutional lethargy in actualizing this massive resource for responding to social needs. Former U.S. Secretary of Health, Education and Welfare, John W. Gardner, in his book *No Easy Victories* (1968) notes that:

> It is apparent that we do best when the problems involved little or no social context. We're skilled in coping with problems with no human ingredient at all, as in the physical sciences. We are fairly good at problems that involve the social element to a limited degree, as in biomedical research. But we are poor at problem-solving that requires revision of social structures, the renewal of institutions, the invention of new arrangements.

In the future, members of the park and recreation profession will have to conceptualize and put into practice a far greater understanding of the process of transforming the currently dormant human energy of our special populations into productive human energy.

Power Conceptualized

The relative "power" of any social or cultural organization might be measured by its ability to: (1) attract participants to engage in its programs; (2) provide the depth and breadth of program opportunities; (3) match the available resources to participant needs; (4) effect higher levels of participatory behavior in participants, i.e. from spectator status to an eventual leadership role, and (5) rise to meet and conquer the current and pending social problems of its citizenry (problem-solving capacity).

2. VALUE

For any social or cultural organization, including parks and recreation, to generate optimal productivity, the aforementioned five factors must be recognized and implemented. Continuing to provide programs and services according to current practices, expressed desires, tradition, or a best guess (Danford, 1953) merely depletes an agency's efficiency rating and overall effectiveness in "human" economic terms.

The Cost of Non-Participation

Though it is difficult to accurately calculate the cost of excluding members of special populations from public-sponsored programs, the following factors may lead administrators, politicians, and professionals to rethink the posture of excluding special populations from the community:

1. *Housing.* The cost of daily institutional care for the retarded, mentally ill, alcoholic, addict, delinquent, aged, etc. far outweigh similar services in the community; the virtues of home ownership by the individual should be explored with all members of special populations. For example, recently a group of four young cerebral palsied men in Minnesota purchased a four-plex apartment and now enjoy the rights, privileges and responsibilities of home ownership, and in addition, are now taxpayers!

2. *Recidivism.* The highest rates of recidivism are associated with large institutional care centers; long-term association with anti-social, maladaptive behavior only tends to foster such behavior in others; institutionalization on a mass scale has failed in America and this failure was documented as far back as 1906 by Clifford Beers (1908) in his book *A Mind That Found Itself.* Institutionalization breeds institutional behavior which is distinctly different from that of the free society. Institutional behavior promotes the high recidivism rates in our "correctional" and "rehabilitation" institutions.

3. *Self-Actualizing Behavior.* Institutional care more often than not promotes a dependent state of living in its population. The very fibers of many large institutions are based on dependent modes of operation. Much failure on the part of the institutionalized is the result of the thoroughly cemented dependent roles nurtured through years of experience in hospitals and asylums. Community-based services tend to promote resource utilization by the individual;; achieving the pinnacle of Maslow's hierarchy of needs is virtually impossible in the institution due to its inherent organizational weaknesses.

4. *Free-time.* A large percentage of the problems of special populations can be related to the abundance of free time and its misuse. Programs planned to meet their needs simply short-circuit many of the recurrent problems. Converting free time from the negative or unproductive roles into satisfying, productive roles is a major factor in advocating participation by special populations in parks and recreation programs.

5. *Human potential.* Exclusionary activity on behalf of any social or cultural agency is difficult to comprehend. Every individual has his/her own highest level of human potential which is not pre-set or measured in normative terms; excluding merely thwarts the individual in his efforts to explore and realize his/her fullest human potential.

Payment: Now or Later

Though the cost of excluding special populations from public programs is difficult to specify, the slogan of one advertiser on American television may say it all, "You can pay me now . . . or pay me later!" I am sure that the cost of paying for institutional based rehabilitative services is much more expensive than preventative or ongoing services.

In addition to the aforementioned points, we should begin to recognize that our special populations have started to "speak for themselves" rather than continuing the role of having others speak for them. Several groups including the blind, aged, and the mentally ill are thoroughly ingrained in this advocacy role. In a recent editorial research report by Hamer (Iowa City Press Citizen, November, 1974), Bruce Ennis of the American Civil Liberties Union, referring to the fundamental rights of mental patients was quoted as saying, "This is clearly going to be one of the most important civil rights issues in the next few years." Hamer continued, saying:

> Almost every American knows someone who is handicapped, and few persons oppose the concept of equal rights for the disabled. However, general indifference and unthinking discrimination are the rule. But proponents of broader rights for the handicapped believe that making changes will benefit all citizens by helping society become more tolerant, more understanding of human differences and more humane.

Including rather than excluding members of special populations in parks, recreation, and leisure programs must become the rule rather than the exception. Mobilization of such a massive reservoir of untapped human energy should not be seen as an impossibility but a distinct possibility! Putting a man on the moon was the technological marvel of the century; full integration and provision of social, cultural, intellectual, and physical activity to our special populations should become one of the "humanistic marvels" of this century.

Basically there are five steps which park, recreation, and leisure agencies can take to tap the existing reservoirs of human energy in our special populations.

Step 1: Assume a Dynamic "Risk-taking" Posture.

At the foundation of many leaders thinking today is an attitude of reservation about starting programs or services for special populations. Many excuses are offered as a front to bide time or avoid facing the issue, but generally the problem is one of taking "risks" -- trying it and possibly liking it! In his article, "The Dignity of Risk and the Mentally Retarded", Perske states:

> The world in which we live is not always safe, secure and predictable. It does not always say "please" or "excuse me." Every day there is a possibility of being thrown up against a situation where we may have to risk everything, even our lives. This is the *real* world. We must work to develop every human resource within us in order to prepare for these days. To deny any retarded person his fair share of risk experiences is to further cripple him for healthy living. Mentally retarded persons, may, can, will, and should respond to risk with full human dignity and courage . . . Where many of us have worked overtime in past years to find clever ways of building the avoidance of risk into the lives of the mentally retarded, now we should work equally hard to help find the proper amount of normal risk for every retarded person. (1972, p. 26)

2. VALUE

Step 2: Utilize a Managerial Style Which is Conducive to Social Action, not Corporate Splendor

Managerial styles will often times dictate the direction and productivity of an organization. It is not usually possible to instill high degrees of humanism and productivity in all employees. What is possible, though, is to establish an operational style which is cognizant of the human needs of workers and, in the case of parks and recreation, the participants.

Managerial staff in parks and recreation must keep in mind that mobilization of human energy resources . . . and after all, we are in the people business . . . calls for a managerial style which leans toward what Blake and Mouton (1964) call "concern for people."

An integral part of the managerial style is the type of leadership exhibited by its staff. Dynamic, creative leadership should be expected, but many times this is not the case.

> I have had ample opportunity to observe the diverse institutions of this society — the colleges and universities, the military services, business corporations, foundations, professions, government agencies and so on. And I must report that even excellent institutions run by excellent human beings are inherently sluggish, *not* hungry for innovation, *not* quick to respond to human need, *not* eager to reshape themselves to meet the challenge of the time. (Cohen, 1969, p. 35)

Step 3: Provide "Normalizing" Experiences and Strive for Full Integration of All Special Populations

"Normal" activities, experiences and opportunities many times will yield "normal" results (if there is such a thing as normal!). What is offered to the mainstream of society should be equally accessible to members of special populations even though they may appear deficient, dysfunctioned or otherwise incapable of achievement. Special programs tend to perpetuate the segregation myth and thwart efforts at full integration.

Today is one day too late to recognize the importance of involving special populations in the mainstream of social and cultural activities. For example, a 1970 Ralph Nader taskforce Report of nursing homes revealed that merely keeping the aged out of institutions was not enough.

> All these efforts, some of which are expensive, are predicated on the belief that a person does not lose his social worth simply because he is old, that the aged can make contributions to society and to themselves, and that these contributions more than pay back the costs of programs to keep them in society. (Townsend, 1971, pp. 149-150)

Integration means the opportunity to freely mingle with other participants, and participate as an active member of the organization. This is pointed out by Verner and White:

> Active members are more apt to have a better perception of the purposes of the organization than inactive members. The degree of activity is related to the importance a member assigns these purposes. Active members are more likely to believe that membership is immediately beneficial and will tend to be better satisfied with their experiences as members.

> Active members feel a greater sense of responsibility to the association and usually believe they exercise a greater influence on decisions. Activity in associations appears to be related to social environment in that active members will have family

. and friends who are participants and they will have a greater sense of identification with the organization. (1965, p. 6)

From a recreational point of view, mainstreaming special populations into social, cultural, physical and intellectual activities is a necessity.

> If the public recreation program is to provide adequate recreation programs and resources for the *total population*, we must realize that there are significant numbers in our communities who will require special programs and it is the communities' responsibility to provide special programs for these special groups. (Park, 1970, p. 25)

Step 4: Hire Members of Special Populations as Permanent, Full-Time Staff

. One of the quickest ways to tap the reservoir of human energy in our special populations is to hire one and establish a "pipeline". The senior citizen, disadvantaged youth, ex-con, physically incapacitated are all potential employees with first hand knowledge of needs, problems, and abilities, of members of special populations. Many times these individuals bring "realism" into the agency — participant relationships.

A 1969 report of the President's Committee on Employment of the Handicapped and the President's Committee on Mental Retardation showed that once given the opportunity to become gainfully employed the mentally retarded have made exceptionally fine work records. This same concept is probably applicable to members of other special populations at even higher levels of employment.

Step 5: Provide the Necessary Tools (i.e.) Program, Staff, Budget, Equipment, Materials, Supplies, etc. to Mobilize the Human Energies Vested in Special Populations.

When oil companies sought rights to the vast oil reservoirs on the North Slope of Alaska, sizeable capital investments were committed in speculation of sizeable returns. Similar investments must be forthcoming from municipal, county, state, federal, private and commercial organizations to stem the tide of human, social and cultural problems faced by members of special populations.

Summary

Special populations constitute a major reservoir of human energy which has yet to be tapped. The seventies and eighties may pose severe physical energy crises but our most difficult crises will be with the mobilization and utilization of human energy.

The price we pay for rehabilitation and exclusionary types of programmatic efforts is at best mind-boggling. Pouring money into leisure education, normalization programs, and major preventative efforts may yield much more in the long run for every dollar invested.

Hesitation on behalf of our leadership, if for only a day, will render obsolete vast reservoirs of once useable human energy. For a moment reflect on the thousands of nursing home residents, incarcerated criminal offenders, mental patients, alcoholics, drug addicts, etc. . . . and the magnitude of our wastage of human energy comes front and center. Continual misuse of this vast reservoir of human energy may eventually render our economy obsolete. Welfare and all its related problems should be a constant reminder of the economic virtues of inclusion versus exclusion, self-actualization versus dependency.

A Community Recreation Program for the Mentally Retarded

Helen J. Mitchell

Helen J. Mitchell is Director, Program on the Mentally Retarded
and Physically Handicapped, D.C. Recreation Department, Washington, D.C.

The development of municipal recreation programming for the mentally retarded — a service which has been among the last to emerge in the vast array of services for the retarded — is an important topic of discussion. This paper focuses upon municipal recreation programming in relation to the development of the D.C. Department of Recreation's programs for the retarded as one method for developing a community program in an urban setting.

Background

In June 1962, Washington, D.C. recreation officials and the Kennedy Foundation formulated plans for a pilot project day camp for the mentally retarded. As a result of this cooperation and other community interest, the Sunny Grove Camp was opened in July 1962. The four-week camp program was operated by the D.C. Department of Recreation and funded by the Kennedy Foundation and Civitans International, Inc. Additional assistance and transportation were provided by Help for Retarded Children, the D.C. Chapter of N.A.R.C. Thirty trainable retarded children selected from the Public Schools' Special Services Program were enrolled in the camp which operated a full day program five days a week. The staff included a director, assistant director, several counselors, and fourteen teenage volunteers.

During the summer of 1963, the same sponsors and the Health and Welfare Council extended the camp operation with increased enrollment. The Recreation Department also initiated the following projects:

1. A six-week recreation program at an elementary school for twenty retarded children between the ages of seven and fifteen years, with a staff of six plus volunteers.

2. A four-week pre-school program for twenty four, five and six year olds at the same facility.

3. A cooperative program with Laurel Children's Center, the District's residential institution, established a four-week day camp for retarded children and adults. Four one-week sessions were conducted with thirty campers in each session. Three members of the recreation staff, with the staff of the Center, conducted the program which has been continued annually at the Center.

In 1963, the Department hired a director-coordinator for mental retarda-

"A Community Recreation Program for the Mentally Retarded," Mary Jo Mitchell, Recreation Director of the Mentally Retarded and Physically Handicapped, *Therapeutic Recreation Journal,* Vol. V, No. 1, 1971. National Therapeutic Recreation Society.

tion. programs. A survey was made of the District of Columbia to determine the number of retarded children and adults residing within the confines of the area. The prime mover for the survey was the development of recreation programs to serve the persons identified. In June of 1964, steps were taken to begin early development of recreation programs for the retarded, utilizing the existing public Recreation Department's staff and facilities.

The survey goal was two-fold: (1) to disclose the number of retarded persons and (2) to obtain information about the kinds of recreation experiences desired for them.

The development of recreation for the retarded in Washington was, in the most liberal sense, a demonstration project. The ultimate goals were to (1) develop, using existing facilities and staff, a comprehensive recreation-oriented opportunity for the mentally retarded, and (2) develop within the complex framework of intra-agency function a system of principles and procedures, which would be guides for the development of multi-agency cooperation in the establishment of such programs.

In the establishment of this program, many unforeseen problems arose, many exciting and rewarding experiences were shared by the participants and staff, and most important, a pattern of program established.

This report will trace the progress made in the development of the recreation program for the mentally retarded of the Nation's Capital from the survey (1963) to the summer of 1965.

Plan for Action

The progress made in other fields and the improved outlook for the retarded were some of the thoughts that prompted the Health and Welfare Council of the National Capitol area to begin the formulation of a long-range, two-phase approach in providing the vehicle and the fuel in the development of recreation programs for the mentally retarded. The fuel, in this case, was the results of the survey; the vehicle to be used was the District of Columbia. Recreation Department. Up to that point, the Recreation Department, like departments all over the Nation, had served the retarded, but not in specific programs.

The Recreation Department, in the summer of 1964, received $27,000 from the Health and Welfare Council to implement the results of the survey in the development of special recreation programs for the mentally retarded. The survey disclosed some 7,000 retarded children and adults residing in the District. As of the 1960 census, there were 763,956 persons residing in the District; of this population, 3 percent would yield some 23,000 which in varying degrees would benefit from special programs. The 7,000 disclosed in the survey did not necessarily include all those in the public and private school programs serving the retarded.

D. C. Department of Recreation — Organizational Structure

Geographically, the District is divided into nine recreation department regions. Each region has a director, assistant director, and the necessary staff to man the playgrounds and community centers located in the various regions. Staff from the regions were selected to receive special training in working with the mentally retarded. A series of courses was developed at the University of Maryland to equip personnel with the necessary tools for effective programming in this special aspect of community service. As staff completed these courses, they were encouraged to initiate programs for the retarded on their own playgrounds and centers. The overall responsibility for program development and staff training rested with the director-coordinator of the recreation programs for the retarded. In addition to the department programs, the director assisted all other district agencies, public and private, in the development of a unified approach in providing additional programs for the mentally retarded. To supplement the staff training and to provide a full program facility, a center was established exclusively for the retarded. This center was designed to operate on a year-round basis and to provide program opportunities for groups of all ages. The center afforded an excellent on-the-job training opportunity for staff of both public and private programs.

Program Development

The survey disclosed some 7,000 retardates. It was felt that of this number there would be some who would not be in any program, and steps were taken to develop program facets to serve them. In order to assess the availability of persons in this group for program, 500 of the 7,000 were sent a brief questionnaire. The 500 names were selected at random and represented a cross-section of the retarded population. Other factors considered were the families' economic conditions, place of residence, and ages of the retarded children. The results of this sample indicated that the bulk of those questioned would be interested in programs in the morning and early afternoon, and those currently enrolled in other programs would be available for Saturday programs. It was evident that many of the retarded were concentrated in certain geographic regions of the District.

The original 500 names plus an additional 1,000 names were located by address on an overlay of the District's postal zones. This overlay was combined with one outlining the nine recreation department regions. The resulting map showing both postal zones and recreation regions enabled us to locate the children in terms of their accessibility to the playgrounds and community centers which could provide special programs. From this system, those areas in which there appeared to be concentrations of retarded individuals were located. The special programs were developed in these regions of greatest concentration.

The staff receiving the university training assigned to the centers and playgrounds which were in the areas of concentration were supplied with lists of children living in these areas. The parents were notified by letter and follow-up phone call regarding a meeting in each center to discuss the new program and to answer any questions. Originally, five playgrounds were selected to begin the program. The selected facilities were equipped to handle up to fifteen participants in one or more of the following groups:

Pre-school age . . . . 4 - 7
School age . . . . 8 - 12
Teenage . . . . 13 - 19
Adult . . . . 20 - Up

Evaluation — First Six Months

Progress made in the first six months was far from encouraging. The five centers had a total enrollment of sixty-six children. The retarded population of the areas in which the centers were located had upward of 1,500 children and adults not in school or in other programs. Throughout these early months, many parents were contacted and informed of the program. Generally, they expressed only a vague interest in the opportunity and were not yet ready to send their children.

Certain common factors became evident regarding the parents of retarded individuals with whom staff were working:

1. Approximately 78 percent of all participants in the program were for the most part of low income status. Those with higher income means tended to place their children in private school programs.

2. Parents of low economic means were highly transient. With a constant state of flux, there was little desire to start their children in the program (by law all children must present themselves for school at age six; however, the school officials did not press the issue when the child had been tested and found to be retarded. Often, he was not placed in a special class and was free to return home). This applied to our program, also. Parents unless forced would not generally try to find a program on their own. Often, a child would attend two or three weeks and then would not be heard of again. Attempts at tracing the child were thwarted by no forwarding address, histories of unpaid rent, etc. One exception to this was a family that moved three times in thirty days, but continued informing the staff of the moves, and kept the child in the program.

3. Those parents who had accepted the fact and understood mental retardation were few (except those parents with children in special classes). This was especially true of the uneducated parents. A great deal of superstition was evident when they did admit their child was a little slow. There was great hesitancy to submit to compulsory testing (public schools); and as a result, many youngsters remained at home with no plan for their education and no encouragement to try. Attendance in the program would identify the child as retarded, and this was the last thing many parents wanted.

4. There were some parents who acknowledged the fact they had a retarded child but did not understand how recreation could help him. This was essentially a problem of selling the public on the values of recreation for the retarded. Other parents questioned the value of additional programs if their child was enrolled in a special school.

5. Perhaps the most important task of all was that of reaching those who would utilize the program and openly desired help for their child. In light of these factors, it was determined that a purposeful pattern of public education and increased focus on recreation for the retarded would aid considerably in reaching more participants who could benefit from the program.

Initially, a series of pictures and articles was run in the three metropolitan newspapers. The articles covered the philosophy of the program and graphically illustrated that children were in the program and parents supported the effort. Data sheets outlining the program, facilities, and locations were made available to all special teachers (public and private), social workers, and welfare workers in the District. Perhaps, the greatest return came from the 300 visiting nurses who frequently came in contact with families with retarded children. The nurses had a rapport with many such families that the other social and welfare agencies failed to achieve.

As parents began responding to this increased effort, tactics were changed in dealing with them. For most of them were inquiring about the "special school": information was provided about the "school." The term recreation for retarded was dropped in initial contacts with parents; however, as parents responded to the program, a gradual plan of parent education helped them become more conversant in identifying the special problems of their children. Once again, the program became recreation for the retarded.

Established Programs

At the end of the first year of operation, fifteen separate facilities were serving the retarded in recreation programs. Nine recreation department centers, three school-based programs, and three settlement houses programs comprised the total effort for special programs at the end of the first year. These fifteen programs were serving a group of retarded individuals in excess of 300. This represented an increase of over 150 participants in a period of sixty days.

It would be hard to single out any particular aspect influencing the increase in effort in the many quarters utilized. The overall effect was quite amazing. The combination of increased public awareness and a new approach in dealing with the parents seemed to contribute measurably to the increase in attendance.

Summary

It was apparent that with time and patience effective programs for the retarded could be established. The progress made in the first year, the new programs developed, and the continued interest on the part of the parents, demonstrated that (with time and understanding) the program was emerging as a valued service. Parents must see the need for this service, and then they must fully trust the department before they can accept the value of this program for their child.

Recommendations

The program, thus far, is serving only a small percentage of the known retarded population residing in the District. If this past year is any indication of future growth, it is conceivable that additional centers could be added in future years to meet the increasing demand for programs. A total of forty special programs (public and private) would be adequate to serve the recreational needs of the retarded of the District of Columbia.

Continued cooperation with the schools would aid in serving those in school programs with recreational opportunities. Within each of the recreation regions, centers should be established to serve those not in school with programs for all age groups, thus minimizing transportation problems. Special consideration should be given the development of additional programs for evening and weekend operation for those in special classes or in the workshops.

Based on this year, it is evident that an intensive program of public and parent education is necessary and should precede any attempt at additional program development. Thus far,

2. VALUE

each of the centers has an active parent group; they should be utilized in reaching other parents or retarded individuals.

It is important to realize that this is only one approach that can be used in developing a program for the retarded and that it is operated in an urban, inner-city setting.

There are several factors to be considered in developing a group program for the mentally retarded:

1. Recognition of the need for recreation services

2. Identification of the population

3. Development of a philosophy, goals and objectives

4. Determination of interest and availability of the retarded population

5. Location and incorporation of available resources

6. Education of parents and publicity of the services and the need for them

7. Staffing and staff training and development

8. Facilities

9. Evaluation

Other Programs

There are several other existing year-round programs for the mentally retarded and other handicapped populations operated by municipal recreation departments. A few of these programs are located in Greensboro, North Carolina; San Francisco and Los Angeles, California; Philadelphia, Pennsylvania; Milwaukee, Wisconsin; Chicago, Illinois; Seattle, Washington; Waterford, Connecticut; Jacksonville, Florida; and Hamilton, Ohio.

There are also numerous summer programs operated throughout the United States, especially camps which have been co-sponsored by the Joseph P. Kennedy, Jr. Foundation.

Available Resources

National Therapeutic Recreation Society — books, publications, consultative services

American Association for Health, Physical Education and Recreation, Unit on Programs for the Handicapped — information sheets

U.S. Department of Health, Education and Welfare, Office of Education, Bureau of Education for the Handicapped

National Association for Retarded Children

Special Olympics Athletes Face Special Medical Needs

Andrew V. Bedo, MD Marilyn Demlow, RN
Patrick Moffit, BS Kenneth W. Kopke, ATC

The first Special Olympics for the Retarded was held eight years ago in Chicago, where 1,000 youngsters competed in Soldiers Field in front of empty stands. In August 1975, 3,200 competitors paraded in little-known Perry Shorts Stadium in Mount Pleasant, Michigan, to the cheers of a crowd of 20,000.

Until the first Special Olympics Games were organized by the Joseph P. Kennedy Foundation, few retarded children and young adults ever took part in a regular program of recreation or sports competition. Forty-five percent of all mentally retarded children received no physical education at all. Many communities actually had ordinances forbidding the retarded from using public gymnasiums, swimming pools, and playgrounds. Only about 25% of the retarded were given as much as 60 minutes of organized recreation per week.

The idea of the Special Olympics grew out of the Kennedy family's belief in the value of sports training and athletic competition. The founder of the games was Eunice Kennedy Shriver, whose sister Rosemary is retarded.

The Special Olympics is the world's largest sports and recreation plan for the mentally retarded, totaling more than 400,000 athletes

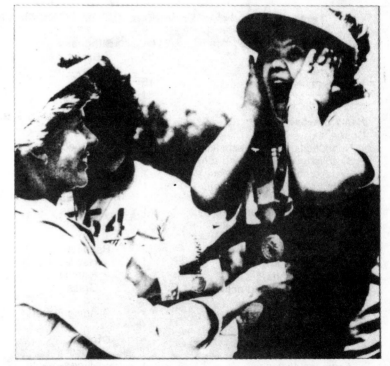

CALIFORNIA SPECIAL OLYMPICS PHOTO
An ecstatic medal winner expresses her joy.

and 150,000 volunteers. Every state has a Special Olympics organization, and more and more foreign countries are joining. At the 1975 games there were competitors from Canada, France, West Germany, Belgium,

"Special Olympics Athletes Face Special Medical Needs," Original article by Andrew V. Bedo, M.D., Marilyn Demlow, RN, Patrick Moffit, BS, Kenneth W. Kopke, ATC. Special Olympics, Inc.

the Philippines, the Bahamas, Mexico, and El Salvador.[1]

The program is open to all retarded 7 years of age and older. Ten official sports are offered: track-and-field, swimming, diving, gymnastics, floor hockey, basketball, ice skating, bowling, volleyball, and wheelchair events. The international games are held every four years. Every state has state games each year. Approximately 20,000 local and area meets were held in 1975. The motto of the program is: "Let me win; but if I cannot win, let me be brave in the attempt."[2]

Central Michigan University (CMU) in Mount Pleasant was chosen to be the site of the 1975 International Games, August 7 through 11. We began preparations for meeting the medical needs of the games early in 1974. John Perry, MD, medical chairman of the Third International Games in Los Angeles, assessed the past medical situation

and submitted his recommendations in a report.[3]

Our decision for a medical plan encompassed:

1. Recruitment of personnel
2. Mission
   A. Anticipation, prevention
   B. Action. Prompt and efficient attention and treatment
   C. Learning experience for all involved[4]

We began by taking stock of the community's medical resources. Unlike some of the previous games, the 1975 Special Olympics were to be played in a small, relatively isolated community. Mount Pleasant is an exurban community of 13,000. During the regular school year, CMU's enrollment totals 15,000 students. The University Health Services (UHS) has a 40-bed inpatient

Table 1. Preexisting Conditions (US and Canadian Participants)

Seizures	**166**	**Blindness**		**6**
Grand mal	120	Bilateral		4
Petit mal	30	Unilateral		2
Unclassified	15			
Psychomotor	1	**Allergies**		**45**
		Drug		
Heart disease	**31**	Penicillin		15
Congenital		Sulfa		2
Nonspecified — no restrictions	17	Demeclocycline		1
Systolic murmur (50-yard run)	1	Dilantin		2
Systolic murmur (self-limiting)	1	Phenobarbital		2
Right carotid systolic murmur —	1	Horse serum		2
no restrictions		Prochlorperazine maleate		1
Septal defect — corrected	1	Iodides		1
Frequent premature beats	1	Aspirin		1
Grade II/III systolic murmur —	1	Iron		1
no exertion permitted		Respiratory		
Post-thoracotomy —	1	Hay fever		4
no restrictions		Asthma		5
"Cardiac" — limited activity,	1	Grass		2
may run 50 yards		Food		3
Cardiac seizures	1	Stinging insects		3
Mitral murmur —	1			
no running		**Other**		**21**
Aortic stenosis	1	Obesity		4
Aortic insufficiency	1	Hypertension		2
Acquired		Chronic otitis media		2
Rheumatic fever (inactive) —	1	Autistic		1
no restrictions		On birth control pill		2
Mitral insufficiency	1	On birth control shot		1
		Duodenal ulcer		2
Diabetes mellitus	**4**	Postcataract surgery		1
Diabetes insipidus	**2**	Sickle cell anemia		1
		Deaf		3
Hernia	**3**	Undescended testicle		1
Inguinal	2	Hemophilia		1
Hiatus	1			
			Total 278	

capacity, x-ray and lab facilities, and five full-time physicians. The Central Michigan Community Hospital has 115 beds, a well-equipped emergency room, x-ray and lab facilities, and a medical staff available for medical, orthopedic, surgical, gynecological, eye, and dental consultation. Consultants were also available via "hot line" to Alma, Midland, and Saginaw. The nearest medical school is in East Lansing. In addition, the Isabella County Ambulance Service stands by at all major events.

We are convinced that in the medical supervision of events for the retarded, we cannot be overstaffed. This is not only because many of the participants have conditions that predispose them to a certain morbidity (seizures, syncope, dehydration, infections, etc), but also because parents, friends, and coaches may become overprotective, especially when far away from home. It is therefore essential to have a physician present at or near each major event to make quick, authoritative decisions.

Our most immediate problem was procuring adequate numbers of volunteer physicians and other health personnel. We accomplished this through a many-pronged approach.

The Michigan chapter of the American Academy of Pediatricians was helpful in contacting colleagues in the state, especially those employed by institutions for the retarded. (The Academy's Committee on Children with Handicaps also sent an observer, who stayed on to help.) Administrators of medical schools and hospitals were contacted by mail, and public notices were posted on school, hospital, and dormitory bulletin boards. Marilyn Demlow, RN, nursing director of the UHS, recruited 50 RNs, LPNs, and aides through letters and personal contacts.[5] Finally, Kenneth Kopke, ATC, head trainer of the CMU varsity sports team, recruited and organized 14 certified and 23 student trainers from eight states. At the final "head count" we had five full-time physicians, six volunteer physicians, one premedical student, and a health education intern from UHS. Moreover, the delegations from California, Florida, and Canada were accompanied by their own medical staffs.

We received help from nonmedical people, too. Members of the local Lions Club donated

time to repair broken glasses and hearing aids. A number of celebrities and entertainers visited the games throughout the week, often giving impromptu performances for bedridden Olympians.

The 1975 games had the largest number of participants ever. In order to anticipate and prevent some problems, an information sheet

Table 2. Total Number and Types of Diagnoses

Abrasions	81
Nose and throat (excl. allergy)	50
Exhaustion (all kinds, mostly heat)	43
Blisters	31
Contusions	25
Sprains	25
Upper respiratory (unclassified)	26
Gastroenteritis	27
Laceration	20
Headache (excl. trauma)	19
Muscle cramps	18
Seizure (grand mal)	15
Epitaxis	10
Sunburn	10
Otitis media	9
Muscle strain	9
Allergic rhinitis	8
Contact dermatitis	4
Otitis externa	4
Head injury	4
Dysmenorrhea	4
Anxiety	3
Syncope	3
Herpes labialis	3
Hyperventilation	3
Fracture (one wrist, two toes)	3
Heat prostration	2
Ingrown toenail	2
Dermatitis medicamentosa	2
Heat rash	2
Lumbosacral strain	2
Asthmatic bronchitis	1
Ludwig's angina	1
Violent behavior	1
Canker sore	1
Puncture wound	1
Chest pain	1
Peptic ulcer	1
Knee instability	1
Morning sickness	1
Hangnail	1
Pain in pinned knee	1
Sutures examined	1
Sutures removed	1
Tendinitis	1
Vaginitis	1
Conjunctivitis	9
Medication supplied	16
Physical examinations performed	2
Total	**509**

Concentration, suspense, and pride are mirrored in the face of a young Special Olympian.

and standing orders were mailed to all participating units. When the records of the participants arrived at our headquarters, a group of volunteers screened them for potentially troublesome conditions, necessary permission and release forms, and the list of medications the participants were using. From the records of US and Canadian participants, we found 278 (8.7%) contestants with preexisting conditions (table 1). Seizures were the most numerous (166), with congenital heart disease in second place (29). We were greatly concerned about the Olympians with aortic lesions, but they were not entered in any running events. Anticipating trouble with a hemophiliac, we withdrew him from the 50-yard dash, permitted him to enter the baseball throw, and stocked the blood bank with factor VIII. We also made certain

that all participants with serious conditions were under constant one-to-one supervision, with their medications available immediately.

As in all previous Olympics, heat exhaustion, dehydration, and sunburn were serious threats. This was offset by providing shade from tents loaned by the National Guard and canopies loaned by local businessmen. The liberal use of sunscreen donated by the manufacturer helped in preventing sunburn. Gallons of electrolyte replacement liquid donated by the manufacturer were placed in every aid station and other locations where people would congregate.

In Mount Pleasant the weather cooperated on August 7 and 8. During the next two days, however, temperatures rose to 95 F. Still, only ten participants became sick enough from heat exhaustion to require admission to the UHS infirmary. They were released in good condition after intravenous fluids and rest.

For the prompt and efficient care of the sick and wounded, first-aid stations were strategically located at poolsides (with resuscitation teams and equipment), gymnasiums, major event areas on the athletic fields, and in the dormitories.[6] Staffed by nurses, LPNs, and aides, the stations were stocked with first-aid equipment obtained from the UHS; supplies were donated by pharmaceutical companies. Copies of the standard operating procedures manual for first aid were also provided.[7] Here patients were evaluated, treated, and either sent back to compete or escorted to the UHS or a collecting station.

Collecting stations were larger, more completely equipped areas located in two major training rooms and served by physicians, nurses, and aides. Here more definitive work was done (suturing, injections, application of splints, etc). The patient was thoroughly evaluated, treated, and either returned to the field or sent on to the UHS.

The UHS served as the evacuation hospital, where the sicker and the more seriously injured were sent for more complete and leisurely evaluation, observation, laboratory and x-ray work, if necessary, and treatment. No patient was allowed to be sent off campus without a physician's orders. For variety and experience, the medical teams were usually rotated from one area to another at half-day intervals.[8]

The concept and role of the athletic trainer was developed by Kenneth W. Kopke.[9] The athletic trainers were the primary care unit on the field, in the gym, and poolside, focusing on the immediate care of injuries. They were eminently qualified for this, having had the experience of working with athletic injuries, in front of crowds, and under pressure from impatient coaches and athletes anxious to return to competition. We had 15 two-man teams, each scheduled to cover an event, who were provided with a field kit and the necessary supplies. All medical personnel wore white T-shirts with the Special Olympics emblem to make them readily identifiable.

For lost, strayed, or confused competitors, a holding area was established at the Health Service recreation room complete with TV sets, toys, and games and supervised by a volunteer.

Our basic record was the emergency medical tag (EMT), an idea borrowed from Army service. Whenever a contestant was seen with a problem, an EMT — actually, a large luggage tag — was attached to the arm. The patient's name, hometown, injury, treatment, and disposition would be written on it. If this was the only treatment needed, the tag was retained for filing. If the patient was sent to a collecting station or to the UHS, the tag accompanied him or her to the next station where further information was added, or the data transferred on to the regular UHS record.[18]

Our standard operating procedure manuals[10] covered the management of the most likely conditions encountered. We stressed the importance of the search for possible underlying difficulties. In addition to the treatment of trauma we emphasized care of patients with seizures, syncope, and severe allergic reactions.

A total of 590 patients were treated at Central Michigan University throughout the seven days of the games, 18.47% of all participants. Included in this number were coaches, chaperones, headquarters personnel, students, and guests. Forty-seven were admitted to the infirmary, and none were treated for more than two days. There were 56 x-rays taken, mainly of the extremities, two of the chest, and one of the skull.

Special Problems

The distribution of injuries and sickness was roughly comparable to that of any other group of youngsters competing on hot days. The main differences were caused by these patients' central nervous system vulnerabilities. There were 15 patients treated for grand mal episodes.

Analysis of our hospital admissions revealed that two competitors collapsed from heat and exhaustion at the mile run, two others at the 440 (one with seizures), one at the 220, and one at the 50-yard dash. This last one was a Filipino youngster sent in as a substitute at the last minute without much training. She was anxious to do well and tried too hard. Naturally she was given a medal, special mention, and a private bedside performance by one of the celebrities. A young champ from Ohio had heat exhaustion and seizures at the high jump. All of these children had microscopic hematuria and a transient elevation in blood pressure. They recovered readily with hydration and rest. It is obvious that track events, especially the long and middle distances, call for special attention.

On opening day six youngsters arrived with pharyngitis, four with otitis media, and six others with various upper respiratory infections. Three others arrived completely exhausted after the long journey. After a good night's rest they were ready to go.

Some competitors reported without their medications (usually anticonvulsants or tranquilizers). Their chaperones either had the prescription and we procured them from our own supplies or one of our physicians made out the prescription and sent it to drugstore. Two children arrived without the mandatory physical exam. To spare them the disappointment of not being able to compete, we performed this for them on our own responsibility.

The second and third days saw the heaviest competition, and obviously, were our busiest. The usual injuries and illnesses (abrasions, contusions, sprains, upper respiratory infections, seizures, and exhaustion) were treated. There was a teenager who during two previous state meets reported to us with signs and symptoms of acute appendicitis and could not compete. When we saw her again she had the usual abdominal complaints and a white count of 12,000. She was observed and given a medal and a special bedside performance.

The last day of the program was a rather anxious one. This was "exploration day." Groups of youngsters were bused to different parts of the state and entertained by the residents with picnics, shows, and other outings. (The Michigan delegation was given a "pig roast" in Mount Pleasant.) On the return of the buses, participants poured into UHS, ten children with various traumata, one with concussion. One child had to be admitted with violent behavior, due to overexcitement. She was "talked down" without the need of any medication. A young woman was brought

in with a rather frightening case of Ludwig's angina. She responded well to millions of units of IV penicillin. Some were exhausted.

We saw 38 patients this last day, but were able to send them home on schedule.

Discussion and Conclusions

By and large the pattern of injuries was similar to any other group of competitors, with the exception of those caused by the competitors' underlying conditions. This is why, from the point of view of the responsible medical team, we could not consider them "just like any other kids, except a little slower." We had to be prepared to anticipate difficulties and be ready to treat them in a hurry. Any major mishap could cause a severe setback to this splendid program.

In our efforts to minister to the sick and injured, we could not take the time for really effective observations on the reactions and abilities of the competitors. We did, however, gather a few impressions. First, we found that mentally retarded, or otherwise handicapped, children do have stamina, courage, and maybe even try too hard.

Specifically, some with Down's syndrome were quite buoyant and made good swimmers. They were strong, and one of them in particular did an outstanding job in floor gymnastics. Others with microcephaly had good speed and balance.

In social situations they acted more or less like other young people. Some of them were more retiring than usual, others did not know when to stop their horseplay. Because of their tendency toward overreaction and a certain lack of judgment, coupled with our moral and legal responsibilities, constant supervision with firm but gentle guidance could not be relaxed.

The most serious aspect of this responsibility is the protection of these young people from pregnancy and VD. Close supervision is mandatory, because retarded or not, young people are very resourceful and have been able to evade chaperones from time immemorial. As supervisors, of course, we must always be mindful of the mental health laws and the participants' civil rights.

In the future we hope to have enough time to make objective and quantitative observations. These observations, properly

'On opening day six youngsters arrived with pharyngitis, four with otitis media, and six others with various upper respiratory infections.'

documented, will be a great help in making these games meaningful not only for the individual participants, but also for communities seeking ways to integrate retarded people into productive and meaningful community life. Medical students and house officers should be encouraged to attend, and be given school or postgraduate credit. From their participation all would benefit.

References

1. Montague RM: Special Olympics. Washington, DC, Special Olympics, Inc.

2. Joseph P. Kennedy Foundation: A New Kind of Joy. Washington, DC, 1976

3. Perry J: Report of the Medical and Emergency Services Committee. Third International (Western) Special Olympics. Washington, DC, Special Olympics, Inc.

4. Bedo AV, Demlow M, Kopke K: Final Report, Medical Staff, International Special Olympics August 7, 1975 - August 11, 1975. Enclosure 14, Washington, DC, Special Olympics, Inc.

5. _____ : Enclosure 14

6. _____ : Nursing Report. Enclosure 15A

7. _____ : Aid Stations. Enclosure 14

8. _____ : Doctor's Schedule. Enclosure 8

9. _____ : Trainer's Report. Enclosure 15B

10. _____ : Standard Operating Procedures. Enclosure 14.

Dr. Bedo is staff physician at the University Health Services and adjunct professor of health education, Central Michigan University, Mount Pleasant, and assistant clinical professor in the Department of Human Development, Michigan State University College of Human Medicine, East Lansing. Ms. Demlow is director of nurses at the University Health Services, Central Michigan University. Mr. Kopke is head trainer of the Central Michigan University varsity sports teams.

During the Fourth International Special Olympics, Dr. Bedo was chairman of the medical staff, Ms. Demlow was director of nurses, Mr. Kopke was head trainer, and Mr. Moffit was a health education intern.

FOCUS... SPECIAL OLYMPICS

1963

The Joseph P. Kennedy, Jr. Foundation and the American Association for Health, Physical Education and Recreation cooperate on a physical fitness program for mentally retarded individuals and offer awards for achievement.

July, 1968

First International Special Olympics Games held at Chicago's Soldier Field.

December, 1968

Senator Kennedy announces establishment of Special Olympics, Inc. The National Association for Retarded Citizens pledges its national support. Don Adams is appointed head coach.

January, 1970

All 50 states, the District of Columbia and Canada have Special Olympics organizations and State Directors. 50,000 athletes are involved.

March, 1970

The National Hockey League Board of Governors announces sponsorship of International Special Olympics Floor Hockey Program.

June, 1970

550 young athletes participate in the First French Special Olympics Games--the first instance of significant participation outside the United States.

August, 1970

150,000 Special Olympians and 65,000 volunteers now involved in more than 1,400 local and area meets. All states hold State Special Olympics Games.

August, 1970

Second International Special Olympics Games take place in Chicago with 2,000 athletes from 50 states, the District of Columbia, Canada, France and Puerto Rico.

December, 1971

U.S. Olympic Committee gives Special Olympics official approval as one of only two organizations entitled to use name "Olympics."

June, 1972

Jean Claude Killy, world champion skier, welcomes 1,500 young French athletes to French Special Olympics Games.

August, 1972

Third International Games open on campus of University of California at Los Angeles with 2,500 participants. Elree Bivens sets mile record of 4 minutes 48 seconds, Texas team sets 440-yard relay mark of 53 seconds.

April, 1973

ABC television broadcasts segment covering Special Olympics on Wide World of Sports.

June, 1973

Pierre Mazeaud, French Minister of Youth and Sports, attends French Special Olympics Games. Spirit and courage of athletes moves him on the spot to offer six silver cups as trophies.

December, 1973

At 4 a.m., in a cold driving rain, three University of Vermont Students complete 41 mile marathon for the benefit of Vermont Special Olympics. One runner remarks, "What with all the problems facing the world, we felt it would be a good idea to generate some enthusiasm for some really deserving people."

January, 1974

More than 300,000 children now active in Special Olympics year round, including 15,000 local meets and games.

April, 1974

Kyle Rote, Jr., winner of the ABC Superstars Competition, contributes $5,000 of his prize money to Special Olympics.

May, 1974

In a mile race during Washington, D.C. Special Olympics Games, two young men leading the field join hands and finish together showing the great friendship that competition develops.

June, 1974

The National Hockey League hosts third annual Floor Hockey Tournament in Winniped, Philadelphia team wins Little Stanley Cup. Team from St. Louis captures Clarence Campbell Bowl.

MILESTONES

July, 1974
400,000 athletes take part in 1974 Special Olympics program showing that participation continues to spread and expand.

December, 1974
The National Basketball Association and the American Basketball Association cooperate to sponsor the National Special Olympics Basketball Program, including exciting Run, Dribble and Shoot competition.

February, 1975
Winner of second Superstars competition, O.J. Simpson, contributes $5,000 of his prize money to Special Olympics following the lead set by Kyle Rote, Jr. a year earlier.

February, 1975
AUTOLITE/FRAM Corporation, a Bendix Company, announces its sponsorship of the 1975 National Run, Dribble and Shoot Contest.

March 1975
First Presidential Premiere for Special Olympics features Barbara Streisand and "Funny Lady." 10 million Americans see TV Special featuring President Ford, Muhammad Ali, Frank Gifford and Special Olympics athletes.

March-April, 1975
3,182 noncommissioned officers run from Washington, D.C. and Los Angeles, California non-stop in a 3,182 mile marathon for Special Olympics. Hundreds of high school and college track and cross country teams, jogging associations, running clubs and concerned volunteers join to help raise funds to send athletes to the International Special Olympics Games.

April, 1975
Mexican athletes compete for the first time in a Special Olympics event held in Nogales, Arizona.

August, 1975
Fourth International Special Olympics Games takes place with 3,200 young athletes participating from ten countries at Central Michigan University.

September, 1975----August, 1976
International expansion occurs from impetus of 1975 International Games. New programs start in Hong Kong, the Bahamas, Honduras, Okinawa and other countries.

January, 1976
More than 500,000 athletes now involved in Special Olympics in the United States and 12 foreign countries.

March, 1976
Superstars Kyle Rote, Jr. and Anne Henning contribute $5,000 each to Special Olympics.

February, 1977
First International Winter Special Olympics brings over 500 athletes to Steamboat Springs, Colorado, to learn to ski and skate.

March, 1977 Grey Advertising volunteers to serve as public service advertising agency for Special Olympics internationally.

July, 1977
Participation in Special Olympics climbs to over 700,000 with increased number of adult participants. 19 countries have Special Olympics.

August, 1977
Bruce Jenner, world's winner in the Olympic Decathalon, becomes Head Coach of Special Olympics track and field activities.

September, 1977
Special Olympics launches worldwide soccer progam with Pele as Head Coach and sponsorship by North American Soccer League.

November, 1977
Governor Carey, Eunice Kennedy Shriver and Dr. Albert Brown announce award of Fifth International Summer Olympics Games in August, 1979 to the State University of New York at Brockport.

August, 1979
Nearly 3500 athletes and their 1000 chaperones joined 3000 parents, friends and relatives in Brockport, New York for the Fifth International Summer Special Olympics Games.

IMPROVED FUNCTIONING OF THE PARTICIPANTS

Recreation and athletics for mentally retarded participants develops self-realization, promotes satisfying human relations, and improves self-confidence. Also of importance is the acceptance of the child by his parents, peers and community. Involvement in Special Olympics removes him from his daily routine and provides the child an opportunity to show his physical prowess. It further allows him to make decisions in a non-threatening environment. In addition to the more obvious advantages associated with physical conditioning of the child, Special Olympics provides opportunities for participants to help other handicapped children and thus experience the sense of importance and accomplishment.

Recreation and physical education program improve the general physical condition of mental retardates, increase their mobility and muscular strength, improve their coordination and self-control, and contribute to their overall sense of security. Research supports the contention that retarded children profit significantly from physical education programs and that muscular fitness in the trainable mental retardate increases with long term training periods. Studies have found that improvements in classroom attitude and behaviors were reported by teachers of excercising retardates. Further, in addition to the physical changes and effects of exercise programs, retardates also acquire an overall sense of security. Mentally retarded adolescents receive a high degree of psychological stimulation.

Coaches, teachers, parents and other persons working with the mentally retarded indicate that they are aware of the mentally retarded child's emotional activities. It has been shown that sports participation by mentally retarded children enhances their self-concept and builds their self-confidence.

If a retardate is active in a sport, no matter how simplified, a common tie with normal people is made. Lead-up skills and modified sports not only provide a tie with normality but also enjoyment through fulfillment of the need to play. This is an extremely important and timely consideration in view of the recent trends in normalization and deinstitutionalization.

Physical activity and play are important aspects of a normal growth pattern. Movement experiences made valuable contributions as children learn to perceive and relate their bodies to the enviroment. Through positive perceptions, confidence is increased in their ability to function motorically, psychologically and socially.

Play and Mentally Retarded Children

Joe L. Frost
University of Texas at Austin

Mentally retarded children typically lack the skills needed to engage in higher level cognitive and social play. When placed on the floor in close proximity to toys, severely retarded children may not move from the position in which they are placed, reach out to examine toys, or imitate the actions of others. The problem is further complicated by the attitudes and actions of people and institutions who care for retarded children. Everyone agrees that retarded children have the same play needs as nonretarded children but retarded children, especially those in training schools, have fewer opportunities to play (Benoit, 1955). This is due to a number of reasons:

- Adults may underestimate the potential of retarded children to develop skills in play

- There has been little thinking and writing on the subject of play and retarded children

- Much of the existing play equipment and materials is questionable for normal children and is unsuitable for the retarded

- Mental retardation is frequently linked with special deficiencies that make play difficult

- An attitude of hopelessness toward teaching play activities to retarded children.

- Ignorance concerning the importance of play in the development of both normal and retarded children

- An overconcern with accident and injury

Once positive attitudes concerning play and retarded children have been developed, parents and care-givers are faced with the task of teaching retarded children how to play. Whereas play, imitation, and exploration occur as a matter of course in normal children, play and other associated behaviors must be systematically planned for and taught to retarded children.

A number of people have studied the play behaviors of mentally retarded children. Some tentative generalizations are available. Social play can be increased by direct teaching, prompting and rehearsing roles, followed by positive reinforcement (Strain, 1975; Paloutgian, Hasagi, Streifel, and Edgar, 1971. Integrating handicapped children into play situations with nonhandicapped or higher-functioning peer models also increases their social play (Morris and Dalker, 1974; Devoney, Guralnick, and Rubin, 1974). Thus, it seems that tools already at our disposal, i.e., direct instruction, modeling, and reinforcement, can be valuable allies in promoting social play among mentally handicapped children. Further, the currently popular concept of mainstreaming or integrating handicapped and nonhandicapped children in the classroom should be extended to the outdoor play environment.

Mentally retarded children should be thoroughly evaluated to determine the extent of any motor or sensory deficit and a review of their behaviors should be conducted. This includes analysis of imitation behaviors, tracking and searching skills, language competencies, and social interaction skills. Additional behaviors that have rarely been measured by researchers and clinicians include frequency of action on play materials and toys; diversity of play behaviors, i.e., frequency of novel responses; range of toys or materials acted on; frequency of interaction between peers and number of different peers interacted with; affective or aggressive behavior during play periods (Wehman, 1975, p. 242).

In working with severely retarded children who have few skills, it may be more appropriate to work on a wide range of parallel activities at a low developmental level, rather than attempting to achieve a high level of sophistication in

"Play and Mentally Retarded Children." Original article by Joe L. Frost, Barry L. Klein. *Children's Play and Playgrounds*. Allyn & Bacon, Inc.

Table 1 Categories of Handicaps and Their Consequences

Category	Specific Handicaps	Social and Personal Consequences
Physical	Crippled Birth defects Blind and partially sighted Neurological disorders Cerebral palsy Epilepsy Health impaired	The child has problems with: Mobility Experiencing the world through all of his senses Mastering his physical and human environments People who are too helpful or too demanding People who do not understand his difficulties in gaining mastery over his world Isolation Diminished energy
Communication	Speech Deaf and hard of hearing Language disorders of childhood Severe language delay Multihandicapped	The child has problems with: Learning or using verbal symbols to think and communicate about his world Isolation Dealing with academic learning which requires the use of verbal symbols
Development and learning	Mental retardation Behavior disorders Specific learning disabilities	The child has problems with: Reduced interest in the world Difficulty in relating positively to children and/or adults Developing internal controls Failure to live up to expectations Rejection and isolation

one play skill, i.e., block design.

Michelman (1974) constructed a detailed "Play Agenda"* for the handicapped child that describes the specifications for designing a play environment, toys appropriate for various cognitive levels, specifications for play experiences, and specifications for activities that promote risk-taking and decision-making abilities.

Specifications for Environment

Play environments for handicapped children should meet the following criteria:

1. provide a match between the child's abilities, interests, and environmental expectations. Play equipment should adjust to more than one purpose, more than one child, and more than one developmental level

2. provide substantial sensory-cultural enrichment that arouses curiosity and stimulates investigation

3. include play materials and activities that meet the requirements of children at different cognitive, kinesthetic, and play stages and foster growth and learning

---

*Adapted from "Play and the Deficit Child" by Shirley S. Michelman. In *Play as Exploratory Learning*, edited by Mary Reilly © 1974, pages 194–205. By permission of the publisher, Sage Publications, Inc. (Beverly Hills/London).

A. At the sensory-motor stage of practice play:

1) toys that appeal to the senses and muscles: soft toys for feeling, squeezing, and throwing; toys for sand and water play; swings, seesaws, slides

2) toys that challenge growing powers: empty containers with removable lids to take off and put on, cartons or boxes to climb upon or into, building blocks

B. At the symbolic, imaginative play stage:

1) toys that strengthen large muscles: wheeled toys, large balls, large hollow blocks

2) toys for stretching the mind and activating problem solving: puzzles; wooden beads for stringing; aquarium, terrarium

3) toys for make-believe, pretending, and practicing grownup roles: dolls, housekeeping equipment and props, dress-up clothes

4) toys for creating, expressing feelings and ideas, and symbolic formation: crayons; chalk; paint, clay; materials for collage and construction; variety of records and percussion instruments

C. For children who are learning to play games with rules:

1) toys, games and apparatus for developing skills, teamwork and group participation: bicycle, skates, sports equipment

3. IMPROVED FUNCTIONING

Adults must be skillful in supporting and extending the play of handicapped children.

2) materials for creating, for practicing risk taking and decision making, and for building confidence and self-esteem: art materials, needlework, carpentry tools, model building, camera, musical instruments

3) materials for stretching the mind: measuring instruments; magnifying glass, microscope; binoculars; hobby sets; board games; games of chance; games that develop specific academic skills

4. offer opportunities for success and evoke confidence and self-esteem

5. include models of adults and older children to imitate and learn from

6. be structured by consistency and pervaded by a spirit of playfulness to encourage adaptation

7. be structured by time and space to help children understand these concepts as they build habit structures for dealing with such realities

Specifications for Experiences

1. Play experiences that correspond as closely as possible to the normal stages of healthy children.

2. Sequences of play activities that alternate group experience with periods set aside for solitary play with materials and ideas allow the child to proceed at his own tempo as he practices basic skills and gains understanding of his environment.

3. Art experiences with sensory media and imaginative play activities enhance a child's capacity for adaptive emotional behavior.

4. Play experiences that provide opportunities for repetition, imitation, and problem solving promote learning and help the handicapped child find order and meaning in the environment.

5. Games with rules of graduated difficulty encourage children to practive the discipline of self-restraint and control of immediate impulse as they submit their behavior to a given task.

6. Experiences that evoke the instinct for workmanship and or sense in mastering things for their own sake, such as making sand castles, painting, and model building enable handicapped children to savor intrinsic satisfaction and reward.

7. Motivation stimuli keyed to the child's interests and developmental level as well as enthusiastic adults are devices that get a play experience started.

8. Variables to be aware of in play experience are:

   A. the degree and range of required rules and the form and source of personal or impersonal controls exercised over the child

   B. the minimum level of ability required to participate in a game

   C. the provisions for verbal or nonverbal interactiveness

   D. the provision for reward, both intrinsic and extrinsic

9. Individual and group variables to be aware of:

   A. the child's readiness, capability, and motivation at the current moment

   B. the degree of self-control available to the child at a given time

   C. the degree of group cohesion, composition, and mood, influence the course of play development

   D. timing and sequence of play experiences are important variables to control

Specifications for Activities that Promote Risk-Taking and Decision-Making Abilities

1. Art activities that encourage experimentation with numerous solutions to a problem involve children in risk taking and decision making.

2. Table games in which errors and wrong decisions are not irreversible.

3. Activities that allow alternative solutions to problems and adults who refrain from making a child's choices encourage decision making and active learning.

4. Creative activities and imaginative play allow children to revise and alter many previously held wrong decisions about themselves.

5. Activities that are dependent upon group choice help handicapped children learn the dynamics of group decision making.

6. Any play activity or game that provides experiences in success promotes feelings of confidence and competence in handicapped children and builds a framework of security from which children draw courage and flexibility for their daily living.

(Photo by Camilla Jessel)

Some of the most satisfying play equipment is constructed from discarded materials.

SPORTS AND THE MENTALLY RETARDED INDIVIDUAL

Mike Nychuk *

To many of us an involvement in organized athletics not only played a major role in our physical development but also in our social and physiological development as well. Having been in an advocacy position for the mentally retarded in their leisure time fulfillment over the past 7 years I can truly say the same goes for this group of people.

In the summer of 1975, under the guidance and financial assistance of the Canadian Special Olympics Inc., and Wintario, a true sports organization was initiated for the mentally retarded. Based as a modular project in trying to motivate communities and mentally retarded citizens to develop and participate in sport and fitness programs, the Ontario Floor Hockey League (OFHL) in its first year, could boast 1,500 players and organizers in well over 65 communities across Ontario. In its second year of operation the numbers reached 2,500 and close to 75 communities involved. Both make and female athletes take part.

The organization itself resembles any other on-going sports governing body here in Ontario or Canada. Although it was a one sport entity when initiated, the league has added to its title (Project "Multi-Sport") which reflects its widening objectives and philosophy. Under this wider approach bowling, swimming and track and field have become strong community programs and based on interest, other sport areas will be initiated through clinics and workshops in the future. The main reason for this development is that the league has provided sufficient communication, local, regional and provincial organization interest, and involvement to warrant a multi-sport operation.

Segregation?

To some this may sound like another truly segregated approach to services for the mentally retarded. It is and it isn't. It is when you consider part of the operations philosophy is "providing a stepping stone of experience and learning to allow that particular individual to graduate to an integrated session". (i.e. local swim team). The experience and knowledge we talk about is not only in the sports skills area; it also deals with the socialization areas as well. It is not a segregated organization in the sense that we use available channels to allow integration to be part of the total organization and participation objectives (i.e. at the 1978 Provincial Championshps five out of the 32 teams in attendance were integrated).

The league has provided something for the mentally retarded that

*Executive Director, Ontario Floor Hockey League. 40 St. Clair Ave. W.,Toronto, Ontario M4V 2M6

was never there before. True, the mentally retarded have had opportunities to run, jump, swim and bowl. But now with the league and its multi-sport aspirations the mentally retarded are being provided with:

1. continuous programs on a regular basis
2. regional and provincial activity outlets
3. a higher ratio of volunteers because of the interest the league has generated
4. higher levels of involvement by other generic agencies (i.e. park and recreation departments, YMCA'S) in local communities
5. a source of identity for both athletes and coaches
6. normal opportunities for athletic development, aspirations and training.
7. a national outlet for the individual to gain confidence, self-esteem, pride, etc.

As far as the writer is concerned, providing normal opportunities for athletic development is one of the most important features of the league. The operation has created a high identity level for the athlete and the coach. The crests, team pictures, player cards, tournaments, regional qualifications, committee meetings, rules and regulations, etc. all add up to something the participants belong to; its theirs, and whatever happens starts with them. It is a participants organization and the athletes are proud because it is their league and they have a players card in their wallet or purse saying they belong to it.

Organization and Leadership

Leadership within the ranks of the league comes from all walks of life. Volunteers range from teachers, parents, counselors, teenagers, mechanics by day - volunteer coach at night, to professional athletes. Presently there are 11 regional coordinators, one in each of the league's regional boundaries. They oversee the activities personally and report to the Executive Director who in turn reports to the league Executive Committee.

The league meets as a provincial concern every January to go over all the good and bad aspects of the organization. There is a standard set of rules and regulations so when a team from Chatam plays a team from Thunder Bay the game is the same and we don't lose the players interest and involvement with the coaches arguing for 2 hours before the game starts.

The league and Project Multi-Sport is and will in fact play a major role in encouraging participation, skill development, confidence building, etc. The role is to provide the outlets necessary for the mentally retarded athlete to fulfill his/her ambitions in the pool, on the court, or wherever sport activity might take place. And in providing these outlets we are allowing the mentally retarded to experience a great variety of new experiences, like what it feels like to fly from Thunder Bay to Toronto for the first time, to meet and enjoy the company of someone who lives 1,000 miles from their home town, to lose or win a game in the Provincial Championships.

Weekly programs, locally, are becoming more orgainized to the point where there are opportunities for the mentally retarded athlete to develop physical skills, sport strategy, leadership capabilities, peer group understanding in team activities, and how to take criticism and respect authority. Communication and cooperation with Parks and Recreation departments, YM-YWCA's, and other generic services are leading to great rewards for the participants. Instead of the church basement, most programs are being conducted in fully organized gymnasiums and instead of having a program once a month it is now once a week. The individual participant is beginning to feel alot healthier because of all the physical activity. The athletes want to come to practice and participate because they enjoy the rewards, esteem, etc.

3. IMPROVED FUNCTIONING

Effect of the Program

As a result of the program, many communities are becoming more and more aware and sensitized to the positive attributes of a mentally retarded person. This is mainly through the media attention the local teams receive, and from the spectators that show up for their home games and tournaments. Through these events, more opportunities are opening for the mentally retarded in the community. The best thing about the outcome of the program is that none of it's tokenism. The mentally retarded are being looked upon as citizens, athletes and contributors to the community's daily life.

There are numerous examples which could be used to depict the effect the OFHL has made on some communities. Timmins, Ontario, for example, has a strong following within their community. Having attended two Provincial Championships has increased awareness within the community and opened a number of doors which were closed at one time to the continuing development of sports in that community.

Thunder Bay has taken the floor hockey program from a segregated approach to a general community program open to anyone. In 1978 they had close to 75 participants of which 25 were people from the community interested in the sport and cared little if nothing that their right winger was mentally retarded.

A city council welcome home and main street parade for the successful Woodstock team, which captured the co-ed championship title in 1978, shows the strong effect the league has provided. People can identify with sports. The identity that the OFHL has created is one which can be summed up by a quote - "hey, they can really play hockey!"

Success can be measured in many ways. One way is in numbers. The league has had two years of operation, each year the number of participants has increased. With the strong initiation of "Project Multi-Sport" in 1978-79, participation numbers should triple. Another indication of success is that on June 1, 2 and 3, 1979 there will be a Provincial Summer Special Olympics in Ontario. Each and every athlete who attends will deserve attending due to his/her involvement locally and his/her performance at a regional qualifying level. In the past there have been provincial, national and international events in which mentally retarded athletes from Ontario have taken part. A problem area has been in the proper selection of athletes for these various levels of competition. Initiation of local, regional and provincial games package will provide the basis for establishing selection for future national and international competitions.

Canadian Implications

Other Provinces in Canada have begun to learn from the Ontario experiences. As a result, a national floor hockey program is not too far off. Canadian Special Olympics, Inc. in the future will continue to encourage local, regional and provincial levels of development in all provinces in Canada. For example, Saskatchewan presently has a Special Olympics Society made up of a great organization and provides a variety of local, regional and provincial incentives and outlets.

The founding organization for all of these efforts has been Canadian Special Olympics Inc. It has promoted a national program of sports training and athletic competition for mentally retarded individuals of all ages, sex, and skill levels over the past several years. Initiating a project such as the floor hockey league in Ontario is only one small area in which C.S.O. has assisted. Many people have felt that C.S.O.'s major concern was staging a one shot, yearly "competition" for retarded individuals. The program in Ontario is an indication that this view is wrong. Stimulation of year-round community based programs in sports and fitness is a major objective of C.S.O. and through a seeding program, Ontario has benefited from this organization's involvement. If the success pattern in Ontario is any indication future sports development for the mentally retarded should expand rapidly and across a broad range of sport activities.

THE RECREATION ADVOCATE:

YOUR LEISURE INSURANCE AGENCY

Andrew Weiner

Purchase of insurance represents a process quite familiar to many of us. The interested party, customer, policy holder, or client, contacts an insurance agent. This agent serves as the personal representative of the company and outlines to the client details involved in policy coverage. These details may include extent of coverage, amount and dates of premium payments, and procedures to be employed in exercising the right to coverage. The policy, as a contract for services, usually identifies the agent as the liaison between company and client. In adopting this role, the agent guarantees the delivery of those services stipulated in the contract.

An analogy may be drawn between insurance services and that system which is responsible for dispensing leisure services to handicapped individuals residing in the community.

Many residential facilities engaged in the rehabilitation of the handicapped pride themselves in offering recreation therapy as an integral component of the treatment milieu. Participation in these programs requires residents to expend huge quantities of time and energy which are channeled into the acquisition of recreative skills; skills are purportedly retained for independent use within the community (Lindley,

1972). Thus, the handicapped individual does pay premiums (time and energy) for which he is entitled to receive services. Services would be identified as special community recreation programs. Therefore, a subsequent failure of the community to provide such services constitutes a breach of contract.

A study of community recreation programs for the handicapped depicts an anemic condition. Only 35 percent of the local park and recreation agencies operating in the U.S. offer programs for the handicapped and mentally retarded (Pomeroy, 1974). Needless to say, the extent of services varies from state to state and corresponds to the size and location of the various municipalities.

In a comprehensive study of community leisure opportunities available to selected special populations in Texas, park and recreation agencies throughout the state were asked about their sponsorship of community services. The survey was designed to investigate the effect of certain variables upon the delivery of leisure services. Notable findings include the following: 1) Of the 78 percent that returned the questionnaire, only half (50 percent) offered special programs under the aegis of the public recreation department, and of those departments providing services, more than half consisted of agencies existing in large urban areas; 2) Many departments relied upon local health and welfare agencies for program support, in the form of knowledge concerning the various behavioral dynamics demonstrated by handicapped individuals. Churches, special interest organizations (*i.e.*, Association for Retarded Children), civic clubs, schools, and other welfare agencies have in many cases assumed some degree of program responsibility while local recreation departments have contributed facilities; 3) The presence of fees and charges were not a deterrent to successful programming while insufficient manpower, lack of knowledge concerning various handicapping conditions, and overly streamlined budgets were real obstacles. Surprisingly enough, lack of transportation was not reported to be a key problem despite the article's contention that most recreation departments do not offer such a service; 4) The types of activities provided by the state institutions and training schools boarding the handicapped correlated significantly, but not highly, with those offered by the public recreation agencies. In view of the emphasis placed upon the handicapped individual's independent performance in the community, the authors suggested that the compatibility existing between institutional and community recreation programs fell far short of the ideal; 5) The final and perhaps most startling statistic was that almost half (42 percent) of the agencies responding indicated that recreation programming for special populations was *not* their responsibility (Hayes and Smith, 1973).

While the above study does not necessarily imply that a situation of the same magnitude exists universally, most professionals will concur that the problem of providing programs for the handicapped is a pervasive one. With the advent of the "economic crunch", the immediate prognosis for increased community recreation services appears guarded at best. This plight leaves professionals with the dilemma of trying to place handicapped individuals into recreation programs which do not exist.

Or do they exist? Perhaps a method garnered from the "Texas Study" may be used to partially alleviate this stressful situation. When certain municipal park and recreation agencies failed to provide the necessary programs *en toto*, the aid of other community agencies was enlisted. Consider a partnership between the recreation department and one of the local health and welfare agencies. The recreation department or school could furnish the facility while the partner agency would provide the information concerning the special population involved in the program. The net result is a combination of resources designed to meet a community need. Therefore, it becomes imperative that professionals dedicated to helping the handicapped, seek alternate avenues of relief.

Yet another obstacle to satisfactory service exists. The organizational bureaucratic maze requires the designation of a guide who will escort the bewildered client through the appropriate channels. This guide would function as an agent, or to be more in accord with the social service vernacular, as a client advocate.

Before generously dispensing roles, duties and responsibilities, a scrutiny of the concept of advocacy and its relation to leisure services is in order.

"Advocacy is an act or process of defending or promoting a cause and the subsequent pleading of that cause." (McCormick, 1970). In analyzing the concept from a practitioner's standpoint, Grosser (1965) views the advocate as a partisan who draws upon his resources to insure a favorable position for his client. Brager (1968), in associating the advocate with the "plight of the disadvantaged," identifies a segment of the population in need of service.

The concept of advocacy is not new to the area of recreation and leisure service. Hillman (1972) editorialized about the need for therapeutic recreators to serve as advocates, stating that only by acquiring a more aggressive posture could recreators insure a humanistic quality in client service. Even prior to this, endorsement of the advocacy relationship between recreator and client was well stated by Dunn (1971), who enumerated the duties performed by those professionals actively engaged in advocacy. These functions included creating and supporting legislation favorable to the leisure needs of the handicapped, testifying at public hearings in order to educate the public regarding the need for increased special programming, communication with elected officials, researching special problems germane to the leisure concerns of the handicapped, implementing and directing special recreation programs, and promoting job opportunities for special populations in the field of leisure services.

Thus, various obstacles which have marred the ability of public recreation agencies to deliver leisure services have prompted professionals to explore other means of providing satisfactory service. Based on the premise that various other local agencies can assist in the promotion of leisure services, the role of recreation advocate can be viewed with perspective. The recreation advocate functions as the client's ticket to available leisure resources.

With this introduction, the stage is set for further examination of the role of the recreation advocate. Let us answer the following questions.

Who will serve as the Recreation Advocate?

The role of recreation advocate should be assumed by a professional possessing considerable knowledge concerning the physical and psychological conditions imposed upon the individual by his handicap. This knowledge is of prime importance when attempting to identify suitable community programs. While a trained recreation therapist would be most desirable for the role, a professional not specifically trained in therapeutics, but demonstrating other necessary qualifications, as outlined below would suffice.

What competencies in addition to recreation therapy skills should an advocate possess?

The advocate should be able to demonstrate many of the competencies traditionally associated with social workers. Most notable among these would be a lucid understanding of the eligibility and operational policies of the various health and welfare agencies. Only armed with this information can the advocate correctly determine the leisure opportunities actually available to his client. An understanding of "where the client is" in relation to his local environment is also of paramount importance. Additional skills include interpersonal communication skills (sys-tematically responding in a helpful manner), interviewing techniques, and an acquaintance with the legal aspects of client-agency relationships. The necessary interpersonal relationship between advocate and client is built on a series of successful transactions. For example, if a client is encountering difficulty in securing services from one of the health or welfare agencies, calls upon the recreation advocate to intercede, and the advocate does so successfully, the facilitative relationship between client and advocate is thereby enhanced. Once rapport is established between the two principals, motivation of the client to participate in recreation programs becomes less difficult. Parenthetically, since a caring and productive relationship can only be fostered through close contact, it has always remained puzzling to this writer how certain professional recreators can claim to have a facilitative relationship with their clients when the extent of their interaction rarely exceeds five hours per week, including active recreational activities. A client's problems do not dramatically disappear upon entering or exiting the gymnasium; rather, such problems linger throughout the activity session, often impeding the client's performance and subsequent enjoyment. Would it not be wiser to deal with the problem immediately, and to postpone the activity programming until the next session?

Where will the advocate be situated?

The most advantageous location for the advocate, assuming the supply is limited, would be in an institution serving the handicapped. It has already been acknowledged via the "Texas Study" that many community recreation departments do not employ a qualified recreation therapist. If a similar predicament exists universally, then the geographical distribution of therapeutic recreators is already highly unbalanced, with a disaproportionately high concentration of therapists operating in institutions. Thus, the institution becomes a de facto center for information and the possible training center for future advocates. A secondary reason for locating the institution relates to logistics, as usually rehabilitation facilities are strategically situated in an attempt to service as large a geographic area as possible.

How are advocacy duties delegated?

Advocacy duties would complement rather than supplant the primary duties involved in administering therapy. Hypothetically, if two or three recreation therapists worked at an institution, each therapist could devote 75 percent of his time to institutional obligations and the remainder to advocacy assignments. Each advocate could assume responsibility for a designated section of the community, city, or state, contingent upon the location of the institution and target population to be served. Further, the quantity of similar facilities existing within the state would have considerable influence upon determining the number of advocates needed.

What are the specific responsibilities of a recreation advocate?

The major responsibilities of the advocate should involve: (1) placement of the client into the appropriate community program; (2) periodic monitoring, via telephone or personal visit, of the client's progress; (3) "running interference" should the client become embroiled in agency "red tape;" (4) evaluating programs through feedback from both client and agency; and (5) educating the public as well as various agencies as to the leisure needs of their clientele. In addition, those activities previously described by Dunn paint a clear picture of recreation advocacy. However, it should be noted that many of the responsibilities mentioned here are situation specific and must be assumed within the scope and range of the advocate's professional environment. Also, the advocate's behavior should be in harmony with his personal value system.

How long should advocacy duties be assumed?

As a general rule, advocacy should be continued for that amount of time required to complete the task. The character of the work is so fluid and subject to so many external variables that arbitrary time limits are unworkable. An anticipated general time limit of a one year follow-up period after initial satisfactory program placement could be established, but would be subject to change, depending on such factors as size of the advocate's case load, mobility of clients, availability of programs and the client's adjustment rate. Hopefully, a one year period of follow-up will be enough time to facilitate the client's independent adjustment in the community. However, until that time arrives, it remains incumbent upon the recreation advocate to serve as his client's leisure insurance agent.

Thus, in return for the client's payment of premiums in the form of time and energy, the recreation advocate should serve as the leisure insurance agent, representing to the client the recreational offerings of community agencies and insuring, via his advocacy role, that both the client and the agencies honor the service contract.

References

Brager, George A., Advocacy and Political Behavior. Social Work, 13:5-15, (April) 1968.

Dunn, Diana R., Advocacy as a Basic Responsibility. *Report of Proceedingis of the National Institute on Program Development in Recreation and Physical Education for Handicapped Children.* John A. Nesbitt (ed.). (April 22): 1971.

Grosser, Charles F., Community Development Programs Serving the Urban Poor. *Social Work,* 10:18, (July) 1965.

Hayes, Gene A. and Dick Smith, Municipal Recreation Services for Special Populations in Texas. *Therapeutic Recreation Journal,* 8:1:23-30, 1973.

Hillman, William A., Jr., Therapeutic Recreation Specialist As Advocate. *Therapeutic Recreation Journal,* 6:2:50, 1972.

Lindley, Donald D., Problems of Integrating Recreation Programs into the Community. *Therapeutic Recreation Journal,* 6:1:8-10, 34, 1972.

McCormick, Mary J., Social Advocacy: A New Dimension in Social Work. *Social Casework,* 51:3-11, (January) 1970.

Pomeroy, Janet, The Handicapped Are Out of Hiding: Implications for Community Recreation. *Therapeutic Recreation Journal,* 8:3:120-128, 1974.

Recreation for the Retarded
One Institution's Approach

NICHOLAS RUSINIAK is recreation supervisor at Southbury Training School, Southbury, Connecticut 06488.

Southbury (Connecticut) Training School currently serves 1,700 retarded people, 80% of whom are over 16 years old and about 70% of whom are moderately to profoundly retarded. Since services are provided individuals who are mildly, moderately, and profoundly afflicted, the staff is concerned with a wide range of individual interests and abilities. Ages of participants, along with degrees and types of mental and/or physical handicapping conditions, help to determine their leisure time activities. For mildly and moderately retarded individuals, recreation may mean a concentrated effort to provide socialization and participation outside the institution and in the community. When programming for severely and profoundly retarded residents, emphasis is generally on motivation, skill building, and behavior shaping so that participants can better adapt to social and physical conditions of the institution.

Opportunities for recreation afforded by the physical aspects of Southbury are good. Every living unit (cottage) has at least one room or area which can be used for play as well as its own outdoor area which is also suitable for activity. Within Southbury's 1,600 acres are two ponds, an outdoor pool, one official size softball field, various sized playing fields equipped with swings, slides, picnic benches, and other outdoor play equipment, an auditorium which seats 600 and doubles as a movie theater, two gymnasiums, a bowling alley, and a snack shop.

A visitor to Southbury won't see a football game or archery or even volleyball, but he will see people in wheelchairs pushing bowling balls off ramps and scoring consistently in the 60s. He will see severely retarded adults forming a circle around a parachute, grasping it, and watching it billow as they raise their arms in unison. Visitors are often amused to see our train bumping along village streets; they are awed by the fact the physically handicapped people and those afflicted by epilepsy are swimming.

By using Southbury's physical strengths and implementing a philosophy of meeting individual leisure time needs, we include seven types of recreational activities in the program.

Special events such as Fourth of July parade, Santa's arrival, Easter egg hunt, soap box derby race and baby buggy parade day, Halloween parade, amateur night, August moon ball, athletic banquet, and New England Scout Jamboree.

Excursions into the community for activities such as plays, movies, athletic events, Connecticut River boat rides, carnivals, and circuses.

Visiting entertainments to Southbury Training School such as circuses, rock and country and western bands, variety shows, plays, and snowmobiling.

Intramural activities such as checkers, regular and wheelchair bowling, pool, and kick-t-ball.

Recreational therapy includes any activity which improves socialization, teaches a skill, motivates interest, and/or increases body awareness, coordination, and balance.

Scouting features Boy Scout, Girl Scout, and Sea Scout troops.

Camping activities vary with the seasons. In summer there may be boating, fishing, picnicking, swimming, miniature golf, and camping; for winter there are sledding, skating, bowling, movies, and bingo.

No matter what the season, each resident is provided some type of activity each day of the year—every resident, every day! At a time when institutions are overcrowded, understaffed, and poorly funded, how can Southbury provide for all its residents?

To operate these programs a better means of scheduling than once existed had to be initiated. At one time we were faced with the impossible task of providing 41 cottages averaging 43 people per building with some type of recreation on a somewhat regular basis with a recreation staff of four full-time and two part-time people. Obviously, consistent high quality programming was impossible; more staff was needed. However, being with the Residential Services Department, we realized that there was available a nucleus of 600 attendants who could be trained and had some time within their normal work day to provide leisure time activities for the people in their charge. It became the duty of the supervisor of recreation to:

Initiate activities suitable to mental and chronological ages of homogeneous groups which aides could supervise for two one-hour periods per day.

Attend in-service training classes to meet new employees, acquaint them with the philosophy of the recreation program, and explain their role as attendants in meeting leisure time needs of residents.

Help train and license cottage personnel to drive one of four large school buses so they could take residents to community activities deemed appropriate and enjoyable by participants and staff.

Provide equipment and supplies to all cottages to meet individual needs and desires of men or women living within each unit. In this way, any cottage could obtain a croquet set, arts and crafts materials, paint sets, bats and balls, yarn and needles, or whatever items were needed for activities.

Organize bowling leagues and have cottage attendants serve as coaches; recreation's only responsibility in this was to keep a tournament board current and to post time and opponents for the next match. Use of cottage attendants as coaches is suitable for any type of league or tournament.

Encourage individual cottage supervisors to initiate and carry out trips, set up intercottage tournaments, provide game times, take walks, and use the lake area, boats, fishing gear, bowling alleys, and gyms.

Use volunteers in all phases of recreational programming.

During the summer slimnastics classes for teenage girls and coed camping on Long Island Sound were initiated; coed recreation programs increased in terms of frequency and numbers of the population served. With cottage personnel providing more and more leisure time activity, the role of the recreation staff became more consulting, coordinating, and directing special events than directing resident programs and activities.

However, the recreation staff was responsible for increased recreation programming and direct services for severely and profoundly retarded residents. Initially there was need to break away from time spent within the confines of the cottage or immediate outdoor area, so bus rides and picnics a few miles from the institution were introduced. Some residents attended on-grounds Saturday morning movies; others took walks with a staff ratio of one to two; many were bused to the pool so 20 or 30 at a time could swim for one to one and a half hours. In the beginning there were problems. For many, bus rides caused motion sickness; some were incontinent in the pool; many could not feed themselves, which made picnicking difficult. But recreational activities coupled with self-care programs alleviated most and entirely extinguished many of the problems.

There was a need for intense, small-group recreation skill training. This was begun by taking a pilot group of six severely retarded men (chronological age 23 to 46), two recreation personnel, and one cottage attendant trained in behavior modification tech-

niques to two-hour recreation periods twice a week. To remind them that something special was about to happen, residents were always groomed and waiting for class to begin. They were driven from their cottage to a recreation room and were involved in such skill building techniques as block building, puzzle building (maximum eight pieces), color discrimination, ball throwing, shooting baskets, kicking a ball, pushing and pulling large objects, riding an adult tricycle, and coloring. After 12 weeks of the program one client was

accepted into the fall school program and possibilities for resident improvement with similar programs was indeed exciting.

In summary, the Southbury experience indicates that, with good organization and program supervision, a recreation staff of six can provide a total recreation program for 1,700 residents. The answer to how this can be done rests with the direct involvement of cottage aides in recreational activities in the cottages, on the grounds, and in the community.

Weight Training for Severely Mentally Retarded Persons

RICHARD A. NESS is director of an
S.R.S. Grant at Denton State School,
Denton, Texas 76202.

A primary goal of physical education programs should be helping each participant become more functional physically within his environment. For many severely mentally retarded individuals, the environment is often an institution. The inherent qualities and administrative structure of state institutions for mentally retarded persons are designed to provide the best possible care within a restricted environment. A major objective of the educational program is ultimately to prepare the resident to leave the institution and live and work in some type of sheltered environment or for independent living.

The mental and often physical inabilities and hardships placed on parents or guardians to care for severely and profoundly retarded individuals are so great that long-term institutionalized placement is often the only realistic solution that will benefit both parent and retarded child. In the institutionalized lifestyle, however, residents are often prevented from participating in many of the developmental physical activities which noninstitutionalized individuals are afforded in environments outside of institutions. Thus, many institutionalized individuals are not only mentally retarded, but almost always physically deficient when compared to individuals of the same chronological age and of normal intelligence.

One way to improve physical abilities is through well-designed, structured programs of physical activity. In the Recreation Department at Denton (Texas) State School for the Mentally Retarded, a strong emphasis has been placed on developing programs which help mentally retarded residents become more functional physically. One such program, weight training, has been used to increase the strength of severely retarded residents.

The weight training program was designed to develop progressively muscular strength of severely retarded students by a system of six resistive type exercises. Exercises were performed on a single unit adult-station multipurpose weight training machine. Although the particular gym machine used has nine lifting stations, only six were used for this program. The six lifting stations designed for total body strength development were leg press, lat pull, bicep curl, standing press, bench press, and sit-up board.

The gym machine afforded three essential factors which contributed greatly to the success of the program. Since weights were lifted by means of lever and pulley actions, there was little opportunity of injury from dropping weights. Once a student developed confidence and felt secure in what he was doing, he could motivate himself to lift even heavier weights. The instructor was able to adjust quickly the weight each student was to lift. thus allowing each student to progress on his own individual program at his own individual rate.

Three problem areas occurred which were commensurate to a student's level of retardation. Initially some students were unable to understand directional movements of push-pull, up-down, and in-out. This problem was intensified when combinations of directions were necessary to complete lifting movements—e.g., push the bar up, pull the bar down, push the pedals in. Additional difficulties were encountered when students were asked to move body parts from different positions such as sitting, standing, or lying on the back.

Two approaches were used to alleviate this problem. First, in extensive practice sessions students used broomsticks and wands to perform lifts from various positions. They had to push or pull the stick up and down or in and out from positions of sitting, standing, and lying on their backs. An instructor manually applied resistance to the broomstick to help a resident understand the direction in which he was to exert force. Another approach was to use the weightlifting machine itself with very light weights. A student was told to push or pull against the resistance so he learned weightlifting movements by moving the bar of the gym machine in the direction of the resistance. In both approaches ample assistance was given by the instructor to ensure that a student was performing correct directional movements.

Another problem area involved the student's comprehension of the number of repetitions he was to do at each lifting station. None of the students was able to count or understand the concept of numbers; ability to attend to a task for a given length of time was minimal. The students could, however, comprehend and follow loud rhythmical music. Therefore, it was decided to use music to signal starting and stopping of the lifting period at each station. When the music started, students would start to lift and they would stop when the music stopped. An instructor determined length of time music played by observing a slower lifter to ensure that he performed at least five repetitions of his lifting movement. In addition, a great deal of verbal encouragement was given by the instructors during each lifting period.

The final problem area occurred at three lifting stations where a student was required to fully extend either his arms or legs. Many students would not extend their limbs through the full range of motion in bench, standing, and leg presses, and thus did not receive full benefit of these lifting motions. A form of spotting was initiated to remedy this problem. An instructor

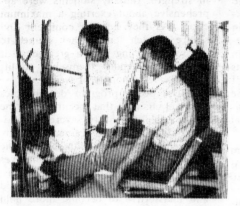

Spotting for the leg press, bench press, and standing press.

Table 1

Weightlifting Station	Average gain in weight lifted per student		
	after 2 months	after 4 months	after 6 months
leg press	26.24 lbs.	47.40 lbs.	73.74 lbs.
lat pull	17.25 lbs.	26.25 lbs.	36.87 lbs.
curl	11.25 lbs.	16.25 lbs.	20.00 lbs.
standing press	9.37 lbs	14.37 lbs.	20.00 lbs.
bench press	4.37 lbs.	12.50 lbs.	18.75 lbs.
sit-up board	Same level	plus 10 degrees	plus 10 degrees

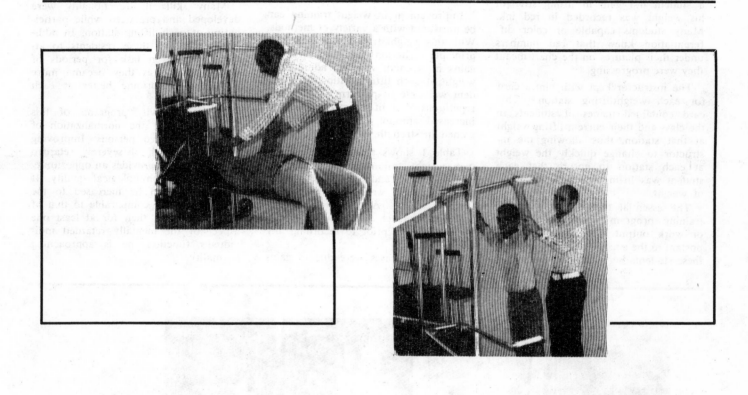

Six students perform at six different lifting stations at the same time.

applied minimal pressure to the fixed joint during the final degrees of extension to ensure that the limb would extend fully (see photographs).

Lifting data were recorded to determine gains in lifting strength and also as an incentive and a reward for these severely retarded individuals. Lifting records of each weight training class were kept on a large chart. Although students were not able to read, most could pick out their own picture on a chart of several pictures. Each student was evaluated at each station monthly to determine gains in lifting strength; a color-coded system was used to record data. If a student did not gain in lifting strength, the same weight was recorded in black ink. However, if a student did gain in lifting strength his weight was recorded in red ink. Many students capable of color differentiation knew that red numbers under their pictures on the chart meant they were progressing.

The instructor kept with him a card for each weightlifting station. This card contained names of students in the class and their current lifting weight at that station, thus allowing the instructor to change quickly the weight at each station to ensure that each student was lifting the proper amount of weight.

The essential theme of this weight training program was that of effort or work output. Scheduling was important to the success of the program as these students performed on the weight machine twice a week. Students were also involved in cardiorespiratory walking and basic movement programs in addition to weight training. By organizing the program in this manner, an attempt was made to keep students from becoming stale in one area of motor activity and also to teach the whole individual rather than emphasize one aspect of his total physiological need.

Weight training classes varied from 10 to 16 students. Each student was involved in approximately 15 to 20 minutes of concentrated circuit type weight training. A group of six students worked at one time at six different lifting stations on the weight machine. This group rotated through all six stations during the lifting period.

Improvement in weight training can be measured with a variety of methods. With this weight training program, the principle criterion used to measure gains in strength was the addition of weight at each lifting station. If a student was able to perform at least five repetitions at a lifting station with an increased amount of weight, he had gained in strength.

Table 1 shows the results of a 16-man weight training class which ran for six months and met twice a week; all participants were classified as severely retarded. A three-week period was used to teach the six weight training movements prior to recording any data.

Not all increases were due to gains in strength. Initially students were apprehensive about exerting a maximum effort. As they became confident and secure at each station, they seemed to enjoy performing with a great deal of effort and extended themselves to lift even greater amounts of weight.

This type of program demonstrates positive changes that occurred in the physical abilities of 16 severely retarded students. Students gained not only in strength, but in additional intrinsic areas such as confidence in themselves and their bodies. This confidence assisted students who had been timid and unassertive to become more bold and self-reliant. Participants also seemed to develop appreciation and better understanding of their bodies and the strength they possessed.

Many skills in directionality were developed and practiced while participating at each lifting station. In addition, ability of these residents to attend to a given task for periods of time increased as they became more intent on performing better at each station.

Physical activity programs of this nature assist in the normalization of mentally retarded persons. Improving physical strength of severely retarded individuals also provides an opportunity to improve a physiological quality. If this quality can be increased to the extent that it is comparable to that of normal persons, then for at least one aspect of the mentally retarded individual's function, he is approaching normality.

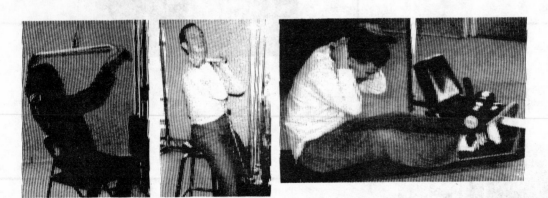

The lat pull (left) is designed to develop the muscles of the upper back, shoulders, and arms. The bicep curl (center) develops the bicep muscles of the arms. The sit-up board (right) is designed to develop the muscles of the abdominal area.

THE POTENTIAL OF PHYSICAL ACTIVITY FOR THE MENTALLY RETARDED CHILD.........

JULIAN U. STEIN

Julian U. Stein is chairman of the AAHPER Task Force on Programs for the Mentally Retarded.

In ancient times, deviates of all types were destroyed. As society became more civilized, the handicapped were spared but segregated; many became wards of the state or were kept in institutions where a life in chains was not uncommon. Even a generation ago, little hope was offered the parents of a mentally retarded child, who was generally relegated to a solitary, sedentary, and unproductive life hidden in an upstairs bedroom or placed behind bars in an institution. Today we can offer a great deal of encouragement and hope to the parents of a retarded child. It has been shown time after time that the retarded can be helped; they can be taught, and they can become productive and contributing members of society. Mental retardation is no longer a taboo subject, to be mentioned in whispers behind closed doors. As the subject of mental retardation has emerged from the darkness of ignorance, prejudice, and active antagonism, an increased understanding of the personal characteristics, abilities, limitations, and the unique needs and problems of the retarded now makes it possible to look for a bright future.

Despite the wealth of information that has been gained from interdisciplinary approaches to research and programing for the retarded, basic knowledge of dealing with the retarded has not been applied.

A visit to some homes for the retarded makes one wonder just how far we actually have moved forward in our understanding and treatment of the mentally retarded. At one institution for the mentally retarded, in a ward containing some 60 eight-to-twelve year old boys, I saw ten or twelve in strait jackets! Why? Because they were exhibiting the same basic drives and fundamental needs for physical activity and exercise that any boy in this chronological age

range exhibits. But the lone attendant, a woman in her sixties, was unable to cope with the energy and exuberance of the youngsters.

Recent trends in research show that the lack of intellectual ability resulting from arrested mental development need not affect the levels of physical fitness and motor development of the retarded. Two studies have shown that the mentally retarded respond and progress as much as normal boys and girls when given specialized training or instruction in a systematic and progressive physical education program.

"The Potential of Physical Activity for the Mentally Retarded Child---Julian U. Stein. *Journal of Health, Physical Education and Recreation.* April 1966. American Alliance for Health, Physical Education and Recreation.

125

3. IMPROVED FUNCTIONING

In one of these studies (Howe, 1957, 1959), normal and retarded boys and girls were given instruction in three motor activities. After ten days of instruction, the normal subjects remained superior in their scores, but both groups showed similar improvement patterns—significant improvement in Burpee squat thrusts, a relatively complex activity, and modest gains on the other two skills, throwing a ball at a target and simple maze tracing.

Recently mentally retarded boys enrolled in a public school special education program showed this same pattern on the AAHPER Youth Fitness Test (Stein, 1965). While normal comparison groups scored significantly higher on both raw and percentile scores based on national age norms, change scores on each of the seven items of fitness were similar and non-significantly related. This study spanned one school year and was organized in such a way that the subjects did not know that they were a part of a research investigation. When the percentile scores for these subjects were compared to the national norms, quartile distributions for both October and May administrations fell into normal distributions in thirteen out of fourteen comparisons; the single significant exception favored the mentally retarded subjects.

Dramatic results were reported in a study involving institutionalized mentally retarded boys 12 to 15 years of age in England (Oliver, 1956, 1957, 1958). All academic subjects except arithmetic and English were replaced for a ten-week period in the experimental group by activities of a physical nature: daily periods of physical education, individual remedial exercises, strengthening activities, and recreative team games. During the same period the control group followed its normal schedule, including only two periods of physical education per week, and daily organized games after school. The experimental group improved significantly in all measures of athletic achievement, physical fitness, and strength. There were also measurable and significant changes in emotional stability, medical evaluation, and personality adjustment, and there were significant increases in the IQ's of 25 percent of the experimental group. No significant improvements in IQ were reported among the control group.

Last year this basic research design was duplicated in Nashville, Tennessee (Corder, 1965). A training group received a daily one-hour period of planned physical education lessons which progressively presented more difficult and challenging activities to the public school special education subjects. After four weeks (20 days) the training group showed significant gain scores over the control group on the full and verbal scales of the Wechsler Intelligence Scale for Children. Progressive and systematic programs of physical education of only 20 days duration thus enhanced the intellectual development of educable mentally retarded boys.

Even severely retarded boys and girls showed significant improvements in muscular fitness strength and endurance through participation in a program involving intensive muscular activity of the shoulders and stressing the development of organic fitness (Hayden, 1964). A wide variety of physical education activities which proved stimulating and beneficial were adapted for use with these severely retarded subjects.

These studies dramatically show the potential of physical education as an important contributor to the total growth, development, and welfare of retarded children of different abilities in a variety of educational, training, and residential settings. This exciting and hopeful trend of recent research is in direct opposition to the results of a group of earlier studies. (For a review of the literature in this field, see Stein, 1963.) These studies indicated that the mentally retarded performed at considerably lower levels than their normal peer comparison groups on tests of motor ability, motor fitness, physical fitness, and physical efficiency. In general, retarded children achieved scores that were between two and four years behind the published age norms for normal children. On the average, retarded children showed only half as much strength, fatigued 30 percent faster, and carried 35 percent more fat than nonretarded children of the same age (Hayden, 1964). How and why is this trend reversing itself?

Analysis of the earlier studies reveals that they were status studies in which a retarded population was selected, trained in the items of the test, tested, and the results reported. No attempts were made in these studies to determine how the retarded would have done after active participation in an organized physical education program. Despite efforts to make certain that the subjects understood the test items and knew how to perform them, serious questions arise as to whether this was the case. Mentally retarded boys and girls do not play spontaneously or innovate as do normal children. They have to be taught to play, whether the play be individual, parallel, or group. Many of the motor skills and abilities that normal children learn from association and play with the gang must be *taught* to the retarded. The retarded have not had the experiences that accrue from opportunities to participate in organized physical education and recreation programs.

Comments by investigators in some of these studies hint that the difference in results of motor performance between retarded and nonretarded boys and girls was brought about through the lack of intellectual ability rather than inherent differences in motor ability. Research backs this stand (Fait and Kupferer, 1956; Asmussen and Heebøll-Nielsen, 1956; Kulcinski, 1945). Several studies have shown that the complexity of muscular movements and the associated intellectual action necessary to carry out these movements were greater factors in limiting the motor performance of the retarded than the lack of motor ability *per se*. Predictions were made as early as 20 years ago (Heath, 1943) that as the intellectual counterpart of a motor act was learned, the resultant performance would became increasingly quick and smooth. Current research is verifying this hypothesis.

Undoubtedly the progress that has been shown by mentally retarded subjects who have participated in planned programs of physical education has accrued through the interplay of a complex of factors: achievement and success (for many it may be the first time they experience the satisfaction of even completing a task), improved confidence, better adjustment, a feeling of importance because of the interest and attention centered on them, increased competitive spirit, increased pride, improved physical condition, more perseverance, and increased desire to perform well. With retarded children, these factors have even greater significance than with the normal population.

Much of an individual's success today is determined by his ability to understand and manipulate verbal symbols. Because the retarded are nonverbal, many have known nothing but failure and frustration as they have wrestled with the abstractions of programs in which success is determined by academic ability. This condition manifests itself in poor learning, inadequate social adjustment, and delayed achievement. Programs and activities in which the retarded child can express himself in nonverbal but concrete, symbolic, and meaningful ways take on even greater meaning. Important contributions to emotional and psychological stability are made through the cathartic values of activity and movement. Preparation for future vocational endeavor and for wholesome participation in recreational activities and wise use of leisure time can also be stimulated through such a program. Greater emphasis needs to be placed on the physical education of mentally retarded children, more time should be devoted to physical activities, and greater demands should be made on each of these children.

Rays of hope are emerging, even for those classified as brain damaged, where large segments of the brain have been destroyed through injury, infection, or disease. The rehabilitation treatment known as patterning, based upon artificially imposing on the damaged brain the motor patterns of movement that the brain cells could not produce themselves, has produced amazing results in patients diagnosed as hopeless by neurosurgeons. As the patient is patterned several times daily, the undamaged parts of the brain gradually take over the work of the damaged sections, making possible movements of the various parts of the body. This rehabilitative therapy is based upon the assumption that all brain cells are educable and that when some of these cells are damaged, those unaffected will gradually, with training, take over the function of the afflicted cells. As motor ability improves, lost sensory perceptions also return. This process has shed new light on the potential for motor development, not only in the brain injured, but for all mentally retarded regardless of cause.

Little has been reported on the recreational interests and leisure time pursuits of the mentally retarded. The few studies (Bobroff, 1956; Peterson and Smith, 1960) dealing with this subject indicated that few retardates know what to do with themselves in their spare time. Fewer mentally retarded adolescents and adults participate in outdoor sports and

activities like hunting, fishing, and boating than members of the nonretarded population. Some report as high as 60 percent of the retarded have no interest in hobbies of any type. Greater numbers of the retarded population spend more time watching television and doing little if anything constructive with their free time. What is being done about this?

The answer is that very little has been done on an organized, concerted, and large scale basis. However, the tide is slowly beginning to turn. Some communities have initiated year round recreation programs for the retarded. Either day or residential

Teaching Suggestions

A study of current practices in teaching physical education to educable mentally retarded children in the schools of Michigan was conducted by Joan Nelson, assistant professor, Ferriss State College, and Gail A. Harris, consultant, Michigan Department of Public Instruction. Their survey indicated that mentally handicapped children participate in most of the activities in which normal children participate. Based on their study, they underscore the importance of the teaching procedures used and suggest the following:

Progress slowly, offering familiar activities first. Use repetition, because these students need reinforcement of learning.
Introduce new activities during the early part of class before the class gets tired.
Be kind, firm, and patient, using a positive approach.
Be clear in directions without talking down to the class. Use concrete examples.
Attempt to keep each child active.
Demonstrate and take part in the activities.
Offer activities which could be useful at recess time, after school hours, and later on in life.
Remember the characteristics of the children and consider individual abilities and attention spans.
Let children compete with themselves. Some simple tests and measurement devices provide an incentive.
Give the children goals in which they can have some measure of success, and use praise as often as possible.
Allow them to have some choice of activities, and allow them to suggest activities.
Include rhythmical activities, such as simple folk and square dancing.
Aid the children in developing skills such as running, jumping, and ball handling.
Correlate good health habits with physical education.
Keep records of physical fitness.
Aim for progression in social and physical skills.

camping for the retarded can now be found in about one-third of the states. Increasing numbers of research projects are being submitted. The impetus behind these programs has come from special interest groups in local communities and national groups such as the National Association for Retarded Children and the Joseph P. Kennedy Jr. Foundation. Conspicuous by its absence to date has been our profes-

3. IMPROVED FUNCTIONING

sion of physical education, a profession that has so much to offer the mentally retarded. Some special educators are now admitting that vigorous physical activity is required as an integral part of the daily education or training program for retardates of all ages. Our neglect cannot continue.

References

Asmussen, E., and Heebøll-Nielsen, K. "Physical Performance and Growth in Children: Influence of Sex, Age, and Intelligence." *Journal of Applied Physiology,* 8:4:371-80, January 1956.

Bobroff, A. "A Survey of Social and Civic Participation of Adults Formerly In Classes for the Mentally Retarded." *American Journal of Mental Deficiency* 61:127-33, 1956.

Corder, W. O. "Effects of Physical Education on the Intellectual, Physical, and Social Development of Educable Mentally Retarded Boys." Unpublished special project, George Peabody College, Nashville, Tennessee, 1965.

Fait, H. F., and Kupferer, H. J. "A Study of Two Motor Achievement Tests and Their Implications in Planning Physical Education Activities for the Mentally Retarded." *American Journal of Mental Deficiency* 60:4 729-732, April 1956.

Hayden, F. J. *Physical Fitness for the Mentally Retarded.* Toronto, Canada: Metropolitan Toronto Association for Retarded Children (186 Beverley Street), 1964. Available from Educational Information Center, Southern Illinois University, Carbondale.

Heath, Jr., S. R. "The Military Use of Railwalking Test as an Index of Locomotor Coordination." *Psychological Bulletin* 40:4:282-84, April 1943.

Howe, C. "A Comparison of Motor Skills of Mentally Retarded and Normal Children." *Exceptional Children* 25:8:352-54, April 1959.

Howe, C. *Motor Characteristics of Mentally Retarded Children.* Doctoral dissertation, State University of Iowa, 1957.

Kulcinski, L. E. "The Relation of Intelligence to the Learning of Fundamental Muscular Skills." *Research Quarterly* 16:4:266-76, December 1945.

Oliver, J. N. "The Effect of Physical Conditioning Exercises and Activities on the Mental Characteristics of Educationally Subnormal Boys." *British Journal of Educational Psychology* 28:155-65, June 1958.

Oliver, J. N. "The Effect of Systematic Physical Conditioning on the Growth of Educationally Subnormal Boys." *Medical Officer* 97:19-22, January 1957.

Oliver, J. N. "The Physical Characteristics of Educationally Subnormal Boys." *Special Schools Journal* 45:29-32, June 1956.

Peterson, L., and Smith, L. L. "The Post School Adjustment of Educable Mentally Retarded Adults and That of Adults of Normal Intelligence." *Exceptional Children* 26:404-408, 1960.

Stein, J. U. "Motor Function and Physical Fitness of the Mentally Retarded: A Critical Review." *Rehabilitation Literature* 24:8:230-42, August 1963.

APE - THE TIP OF THE ICEBURG

Robert E. Cipriano, Ed.D.
and Lisette Walter

The purpose of this one year study was to develop and conduct a diagnostic-prescriptive physical education program for elementary school children as a basis for accurately ascertaining the effect(s) of such a program in enhancing the functioning ability of these students. The primary objective was to determine if an individualized, person-centered diagnostic-prescriptive physical education program could transfer beneficial effects that could contribute to adjustment to the environment in which children live, learn and play. The overall purpose was an attempt to accurately measure if an Adapted Physical Education (APE) program could effect the growth and development of children in the following four areas: (1) Intelligence, (2) Perceptual-Motor, (3) Self-Concept, and (4) Classroom Behavior.

State of the Art

Research generally cannot whole-heartedly support the contention that an APE program can have positive transfer effects. Seefeldt (1972), in discussing transfer of learning in an APE program, wrote that "The paradox we face is there is abundant testimony regarding the effectiveness of perceptual-motor programs in the enhancement of academic achievement but little research evidence to support such a claim." Cratty (1969) failed to detect any improvement in self-concept in mentally retarded children who demonstrated significant improvement in physical proficiency resulting from a formal exercise program. They were unable to transfer their improved physical skills to their self-concept. Lund-gren, et al. (1969) indicated that there was evidence of beneficial effects of exercise programs on IQ but it has not been proven. Oliver's (1958) study, whereby gains in IQ were reported, was not an objective study because no provision was made for the Hawthorne effect. This study attempted to develop an experimental design for implementation in a school system that would yield significant data relative to the merits of an APE program.

The methodology followed in this study was divided into the following five phases:

(1) administration of motor development test
(2) selection of target population
(3) pre-tests
(4) individualized diagnostic-prescriptive APE program
(5) re-administration of tests.

Students in grades 1-6 (N = 1,915) were tested to determine their performance in the area of motor development. The Schilling Test was the instrument used to ascertain student's performance. Those students who scored poorly (i.e with the bottom 20 percentile) on one of the factors measured in the test were evaluated, via the use of standardized tests, in the following areas: (1) motor development, (2) self-concept, (3) mental ability, and (4) classroom behavior. The tests used in this study were, respectively; (1) The Schilling Test, (2) Martinique Self-Concept, (3) Otis-Lennon Mental Ability, and (4) Classroom Behavior Rating Scale. The purpose of these tests was to ascertain student's performances in the above-indicated four areas.

Students were placed in an experimental group or a control group. Placement criteria were established (e.g. age, sex, socio-economic background, score on Schilling Test, etc.) to assure that both groups were as identical to each other as possible. The control group received their regular physical education according to the following configuration:

(1) students in grades 1, 2 and 3 received regular physical education two times per week for a total of 40 minutes per week
(2) students in grades 4, 5 and 6 received regular physical education two times per week for a total of 60 minutes per week.

The experimental group was placed in a prescriptive physical education program designed to facilitate the growth and development of students in those areas of demonstrated weaknesses. In addition to regular physical education, the experimental group had an APE program three times per week for a total of 75 minutes. Students were involved in the program for six months – November to May. It was hypothesized that these functional experiences, based upon real success and full participation, would help the student's self-concept and growth and development. The actual activities offered participants were based upon results of the test for motor development.

Students were reevaluated, via the use of the same standardized tests previously administered, to determine changes in areas previously articulated.

3. IMPROVED FUNCTIONING

Results and Interpretations

GROUPS	Schilling Test Motor Control		Otis-Lennon Mental Ability		Martinique Self-Concept	
Boys grades 4, 5 & 6	t = 2.7	.01 level*	t = no significance		t = 1.8	.05 level
Girls grades 4, 5 & 6	t = 3.63	.005 level	t = 2	.05 level	t = 2.72	.01 level
Boys grades 1, 2 & 3	t = 6.42	.005 level	t = 2.68	.01 level	t = 2.06	.025 level
Girls grades 1, 2 & 3	t = 2.5	.01 level	t = 3.01	.005 level	t = 4.05	.001 level

The differences found to exist in pre- and post-test results may be logically attributed, in part, to inclusion in the APE program. A t score (i.e. the difference between scores of groups on post-tests) was arrived at for each area measured.

Analysis
- Students participating in the APE program improved significantly in the areas of perceptual-motor, intelligence and self-concept.
- The results of the Classroom Behavior Rating Scale could not be interpreted because not enough responses were collected and tabulated. The authors conducted a rather subjective analysis of the student's performance in the classroom. Teachers overwhelmingly indicated that those youngsters included in the APE program improved their overall performance in the classroom. However, because of the above-alluded to delimitations, this claim cannot be substantiated.
- Areas of greatest change in motor control:
  1. lower grade boys
  2. upper grade girls
  3. lower grade girls
  4. upper grade boys
- Areas of greatest change in mental ability:
  1. lower grade girls
  2. lower grade boys
  3. upper grade girls
  4. upper grade boys
- Areas of greatest change in self-concept:
  1. lower grade girls
  2. upper grade girls
  3. lower grade boys
  4. upper grade boys

Standards of behavior for gross motor development can be found in any child development or motor learning text. Michele is expected to be able to skip by 5½, but Bob, not until 7. Jennifer can hop and jump forward and backward with no problem, in the first grade, but not her classmate Ray. Why is this? Is it because Ray does not play jump rope or hopscotch, or is it because he is not developmentally ready for the skills required to play those games?

How often, as professionals, do we verbalize the statement, 'Children develop at their own rate, and there is no such thing as 'normal'?" As educators, do we tend to ignore the statement and prepare lessons geared for the "total group" and possibly for the "upper stratum of the developmental spectrum"? In essence, have we truly taken notice of the Bob's and Ray's in our classes, who by their withdrawal or refusal to participate are saying to us — "I can't play your games."

How do we reach these students? What can we do to help? We strongly contend that there is a way to truly individualize our physical education classes and allow each child a right to his natural heritage — the right to play! A diagnostic-prescriptive approach to our teaching methodologies can enhance the growth and development of our students. After all, in the final analysis, isn't this what we are really all about?

Bibliography

Cratty, B.J. *Developmental Sequences of Perceptual-Motor Tasks, Movement Activities for Neurologically Handicapped and Retarded Children and Youth.* Educational Activities, Inc., Freeport, New York, (1969), p. 88.

Lundgred, S., and others. "Betydelsen AV Fysisk Training Pa Fritiden Vid Sarskoleinternat"; translation: "The Importance of Physical Training at a Home for Mentally Retarded Youngsters". *Psykisk Utveckling Hamning,* (1969), 71:3, pp. 1-11.

Oliver, J.N. "The Effects of Physical Conditioning Exercises and Activities on the Mental Characteristics of Educationally Sub-Normal Boys." *British Journal of Educational Psychology.* (1958), 28, pp. 155-165.

Seefeldt, V. "Substantive issues in perceptual motor development." Symposium on research methodology in perceptual-motor development presented at Springfield College, Springfield, Massachusetts, May 12-13, 1972.

Sport, Myth, and the Handicapped Athlete

Richard E. Orr

Richard E. Orr is in the Department of Health and Physical Education, University of Houston, Houston, TX 77004.

Myth, superstition, and sports control over the individual have an intriguing place in our society. These are observable and common influencing factors on the athlete, coach, spectators, and paying public. They are areas of discussion, argument, and research for control and understanding—because of the pervasiveness of sport. However, this creates a major problem since the sport realm is ruled by the skilled athlete and his/her associated performance standards. There is much ignorance concerning several special groups, particularly, handicapped athletes, who are involved in athletic competition from the most basic forms to the international level. These participants are subject to the control of myths created and perpetuated by society. The concern of this paper is the identification of a primary sports myth affecting the handicapped athlete and illustration of its relationship to the realities of this group in sport.

The imposed myth is that the handicapped person participating in sports is inferior and different from the so called "normal" athlete. The reality is that while the handicapped person usually does not have equal marks in performance of a quantitative nature, the qualitative performance may equal or surpass any other athlete. The effect of the myth has been to obstruct opportunity for the handicapped as time, energy, and funds have been funneled in other directions.

Origin and Perpetuation

In the educational setting, the handicapped potential athlete has traditionally been separated from the mainstream and placed in special education. This has created categorization and stereotyping of a group and is the basis for myth. The literature in adapted physical education recognized and confirmed this separation. Concern for the handicapped individual was shown, but the concern led to involvement only by those with expertise in dealing with a special group.

Separation in itself serves as a catalyst in maintaining the myth of inferiority. People follow their beliefs until exposure or new knowledge is sufficient to overcome misinformation. For example, the experts believed that mentally retarded children could not run, swim, travel, or successfully participate in athletic competition. Then the Kennedy Foundation organized the first Special Olympics in 1968, and today 50 states are involved. Early modern Olympic marks have been attained and this group of handicapped children has achieved visibility and a new acceptance.

For the physically handicapped an avenue of competition has been wheelchair contests. Separation has come both from facility availability and educational isolation and from the development of disability at a later age, such as with military veterans. Performance is away from society's mainstream of observation. It is doubtful that the average person is aware of the National Wheelchair Athletic Association, the variety of its events, and the international opportunities for this group. These people have not had public exposure because, as a group, they lack support of the level of the Special Olympics.

Sport literature has isolated handicapped athletes by avoiding their needs in seeking a more lucrative field and a wider reading public. Someone who wants to improve performance can find innumerable coaching and training sources for athletic events from throwing the javelin, using the whip kick in swimming, shooting basketballs, to throwing darts. However, these are designed for the normal or superior athlete and ignore the amputee, the cerebral palsied, the blind, and the deaf. The literature available for this group is limited.

The lack of written instructional aids appropriate to the handicapped retards athletic development and progression. Thus, further support is given to the myth as performance continues to be below potential because training is not equal to that of the skilled nonhandicapped performer.

A further hindrance to overcoming the myth is the problem of time. Establishing the handicapped person in the mainstream of sports and competition requires considerable planning, effort, and

"Sport Myth and the Handicapped Athlete, Richard E. Orr, *Journal of Physical Education and Recreation,* Vol. 50, No. 3, March 1979. American Alliance for Health, Physical Education and Recreation.

131

3. IMPROVED FUNCTIONING

education of those now in administrative, coaching, or supporting positions.

The handicapped individual has the same needs for opportunity and expression of self that exist for the normal person. The existing myth—and its resulting expression in reality—have been a major obstacle to opportunity for success or failure in the sport world. It is a denial of the right to strive toward excellence in a competitive atmosphere where a person might be measured against many forces, including oneself.

Reality vs. Myth

If our public laws state the right of the handicapped individual to equal education and job opportunity and like treatment of all persons in all circumstances then it must be assumed this identified group is equal to all others. It may also be assumed that they have the same potential for performance abilities, and society's definition of sports may need reevaluation or clarification.

The laws support the educational research showing the need for elimination of student sorting and emphasize the need for students to strive to achieve their potential and overcome the myth of any inabilities. The lack of evidence for separation as promoted in the myth was supported in the following statement:

> Educational research increasingly has undermined one of the essential premises of sorting: that it benefits students. The research concerning the educational effects of ability grouping and special education reveals that classification, as it is typically employed, does not promote individualized student learning, permit more effective teaching to groups of students of relatively similar ability or, indeed, accomplish any of the things it is ostensibly meant to do.[1]

Studies should be undertaken to establish the relationship of the handicapped person to sport and determine a relationship to the "normal" athlete in quality of performance. Emphasis must be given to all avenues available for dealing with these elements if understanding of the handicapped person to sport is to be strong enough to overcome myth.

In sports each performer must conform to rule-governed tasks and be creative within the boundaries of play if the task is to be accomplished. Rules exist for the handicapped which are appropriate for their disabilities and which require many levels of performance for meeting the stated standards. Who is to say that the accomplishment of the task is any less for the handicapped than for the normal performer?

Sport requires effective organization of actions, on a continuum ranging from mental control to physical control. The strategies, development of skills, and other abilities required by the rules of the sport involve any given degree of difficulty. The development of muscular skill and understanding of objectives may take as long and require as much effort for the mentally retarded child running a 100 yard dash in 30 seconds as for the "normal" sprinter running the 100 meters in 10.1 seconds. Again, who can specify which performer demonstrated the better quality of performance related to body potential?

Sport requires movement and attempts at movement of objects in space. Ten wheelchairs on a basketball court are propelled in intricate patterns that relate to individuals, teams, balls, officials, boundaries, and game requirements. Considering the limitations of performers, this is no less effective in object movement than 10 specialized and highly trained athletes, with full muscle capabilities, who have no worry over the size and space requirements of chairs.

Sport rules are the same in all sports for all performers in the sense that they evaluate the athlete's performance of the task at hand. Sport rules prescribe a penalty for failure in assigned tasks. This is often identification as the loser or the nonachiever. No athlete in society can be superior to this relationship with sport whether handicapped or not. The emotional trauma related to winning or losing can be painful or pleasant on any level; it is dependent only on individual involvement and temperament as a moment of opportunity arises.

Sport offers the opportunity for self-expression within a specified arena. The individual's statement of self may relate to environment, interpersonal relationships, personal condition, or whatever that individual chooses. The fact that spectators may not understand or appreciate that statement is not as important as the fact that the statement was made. This results in an equality of athletes in sport, without the stigma of inferiority.

Another element of sport that ties all athletes together and refutes the myth of handicapped inferiority is that each athlete involves him or her self in sport or athletic competition because it is a meaningful involvement. Only the athletes themselves can establish this meaning.

No one can deny them the right or impose limitations on the depth and quality of that meaning.

Given the elements of sport and the rules of performance, all athletes must prepare for participation and find that sport which is appropriate for their individual needs. Training and skill development must occur to some degree. Classification for events by ability levels does not mean that the quality of performance in relation to human potential will be lower. They simply exist for all people to provide maximum opportunity for participation at a level that will create the best possible performance achievements.

If sport is considered an area for allowing the individual to reach maximum potential with whatever abilities are available, then it is appropriate to consider the potential of all athletes in relationship to historical perspectives and philosophies. Handicapped athletes, in their pursuit of sport, may not be inferior, may not be equal. Rather, this athlete may be the closest to realizing the Greek philosophy of the sporting ideal of the 5th Century B.C. that presupposed "an awareness of the value of man, a belief in his freedom and his merit, a consciousness of his responsibilities and, finally, an acceptance of his democratic right to participate in public affairs."[2]

For the handicapped athlete, sport offers the potential for a total understanding of oneself. In the ancient Greek philosophy: "education entailed the cultivation of the whole man, and could not be divided into physical and mental education, because the man can not exist without the body, and the body has no meaning without the mind."[3] Handicapped athletes can use sport to explore the potential of their bodies and the control and influence their minds have training and developing muscular activities. Their limitations in the sport environment stress their individual wholeness and can lead to a deeper appreciation of movement with its aesthetic and meaningful qualities.

To test these hypotheses, a semantic differential questionnaire was given to handicapped students at the University of Houston. The group was limited, but it seemed important to begin somewhere to see if this area was worth pursuing. The results showed that the handicapped athlete assigned a high value to aesthetic appreciation and participation in sport, indicating that sport and its associated movement may be one of the prime vehicles to attaining a better understanding of movement components. Combine this with the understanding these people have of themselves and their limitations, and it may be found that they can evaluate and draw deeper and more intrinsic values from movement and activity than the non-handicapped individual, who participates easily in activity. This stands as another argument against the myth of handicapped inferiority in sport.

As ignorance is overcome, a respect for the ability of the handicapped in sport will, hopefully, develop. This may come about with mainstreaming, more contests with associated publicity and greater

exposure, and greater acceptance for individual potential by society. Understanding of the depth and quality of competition and movement of handicapped competitors can occur.

Each person has the right to seek meaning in sport with the understanding that performance is first for the individual. Then qualitative and quantitative standards may be set and reviewed by others. However, the final judgment of the emotional, intellectual, and physical performance can only be truly understood by the individual in relationship with personal potential and ability.

The myth of handicapped inferiority exists through ignorance. We hope it will dissipate through the imaginative consideration of human beings pursuing individual performance standards and internal meaning.

[1] Kirp, David L. Student Classification, Public Policy and the Courts. *Harvard Educational Review*, 1974.

[2] Christopoulos, George A. and Bastias, John C. *The Olympic Games*. Athens, Greece: Ekdotike Athenon S. A., 1976.

[3] Christopoulos, op. cit.

Mainstreaming at Dae Valley Camp

On this 23 acre farm mainstreaming has been the instructional proce- dure for eleven summers of day camping.

BETTY H. OWEN is an assistant professor of health, physical education and recreation in the College of Education at Memphis State University, Memphis, Tennessee 38- 152.

Through this "mixing bowl," many rewarding incidents have been observed—trainable children sign- ing in order to communicate with the hearing impaired; hearing im- paired campers helping visually im- paired children with horsemanship skills; and six- and seven-year-old normal campers helping adult trainables with lunches. The bar- riers of sex, age, race, and ability are broken down as the children demonstrate acceptance and toler- ance of one another.

During the 1977 seven-week summer session, 126 campers, ages 4-22, attended Dae Valley Camp, a 23-acre farm near Memphis. Twenty-six of the campers were four to six years of age, and 68 campers were there for their first summer, while 58 were old timers. Many have attended this day camp for over six years and two have come for 10 years. The enrollment for each week varies between 50 and 70. The instructional groups have 8-15 campers.

According to the educational classifications of the 126 campers, 25 were normal attending regular graded classes, 36 were in resource or self-contained local classes or the state residential school for the hearing impaired (one camper is visually and hearing impaired), 40 campers were from trainable or educable classes (of this number the majority were trainable and five were multiple-handicapped), 5 were from the center for the autistic, 3 campers were physically handicapped, and 14 were classified as having specific learning disabilities.

Ability rather than class or label is used in grouping children for instruction. The highest functioning group has been composed of 10-12-year old visually impaired, learning disabled, hearing impaired, and normal campers, and older retardates. For the past three summers our best helpers, swimmers, and riders have been a 19-year old Down's girl, four hearing impaired children, and one learning disabled camper. Campers are grouped for instruction by age and performance level. The primary gauges are the ability to follow directions and skill in riding and swimming.

The high group members are able to swim in deep water on their front and back; they can handle a horse in the arena at a trot or canter and on a trail ride and follow instructional directions. Campers of the middle group are able to swim in shallow water, mount and dismount without assistance, rein a horse in the arena at a walk, and follow instructional directions. The lowest groups are composed of those children who need help in the self-care skills of dressing, must be assisted in the pool and in mounting or dismounting a horse, need to be led in the arena, and are unable to follow instructional directions.

As enrollment varies from week to week, so do group members. There are usually two to four high or middle instructional groups and two to three lower groups as age is also used to determine group placement. Grouping is fluid and the children are moved from a higher or lower group when their needs and achievements indicate a change.

The camp usually has 10 to 12 salaried staff members and additional volunteers. The 1977 staff included five certified teachers. Susan Wilson, swimming instructor; Steve Winnette, sports instructor; Sara Dickey, crafts instructor and academic tutor, Ted Rainey, lower group instructor; and Betty Owen, owner-director and riding instructor. Assisting staff members are college and high school students, most of whom have been campers. The college students have been majors in recreation or special education and act as group leaders and assist in the instructional periods.

The primary goals of the camp are achievement and fun. In order to reach these goals, the campers are encouraged to try many types of activities. Emphasis is placed on one-step-at-a-time achievement whether it be conquering the fear of touching a horse, sitting on the side of the pool, or crawling up the creek bank—to riding at a canter, learning the breast stroke, or being timed on a creek bank obstacle course. The campers are given verbal and kinesthetic assistance to help create confidence and to get the "feel" of each skill.

A great variety of activities are offered so that every individual has his/her "sport." Generally, if an activity involves being climbed or balanced upon, struck, thrown, shot, pushed, pulled, rolled, ridden, or jumped on, over, or in—it has been tried with the campers.

Instruction has been given in using and playing with the hoppity hops, scooter boards, roller skates, the slip and slide, rope swings with and without seat supports, grapeveine swings, balancing and walking on electric cable spools, beams or logs, traveling on a hand monorail, climbing trees, jungle gyms and tree houses; also, campers have ridden on a farm trailer pulled by a tractor, a go-cart, pony cart, and a slide pulled by a mule.

Game and sport type activities have included boxing, tennis, paddle tennis, pitch and putt golf, softball, bowling, billiards, badminton, table tennis, air and box hockey, croquet, soccer, low organizational games and relays, and commercial table games. Campers have been encouraged to manipulate and perform skills with bean bags, beach balls, wands, tires, innertubes, scoops, playground balls, hoops, parachutes, frisbees, and ropes. Marksmanship with the bow and BB guns has been a favorite activity of the campers.

The campers clamor to go to the "ditch" where they climb up and down the banks and hills, play in the sand, swing on the ropes and grapevines, and hike through woods, underbrush and over rough terrain. Imaginations soar as they play cowboys, soldiers, and "Tarzan." This natural playground is actually formed by a creek which winds along the back boundary of the farm. Campers particularly like to go there after a rain, then they are able to get extremely dirty by sliding down the rain slick banks and wading in shallow water.

Rhythmic activities such as folk and square dance, singing games, lummi sticks, singing by voice and signs, basic movements to music, and cheerleading routines have been presented and enjoyed.

Bike riding in the arena and on the wooded trails has been an exciting event with the campers and a favorite of the hearing impaired as they are completely safe from traffic. The high and middle groups also compete in races, barrel racing, and pole bending on the bikes.

The "meat" of the instructional program includes trampoline, swimming, crafts, academic tutoring, horsemanship, and exposure to a variety of animals (donkeys, cats, collies, chickens, goats, and ducks in addition to the ponies and horses). Daily instruction is given in these activities. The greatest contributions which have been observed in using the trampoline have been the fun of jumping, improvement in following directions in performing sequence jump commands, and improved balance among the cerebral palsied campers. Most campers learn to perform the basic knee, seat, and front drops.

Swimming instruction and an afternoon free swim are provided each day. The low groups need one-to-one assistance for they are often young and very fearful. Of the children who came for at least two weeks, there were less than ten who were unable to swim on their fronts in shallow water and all had progressed. In experimenting with different methods, we found that a rope around the waist of a child in deep water is an excellent confidence booster. The child is free to perform alone with no artificial floatation and is also completely safe. In shallow water, milk jugs and a broom stick make excellent kickboards and milk jugs are great water toys.

In crafts, the campers have made plaster of paris molds, wood cut-outs for necklaces and key chains, braiding, beading, macrame, clay, and will often choose to clean the barn stalls or saddles. We found that the most meaningful projects for these children are those which can be completed in a crafts period.

Tutoring in academic subjects or in communication skills is arranged for the campers upon parental request. The majority of these children have short attention spans and have had difficulty in school with academics. The tutoring sessions are from 30-60 minutes in length and are highly individualized. The situation is far from being free from distraction. They sit at a picnic table in the open while those not being tutored have an after lunch recess. It has been observed that the children's attention does not wander even when a goat jumps onto the table.

In addition to learning to ride a horse, the children have learned to control their hyperactivity, speak calmly, recognize the left and right sides of their bodies and their mounts, trust and help one another in mounting and being led; they have also learned to be concerned about the well being of animals. Instructional periods are structured and the children are always closely supervised. Good behavior and consideration of others is expected.

The injury rate over the years has been remarkably low when the types and numbers of children and the types of activities are considered. Six campers have been injured seriously enough for medical attention; one camper broke an ankle walking across a pasture; one camper had to have stitches when he got too close to a golf club which was swung too high; one camper knocked out a tooth while climbing onto the trampoline; and three have had broken arms falling from a rope swing, a standing horse, and a log beam.

Primarily the camp is financed by fees paid by parents. Children bring their lunches from home and pay a camp fee of $25 a week. The bus fee is $6 a week and the tutoring fee is $3 per subject per week. The East Memphis Exchange Club sponsors the hearing impaired campers and at various times other agencies sponsor one or two children.

The campers are allowed to group themselves on the bus, at lunch, at recess, on field trips, for free swim, and on the hikes to the "ditch." Many warm friendships develop between the different classifications of children. Also, each camper is guided to think of the land, animals, and equipment as his/hers. Everyone is asked to help perform some service for another camper or the staff. The response of the children has been rewarding and satisfying. The camp, horses, and other animals receive Christmas cards. Campers who have outgrown the camp return to visit and many do volunteer work during the camp season and during the off seasons. Two ex-campers, aged 16 and 17, designed and built a 20 by 40 foot crafts building on weekends and holidays throughout 1976 and part of 1977.

According to a survey of the parents, campers, and staff, it is agreed that mainstreaming is the way life is and contributes toward creating leadership roles for all of the classifications of campers, greater understanding and acceptance of their own problems and those of others, improved self concepts and confidence, independence, a sense of belonging, and a relaxed and happy individual.

HANDS ACROSS the BORDER

Judy Newman
Arizona Training Program at Tucson
29th Street and Swan Road
Tucson, Arizona 85711

An experimental 10-week swim therapy and recreational swim program for children with various handicapping conditions was developed at the Arizona Training Program (Tucson) during the summer of 1974. Thirty-seven children from Nogales (Sonora), Mexico were bused (approximately 50 miles to Tucson) each Saturday for swim patterning and recreational swimming. Among the participants ages 4 to 16 were physically impaired, mentally retarded, and multiple involved children. Parents accompanying their children were given a training course in swim patterning and basic techniques for working with the children. Directors of the Rehabilitation Center for Physically Handicapped and Mentally Incapacitated Children of Nogales also attended each Saturday.

None of the children spoke or understood English; staff and volunteers did not understand or speak Spanish. The first session was hectic. Children were bewildered and frightened; they kicked, cried, scratched, and wanted no part of the program. Volunteers spent the first session playing with children, trying to calm them and help them adjust to water and the strange environment. To be sure children went home with a happy feeling, a picnic at the park was held after the swim session.

"Hands Across the Boarder," Judy Newman. *Challenge.* Vol. 10, No. 3. April/May 1975. American Alliance for Health, Physical Education and Recreation.

3. IMPROVED FUNCTIONING

weighed red tape necessary to get this program going. By the final session, all children were blowing bubbles with faces in the water, doing elementary swim strokes, either in or out of a swim tube, and loving every minute of it.

Two men, not instructors, wanted to help and soon became favorites of the children as they played games and showed a sincere interest in each child as an individual. They towed children around the pool in swim tubes or kickboards. Without exception, everyone involved in this special program thought it was one of the most rewarding experiences of their lives.

People of Nogales are very excited about having their own program in a therapeutic pool now being planned. The author will go to Mexico to conduct extensive training programs for instructors, parents, and volunteers. She will evaluate children and plan individual programs for each child.

Children are children no matter where they are found. Unfortunately, many children are forgotten, relegated to passive inactivity, denied opportunities afforded their peers. This situation is not limited to children from any one country, state, or locality—some children everywhere are forgotten. If an individual gives even one impaired, disabled, or handicapped child a reason for being happy, his life has also been enriched.

Many changes were made before the second session. Staff and volunteers met to learn Spanish words necessary to communicate with the children. *Sopla* (blow), *voca* (mouth), *brazo* (arm), *mano* (hand), *sientate* (sit), *parate* (stand up), *naden* (you swim), *despacio* (slow down), *muy bien* (very good), *salpicar* (splash) were learned and used! The children soon overcame their initial fear of water and of strangers working with them and really entered into the spirit of the program.

All children were evaluated by the author who developed individual programs so progress could be determined and reported. Each child received one-half hour of instruction or training and one-half hour play time. Discipline was no problem as Mexican children are extremely well behaved.

Much advance planning was necessary. For example, visas for children and adults crossing the border and letters to officials concerning such details as program costs and insurance were necessary. Each child had a 4x5 card with name, age, diagnosis, and picture on it. Details required several months of work prior to the beginning of the program. Several staff members from Arizona Training Program, American Red Cross, YMCA, and Parks and Recreation Department donated time. All attended a 16 hour training course for handicapped swimming given at the Center. However, final results far out-

The first step in training is to teach swim patterning movements to make Elvira water safe with supervision. Ten weeks later, she can do a standing dive in deep water without assistance.

Aquatics for the Handicapped

WILLIAM T. MUHL, retired principal of the William T. Muhl Center for the Handicapped, lives at 1112 N. Winnebago Street, Rockford, Illinois 61103.

Increased attention is being given to providing aquatic activity, particularly swimming, for the handicapped. Various approaches are being used to obtain certain objectives, depending upon the training and experience of those responsible for the program.

The therapeutic approach may be either physical or mental, although we usually see it in its physical aspect. It may be a form of physical manipulation while the person is in the water, hydrotherapy, hydrogymnastics, or convalescent swimming. The ultimate objective is to provide an improved or greater range of movement and use and increase strength and endurance, and to restore the affected parts to as near normal as possible. Often this involves a whole series of unrelated movements for the submerged parts.

The rehabilitative approach is an attempt to restore disabled or limited parts of the body to the greatest usefulness of which they are capable, through modification or adaptation of recognized styles of swimming strokes. These swimming movements are related and, when learned, result in skills that provide functional outlets.

The recreational approach combines instruction and play to provide types of activity which contribute to the total welfare of the individual and afford opportunity to socialize with peers and learn a series of life skills.

The educational appoach is usually a formal instructional approach following a planned sequence of steps integrated with games, directly related to the level of skill attained, to provide skills for fitness, recreation, and safety about the water.

Each approach has its proponents who are specifically concerned with their own areas as they interpret them in terms of meeting the needs of the handicapped. It is easy to become so involved and concerned in the intricacies of the program as to lose sight of the ultimate objective — preparing the handicapped through aquatics to be contributing members of society.

There is much to-do over exact categorization of handicapped people. But the handicapped child is first a *child,* with all the basic needs of any child, although limited by the handicapping condition. From the

---

Aquatics is the ideal kind of activity to meet most of the physical needs of handicapped people.

---

beginning this child grows neurologically, physically, mentally, and socially through prescribed stages, spurts, and patterns. At each of these stages he has to meet these basic needs with sufficient organized physical activity to provide the basis for future growth. We need to be much more concerned with these needs and then interpret our present knowledge of the handicapped in terms of meeting them. We must accept the children where they are at the moment, analyze what they have to work with,

and then take them along as far as they can go—and then a little bit farther. These needs have been expressed in many ways, but as I see them in terms of aquatics they include:

1. The need to be myself—not to be pushed into something I am not. When I am ready, let me fully participate in all aquatics.

2. The need for freedom from labels—not to be prejudiced by preconceived stereotyped limitations. Instead, ask me what can I do.

3. The need for motivation—to have someone answer my questions and help me open the door to aquatics, to show me how to apply myself.

4. The need fo self-achievement—to be able to progress at my own speed and within the framework of my own abilities.

5. The need for time—to learn at my own pace and be given the time to absorb what I have learned.

6. The need for freedom from anxiety—to have a sufficient number of successes outnumbering the failures so that I may improve my own confidence and grow within my ability to cope with the aquatic experiences ahead of me.

7. The need for high adventure and risk—the stimulating challenge of being able to do something for the first time.

8. The need for contest—to compete successfully against myself and then against others, the stimulus of good healthy competition so that I may rate myself and in turn be rated in the eyes of my peers.

"Acquatics for the Handicapped," William T. Mull, *Journal of Physical Education and Recreation.* Vol. 47, No. 2, February 1976. °American Alliance for Health, Physical Education and Recreation.

139

9. The need for rhythmic action—many of the body's actions are dependent upon specific rhythms and certainly nothing is more rhythmical than a style of swimming beautifully in a relaxed and smooth fashion.

10. The need for social competence—to be accepted for what I can do in swimming and not for what I know, and thus to be welcome to my peers.

11. The need for a picture of myself which I can like—to be a person of worth, one whom people can like and accept. To meet these needs through an aquatic program, we have four general objectives: to teach the child to swim or to swim better, to help build and maintain physical fitness, to improve morale and self-concept, and to provide life skills.

From the first time the child approaches the swimming area and the water, and in every subsequent session, there are certain basic safety skills to be taught. There is no specific order or timing for teaching these skills but they should be introduced as early as possible and, when mastered, should be reviewed often enough to become a part of the child's way of life.

Handicapped children encounter the same basic problems in learning to swim as normal children. They must make the necessary physical and mental adjustments to the water so that they can relax, be comfortable, enjoy the water, and have an attitude of readiness. They must learn how to maintain a good working position in the water. With the handicapped this frequently involves much adjustment of positions, parts of the body, and patterns of movement. They must get enough practice so a good pattern of movement can be developed to the point where there is no longer a need to concentrate on the exacting component parts.

As we consider an aquatic program for each type of handicapping condi-

tion we quickly see that there is no "typical" pattern of instruction because of the many variables within each condition. However, as a general rule, we can start with the accepted swimming approaches and progressions. In most cases the handicapped are more like the "normal" than the normal are like themselves. We may have to instruct on a one for one ratio and then progress to a one for several before we can get to a one for class situation. We often find that because of the limitations of the child we have to modify and adapt the skill, to change our methods of communication, to recognize that success comes early and quickly but progress may be slow. The more we approach that instruction from the normal expectations, the great-

It is easy to become so involved in the intricacies of the program as to lose sight of the ultimate objective—preparing the handicapped through aquatics to live as contributing members of society.

er the response will be. The voice and attitude of the instructor should be one of quiet confidence, assurance, and patience, while saving the "command" for emergencies.

As guidelines for ourselves we must continually *strive* for the best for each child, *seek* the method for each to succeed, *find* those teachable moments, and *not yield* to discouragement. The future is today's challenge and opportunity, the need is

here today. How will you serve and what will you do to meet this need?

I see aquatic activity in its broadest sense as a phase of general education which uses these aquatic motor activities and related experiences as a means of developing integrated individuals mentally, physically, morally, and socially, so that they can find their place as contributing members of society within their capacities. When they have reached this point, they are no longer handicapped.

Yes, aquatics can be considered the almost ideal type of activity to meet most of the physical needs of handicapped people. There is a never-ending challenge which can be presented through the full range of aquatics. Competition, synchronized swimming, skin and scuba diving, water skiing, surfing, games, stunts, pageants, along with boating, canoeing, and sailing all present endless opportunity for successful participation. Each of you, in your own way, must decide whether you will approach this from the therapeutic, rehabilitative, recreational, or educational aspect—or will these be so interwoven that we just concern ourselves with the needs and progress of the child through successful participation?

I am continually reminded of how wonderfully exciting it is to look at aquatic participation through the eyes of an eager child faced with the many opportunities presented in successful activity: innocent curiosity, creative exploration, dynamic enthusiasm, boundless energy, acceptable challenge—all followed by the winsome smile and the glowing light of any success.

The children are here, the need is now, you have the knowledge. Will you produce for them and are you really providing equal opportunity for their full participation in special groups as well as in peer groups, or do we continue to shortchange these handicapped children?

CROSS COUNTRY SKIING
for the
MENTALLY HANDICAPPED

Nola Sinclair
Physical Education Instructor
Riverview School
Manitowoc, Wisconsin

Cross country skiing is a fast-growing and popular winter activity. Benefits from this lifetime sport include increased strength, endurance, balance, coordination, and appreciation for nature's winter beauty. Equipment can be obtained with relatively little expense.

Riverview School, a public school for mentally handicapped children in Manitowoc, Wisconsin, initiated a cross country program for intermediate and junior high school aged mildly retarded (educable) students during the 1973-74 school year. A local ski hill and ski shop owner donated 20 pairs of old, wooden, downhill (Alpine) skis and helped staff and students convert them into cross country skis. Metal edges were sawed

off to make skis lighter and thinner. Special cross country bindings that fit regular outdoor boots or overshoes and poles were purchased at cost from the same ski shop owner. Students in industrial arts education classes and several staff members dismantled bindings, sawed skis, and mounted new bindings.

To facilitate fitting, skis and poles were marked. Bindings were sized small, medium, and large. Size was determined according to probable shoe sizes of these intermediate and junior high school students. Small bindings were mounted on short skis, medium on medium-length skis and large on long skis. Colored plastic tape with the letters

S, (small), M (medium), and L (large) were attached to the respectively sized skis. A number or letter at the toe of each pair of skis distinguished one pair from another.

Poles came in sizes 48 inches through 56 inches. Colored plastic tape placed on shafts distinguished various sizes. As students were fitted, the ski number and pole color were recorded. Students used the same equipment throughout the unit. By snowfall, skis were usable and the program began.

Prerequisite to cross country skiing seemed to be, *if you can walk you can cross country ski.* This rule was appropriate for the Riverview students with the exception of students who had difficulty

"Cross Country Skiing for the Mentally Handicapped," Nola Sinclair, *Challenge,* Vol. 10, No. 1, January 1975.
American Alliance for Health, Physical Education and Recreation.

141

3. IMPROVED FUNCTIONING

MONDAY	TUESDAY	WEDNESDAY	THURSDAY	FRIDAY
Orientation What is cross country Safety Care of equipment Clothes Waxing Fitting	*Free Exploration*	*New Skill* Moving in place Falls Getting up	*New Skill* Moving in place Step turns	*New Skill* Moving on flat land Diagonal stride
New Skill Moving on flat land Diagonal stride	*New Skill* Moving on flat land Double poling	*New Skill* Moving uphill Side stepping	*New Skill* Moving downhill Straight run Moving uphill Straight uphill	*New Skill* Moving downhill Traverse Moving uphill Traverse
New Skill Moving uphill Herringbone	*New Skill* Moving downhill Snow plow	*New Skill* Moving downhill Step turn	Given a marked trail on and near the school playground area, students move as. far as	possible during the first half of the class period and return during the latter half.

maintaining balance while walking on snow. With some adaptions in equipment students with crutches also participated. A basket similar to those found at the end of a ski pole was attached to the crutch tip to prevent it from pushing deep into the snow.

Student orientation included discussions of cross country skiing, safety and care of equipment, proper clothing, plus the how and why of waxing skis. Students also learned how to fit themselves properly with the correct size poles and skis.

During the first lessons on the snow, students simply explored what they were able to do on skis. Individual exploration gave students practice in standing after a spill, adjusting body positions for maintaining balance, and putting on and adjusting bindings.

As students became more accustomed to movement on skis, various skills were introduced and practiced. Because of vast differences in balance, coordination, and skill acquisition, much time was spent in free exploration and practice of given skills. Students were able to benefit from individual assistance and each progressed at his own rate. Talented youngsters were not stifled and slower students not frustrated by unrealistic expectations.

The unit ended with a cross country trail hike. Given a marked trail on and near the school playground area, students moved as far as possible in the first half of the class period and returned during the latter half. This gave students a real cross country experience.

The following is a three-week cross country skiing unit designed for beginning educable mentally handicapped skiers; each lesson is designed for 40 minutes. With the exception of the first two and last two lessons, the time schedule is: 1. 5-10 minutes to obtain equipment; 2. 5 minutes for exploration and practice; 3. 10 minutes for discussion and demonstration of new skill; 4. 10 minutes for exploration and practice; 5. 5 minutes to return equipment.

Suggested references:
Baldwin, Edward R. *The Cross Country Skiing Handbook.* Toronto. Ontario: Pargurian Press Limited. 1972.
Bennett, Margaret. *Crosscountry Skiing for the Fun of It.* New York: Dodd, Mead & Company. 1973.
Toker, Art. and Luray, Martin. *The Complete Guide to Cross Country Skiing and Touring.* New York: Holt, Rinehart, Winston. 1973.
United States Skiing Association. Rocky Mountain Division, Ski Touring Sub Committee. *RMD Ski Touring Instructors Manual.*

THE IMPACT OF SPECIAL OLYMPICS ON PARTICIPANTS, PARENTS AND THE COMMUNITY

A three year research project conducted by
Texas Tech University
Funded by the Joseph P. Kennedy, Jr. Foundation
and
Special Olympics, Inc.

THE IMPACT OF SPECIAL OLYMPICS ON
PARTICIPANTS, PARENTS, AND THE COMMUNITY

The following report highlights the major results of a three-year investigation of the impact of Special Olympics programs on participants, parents, and the community. This investigation was conducted by the Research and Training Center at Texas Tech University, Lubbock, Texas, and funded by the Joseph P. Kennedy Jr. Foundation and Special Olympics, Inc.

The over-all aims of the research were to:

I.   determine the physical, social, emotional and psychological effects of Special Olympics upon its mentally retarded participants,

II.   determine the impact of Special Olympics upon participating communities, and

III. determine the effectiveness and quality of Special Olympics programs

Previous Special Olympics Research

Past research dealing specifically with Special Olympics (Brower, 1969; Cratty, 1972; Rarick, 1971) suggests that the program is benefitting participants. However, respondents have consisted of rather select groups of individuals (members of the National Association for Retarded Citizens, parents, and teachers of participants), and their opinions would not necessarily be applicable to the population as a whole. Further, program impact has been assessed in terms of parents' or teachers' perceptions of participant change rather than through direct measurement. Finally, since the respondents were directly asked questions regarding the Special Olympics program and were thus aware of the focus of interest of the investigators, their appraisals of the need for such programs might well have influenced their evaluations of program effectiveness. It is important to obtain measures of program impact from parents, teachers, and civic leaders which are free of this bias.

Purpose of this Study

The purpose of this research was to assess the impact of Special Olympics upon the participants, their parents, and the community in a way that would permit less equivocal interpretation of findings and would also include a wider range of measures than has been employed in the past. Such an assessment involved determining what changes can be attributed to the program itself rather than to other events occurring at home, at school, in the community, and even at the state and federal level. Thus, the investigators elected to conduct an experimental study of the impact of Special Olympics, beginning with locations which had no program, accumulating baserate data in these areas, establishing programs in some areas but not others, and continuing to collect measures in all locations for a sufficient time period to detect changes which might occur as a result of the program. Measures were expanded from previous studies to include not only reports from parents and teachers but direct assessment of participants and measures of community attitudes. The specific objectives of this study were:

A. To assess the impact of a Special Olympics Program on the participants in terms of physical ability, achievement, self-perception, behavior (in the classroom and at home), and interaction with peers.

B. To assess the impact of a Special Olympics Program on parents', teachers', and other community members' attitudes and perceptions of retarded individuals.

C. To determine whether Special Olympics, through changes in attitudes of employers, administrators, and local policy-makers, leads to an increased awareness of the needs of the retarded and thus, potentially to more and better services for them.

Research Design

Communities. Four communities were selected which met the following criteria: a) the absence of Special Olympics program; b) cooperation of the school system for testing students; c) location within reasonable traveling distance of Lubbock, Texas; and d) approximate equivalence of population size. Two of these communities were in the state of Texas, and two in New Mexico.

Students. Lists were obtained from the schools of all students in each community who would be eligible for Special Olympics between the ages of 7 and 21 (IQ 75 or below). Letters were then sent to parents which described the project as a study of children's progress in school and which included consent forms to be signed and returned by the parent. Consent was obtained for a total of 224 students, the number in each community ranging from 50 to 61.

Parents and Teachers. During the course of the study, information regarding student progress was requested from parents and also from a teacher who was most familiar with each student. Parents were contacted annually, and teachers semiannually.

Community Leaders. Lists of approximately twenty organizations were obtained from the Chambers of Commerce in each community. One major office-holder of each organization was contacted and asked to provide information regarding organization activities and personal attitudes toward the retarded each year of the study.

General Public. A sample of approximately 150 names was selected from current telephone directories from each community for each year of the study. The names (plus a comparable number of alternates) were selected by flipping a coin and choosing the name on which it landed. Alternates were contacted only if no response was obtained from the original number after several attempts. Although some attempt was made during the second and third years to equalize the number of male and female respondents interviewed, the most common procedure was to interview the individual who answered the phone if he or she were over 16 years of age.

Time Schedule of the Study. Baseline measures were obtained in all four communities in 1975. Special Olympics programs were then organized in communities 2 and 4, while communities 1 and 3 served as controls (no Special Olympics programs). Special Olympics programs were provided over a full year in community 2 in 1975-6, and over a half-year period in community 4 in 1976. Repeated measures were obtained in all four communities in 1976, and final measures obtained in 1977. Table I summarizes the organization of the study.

After all the data was collected, mean values and mean differences were calculated and subjected to standard tests of statistical significance (t-tests and analysis of variance and covariance).

Results: Physical Activities Summary

Teachers of children in both the experimental and control communities were asked to complete a form indicating the type of physical education-recreation activities they had in their program. In the absence of Special Olympic programs, there was considerable evidence that quality physical education programs are not routinely provided for mentally retarded students. Results indicated that mentally retarded children in communities where Special Olympics programs had been established participated in a greater variety of physical education activities than did children in the control communities.

This evidence indicates that one of the primary goals of the Special Olympics program -- to either establish or improve physical education programs for the retarded -- is being accomplished.

Results: Psychological Tests of Children and Ratings Supplied by Teachers

There were a total of thirty scores derived from the psychological tests and teacher rating scales. The differences between pre-test and post-test scores were analyzed to determine any improvements made during the course of the study.

The children who participated in Special Olympics improved significantly compared with control children in two areas. First was the children's attitudes toward school and physical education activities, as indicated by their responses to a seven item questionnaire. Experimental children were more likely to agree that they, "like other children at school", and less likely to agree that, "school is a sad place to be", following participation in Special Olympics.[1]

---

[1] Children in the control communities had higher school-attitude scores than the experimental children at the time of the pre-test and these scores decreased slightly on post-test assessments. The experimental children, although remaining somewhat lower than controls on the post-test, showed an increase in scores over time. (See Table II).

Table I
Organization of Impact Study

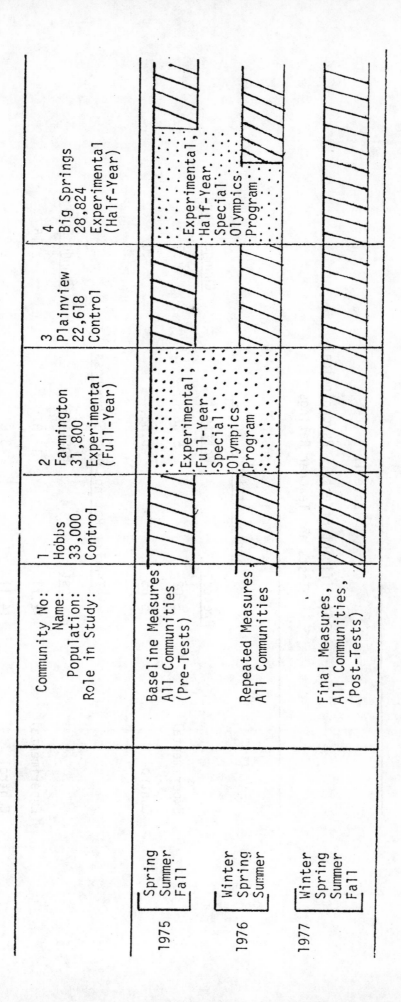

Table II

Significant Effects: Psychological
Tests and Teacher Ratings

School Attitude Scale

	Pretest	Posttest	Change Score
Experimental	5.02	5.36	+.36
Control	5.65	5.58	-.07

Teacher Ratings of PE Progress

	Pretest	Posttest	Change Score
Experimental	12.71	14.87	+2.16
Control	14.11	13.84	-2.27

The second area in which there was significant improvement of Special Olympics participants was progress in physical skills as rated by teachers. Teachers were asked to rate each child's degree of improvement in a variety of skills including baseball throwing, running and jumping. A summary score of these skill ratings indicated that teachers observed more progress among experimental students than among controls.

An analysis of the different effects of the full-year versus the half-year Special Olympics program indicated that the areas of improvement reported above were due primarily to participants in the full-year program; there were no significant gains found among students in the half-year program compared with controls.

Discussion of Psychological Tests and Teacher Ratings

The finding that Special Olympics produces improved attitudes toward school is an important one. These changes may result from feelings of success and achievement not previously associated with school activities, or possibly from the increased attention associated with Special Olympics training and competetion activities. In either case, however, a program which has the capability of providing a more positive school experience for these retarded children can be considered worthwhile.

The most important implication of these findings for program implementation involves the issue of a full-year versus half-year Special Olympics program. Since the changes observed were restricted to the community which conducted Special Olympics activities from September through May rather than during the Spring months only, program planners should attempt to involve students in full-year programs in order to realize maximum benefits from the program.

Results: Physical Fitness Measures

Four individual physical fitness measures were collected on each student: Softball throw (distance); Situps (number-in one minute); Shuttle run (time); and Standing Long Jump (distance).

Each student in all four communities was tested on the above measures at the beginning of the study (pretest score) and again at the end of the study (post-test score). Scores from participants in the full-year and the half-year experimental groups were combined as were scores from participants in both control communities. The mean percent change was then calculated for all students in Special Olympics programs (experimental), and for all students not in Special Olympics programs (control). The results were also separately analyzed for male and female students.

Results: Overall Physical Fitness

Table III shows that participants, both male and female, made significant and substantial gains in the softball throw test. Conversely, the performance of control students actually decreased slightly. Although the other physical fitness measures did not show statistically significant differences between the improvement of experimental and control groups, the experimental groups did show an improvement in several of the measures, especially the long jump.

Table III

PRETEST AND ADJUSTED-POSTTEST MEANS FOR FOUR PHYSICAL FITNESS MEASURES

		MALES			FEMALES			TOTAL		
		Pretest	Adjusted Posttest	% Change	Pretest	Adjusted Posttest	% Change	Pretest	Adjusted Posttest	% Change
Softball Throw	Experimental	600.9	763.55	27.2	379.58	623.22	64.2	509.29	705.77	38.6
	Control	928.02	897.62	-3.3	557.88	553.51	-.8	783.81	763.55	-2.6
Shuttle Run	Experimental	13.89	12.97	-7.3	16.09	13.17	-18.2	14.79	13.05	-11.8
	Control	11.90	13.07	9.8	12.85	11.79	-8.2	12.27	12.57	2.4
Situps	Experimental	12.47	14.65	17.5	14.33	15.29	6.7	13.22	14.94	13
	Control	15.45	16.29	5.4	11.03	10.93	-.9	13.73	14.20	3.4
Long Jump	Experimental	30.96	40.24	3.0	30.92	40.34	30.5	30.94	40.28	30.2
	Control	43.06	44.88	4.2	37.26	32.79	-.12	40.84	40.18	-1.6

Results: Individual Physical Fitness Measures (Figure 1)

Softball throw: The total experimental group (males and females) showed a gain in distance thrown of 38.6% (509 to 706 in. on the average) compared to a decline of 2.6% for the control group.

The total group of experimental females showed a mean gain of 64.2% compared to the controls who showed a mean decline of 0.8%. The total group of experimental males showed a mean percent gain of 27.2% compared to the control males, 3.3% decline. The subjects in the full year program showed greater gains than those in the half-year program.

Situps: The experimental group as a whole gained 13.0% in situps in one minute compared to a 3.4% gain for the total control group. The male experimental group made significantly higher gains in situps than did their matched controls, 17.5% and 5.4% respectively; and the female experimental students also showed higher gain than their controls (6.7% and 0.9%, respectively). The overall gains shown by the subjects in the full-year program were significantly greater than those shown by the subjects in the half-year program.

Shuttle run: Gain in the shuttle run is defined as a <u>decrease</u> in the time to run the course. The total experimental group (males and females) had a mean improvement (decrease in elapsed time) of 11.8% compared to a 2.5% decline for the control group. The experimental males showed a mean gain of 7.3% compared to the control males who showed a decline of 9.8%. However, the experimental females showed an overall gain of 18.1% compared to a 8.2% gain for their controls. The total full-year group (male and female)showed a greater gain in shuttle run performance than did the half-year group.

Standing long jump: The total experimental group (males and females) showed a 30.2% gain in distance jumped which can be compared with a 1.6% decline shown by the total control group. The experimental males showed a 30.0% gin in performance compared to a 4.2% gain for the control males, and the experimental females showed 30.5% gain compared to a -0.1% decline for the control students. The students in the full-year program showed greater gains than students in the half-year program.

Results: Summary of Physical Fitness Measures

In general the analysis of percent change in performance yielded the following results:

1. Experimental students made higher gains than did their matched controls.

2. Full-year program participants in the experimental group made larger percent gains than did students in the half-year program.

The large number of comparisons in which experimental students exceeded the gain shown by control students can be interpreted as a strong trend indicating that Special Olympics involvement leads to larger gains on these measures of <u>physical performance</u> than no Special Olympics involvement.

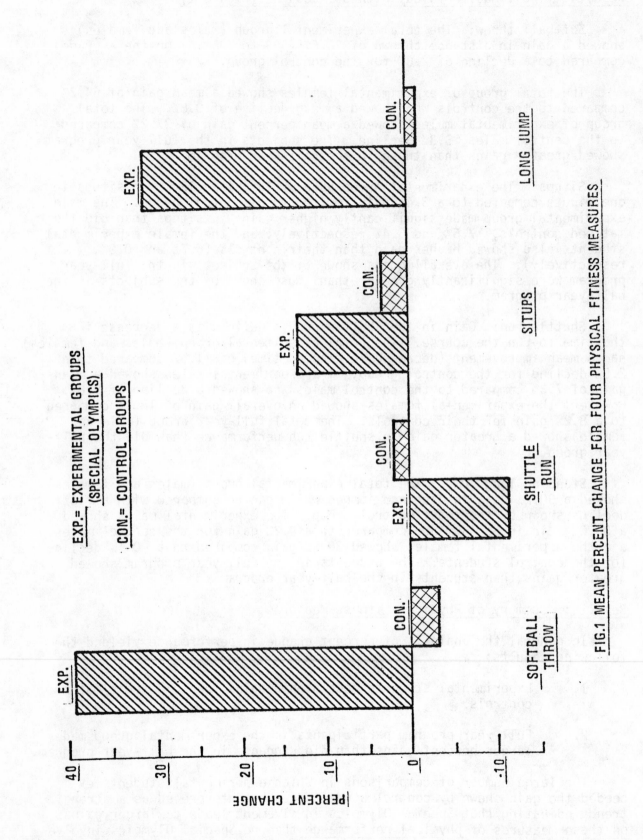

FIG.1 MEAN PERCENT CHANGE FOR FOUR PHYSICAL FITNESS MEASURES

The evidence in favor of Special Olympics involvement is further buttressed by the findings that full-year participants (who had the most Special Olympics involvement) show greater gains than the half-year participants. The results of percent change scores show that, except for the situps measure with female students, the full-year participants showed greater gains than the half-year participants.

Results: Parent Rating

Data was collected from parents on three occasions. On the first occasion, a sample of parents were interviewed and the remainder were sent questionnaires through the mail. On the second and third occasions, all parents were sent mail questionnaires.

In order to assess change in parents ratings, only those parents who completed the questionnaire on both occasions 1 and 3 were included in the analysis. Difference scores between occasions 1 and 3 were computed for six summary scores, each of which were computed from a number of individual items. These were: the child's self esteem, recent improvement in the parent's behavior, the child's physical skills, and recent improvement in physical skills. Comparisons were then made between parents of Special Olympics participants and parents of non-participants (control group). (See Figure II).

Significant improvement was reported by parents of Special Olympics participants compared with control group parents in the following areas: a) the behavior of the parent toward the child; b) the child's recent improvement in physical skills; and, c) the child's self esteem. For example, parents of participants were more likely to agree that, "My child seems to like himself-herself" than were parents of nonparticipants on the post-test compared with pre-test measures. They were also more likely to agree that, "I think I am doing a pretty good job as a parent", and less likely to "become irritated with my child" or to "feel that I need outside help with my child". The other three summary scores also showed positive change for experimental compared with control parents.

A larger number of parents of Special Olympics participants than controls indicated that their child was more interested in sports than in the past (69% for participants, 40% for controls). Finally, parents in the experimental communities were better able to identify Special Olympics when asked if they'd ever heard of it (87% versus 39%) and were also better able to name the activities of the Special Olympics programs (51% versus 15%).

Discussion of Parent Ratings

Parents proved to be an extremely valuable source of information for this study by confirming the teachers' rating. Compared with parents in control communities, parents of Special Olympics participants reported that their children:

- showed greater progress in developing physical skills;
- appeared more interested in sports;
- showed greater improvement in self-esteem.

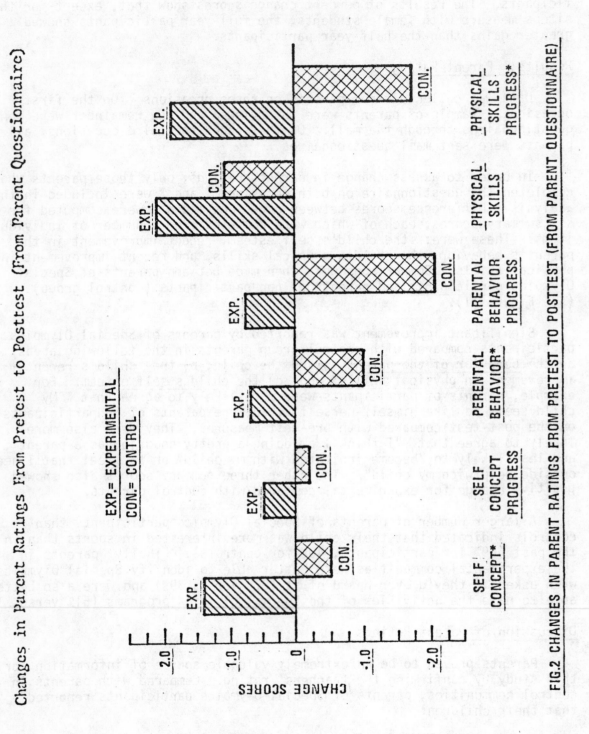

Figure 2

Changes in Parent Ratings From Pretest to Posttest (From Parent Questionnaire)

FIG.2 CHANGES IN PARENT RATINGS FROM PRETEST TO POSTTEST (FROM PARENT QUESTIONNAIRE)

One of the most interesting results of the parent questionnaires was that parents of participants increased more than non-participants in the degree to which they viewed themselves as good parents. There are a number of possible explanations for this finding. First, feelings of being a better parent may result from increased time and attention devoted to the child through parental participation in Special Olympics practice sessions and competitions. Even transporting children to Special Olympics events may represent increased contact with the child for some parents. Secondly, the fact of a community program designed specifically for their child may have reduced the expressed need for "outside help" in the experimental groups. Finally, it is possible that participation in Special Olympics altered the behavior of the participants at home in a positive way. The fact that parents of participants reported that they became less irritated with their children than in the past suggests that the children's disturbing behavior patterns might have diminished under the influence of the Special Olympics programs.

Results: General Public Attitudes Survey

Analysis of the results of telephone interviews compared the responses of the general public in the full-year experimental community with one of the control communities. The pre-test data was collected prior to program initiation, and the post-test data was collected at the end of the second year of the Special Olympics program. Approximately 120 randomly selected individuals were interviewed in each community on each occasion.

Questions asked concerned attitudes toward the retarded, awareness of programs for the handicapped, awareness of Special Olympics, community service of the interviewee, and demographic data (Table IV).

Prior to program initiation, there were no differences between the experimental and control communities in their knowledge of Special Olympics (39% and 38% respectively could identify Special Olympics). However, on the post-test, significantly more individuals in the experimental community indicated that they had heard of the Special Olympics program (68% versus 40% controls).

Furthermore, the results suggest that in many areas there were in fact more positive attitudes toward the retarded following the implementation of a Special Olympics program. For example, although there were no differences between communities in these areas on the pre-test, post-test interviews indicated that more individuals in the experimental community believed that the retarded can learn to live normal lives, that most would make good employees, most would make good husbands or wives and good parents, and most should play on regular sports teams. Overall, there was significant improvement in attitudes toward the retarded in the experimental compared with the control community on nine of the sixteen attitude items. Therefore, the evidence strongly suggests that the fact of having a Special Olympics program in a community does have a positive effect upon community attitudes.

Discussion of General Public Attitude Survey

Many programs require community support in the form of donations of time or money to be viable, and others, such as community group homes,

Table IV

Attitudes Toward the Retarded as Expressed By
The General Public During Phone Interviews

Items Indicating More Positive Attitudes in the Experimental Compared with the Control Community on the Posttest			
Item		Pretest % Who Agreed	Posttest % Who Agreed
Most retarded can learn to live normal lives	Experimental	39.8	48.2*
	Control	36.7	32.9
Most retarded would make good employees	Experimental	25.5	42.2*
	Control	26.2	24.7
Most retarded would make good parents	Experimental	9.7	23.7*
	Control	10.5	6.7
Most retarded would make good husbands or wives	Experimental	13.8	37.6
	Control	15.1	11.2
Most retarded should drive a car	Experimental	3.1	18.1*
	Control	6.3	4.3
Most retarded should vote	Experimental	27.8	41.5*
	Control	17.1	22.6
Most retarded should marry	Experimental	18.1	39.8*
	Control	17.6	12.1
Most retarded should play on regular sports teams	Experimental	36.4	44.4*
	Control	35.1	27.7
Few retarded look different from other people	Experimental	38.5	37.4*
	Control	35.4	24.5

Table IV
(cont'd)

Items Indicating More Positive Attitudes in the Experimental Compared with the Control Community on the Posttest

Item		Pretest % Who Agreed	Posttest % Who Agreed
Most retarded can participate in most sports	Experimental	30.2	34.9
	Control	30.2	24.2
Most retarded can be self supporting	Experimental	22.4	23.8
	Control	28.7	16.1

Items Indicating a Positive Change for Both Groups, No Change, or a Reversal (last item)

Item		Pretest % Who Agreed	Posttest % Who Agreed
Most retarded would make good neighbors	Experimental	63.9	69.4
	Control	50.5	57.4
Most retarded should use public playgrounds	Experimental	76.5	80.2
	Control	68.8	78.1
Few retarded are mentally insane	Experimental	85.5	88.2
	Control	83.3	92.7
Most retarded should go downtown alone	Experimental	25.7	25.5
	Control	24.5	23.9
Few retarded are not able to be physically active	Experimental	72.9	68.8*
	Control	70.0	83.5

* Differences between groups statistically significant ($p < .05$)

require public acceptance. Therefore, any program which has the potential of changing attitudes performs the service of paving the way for additional programs. Since Special Olympics appears to have this potential for positive attitude change, it should be considered as a good first step in locations which do not yet have many community programs for the retarded. Unlike programs such as community homes, Special Olympics is non-threatening to the public, yet at the same time it serves the role of educating the public regarding the capability of many retarded persons to lead normal lives in the community.

Results: Community Leaders Survey

The representatives of major organizations in each community were asked about their knowledge of Special Olympics, their organizations' involvement with the retarded, their assessment of their community's attitudes toward the retarded, and their own attitudes toward the retarded. Personal interviews were conducted with representatives the first year, and mail questionnaires were used in subsequent years.

The only significant differences obtained in these analyses was in the organizations representatives' ability to identify the Special Olympics program. On the post-test, 89% in the experimental communities versus 59% in the control communities had heard of the program. These post-test differences are thus due to an increase in knowledge in the experimental communities.

Discussion of Community Leaders Survey

The responses of these community leaders indicated very positive attitudes toward the retarded, even in the control communities, which probably accounts for the failure to find differences between the responses of those in the experimental and control communities. Despite the positive attitudes and knowledge expressed, it was discouraging that community organizations did not involve themselves with Special Olympics or the retarded. If Special Olympics does serve to stimulate a community to increase programming, then it would be expected that organizational involvement with the retarded would eventually increase.

Results: Newspaper Analysis

Newspapers from each of the four communities were monitored throughout 1976 and from January through June of 1977. Articles were tabulated which dealt with Special Olympics in particular or with mental retardation in general (Figures III).

It is notable that the full-year experimental community had approximately twice as many articles on retardation and the Special Olympics appearing in its newspaper than was true of the control communities, and there is a significantly greater number in the full-year compared with the half-year program.

Discussion of Newspaper Analysis

These newspaper articles counts can be viewed in several ways. The articles dealing specifically with Special Olympics can be used to support

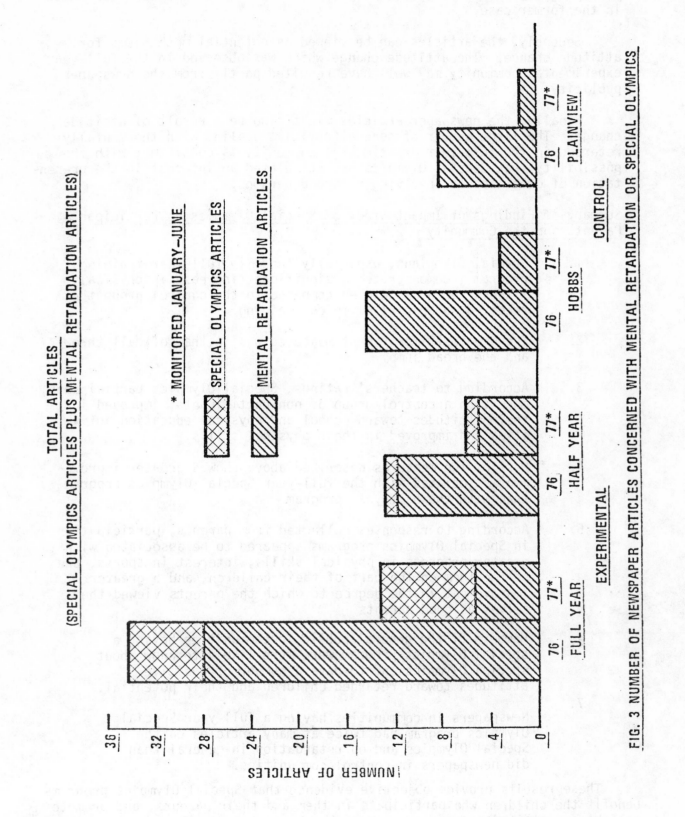

FIG. 3 NUMBER OF NEWSPAPER ARTICLES CONCERNED WITH MENTAL RETARDATION OR SPECIAL OLYMPICS

159

the effectiveness of program implementation, since this kind of publicity would be expected in recruiting community support for the program. In this respect, the full-year program was much more effective than the half-year program, probably because many more newsworthy events were conducted in the former case.

Secondly, the articles can be viewed as potential mechanisms for attitude change. The attitude change which was observed in the full-year experimental community may well have resulted partly from the newspaper publicity.

Finally, the newspaper articles might also be a result of attitude change. The large number of general articles dealing with the mentally retarded in the full-year experimental community is consistent with the possibility that Special Olympics has stimulated an interest in the presentation of other issues involving retarded persons.

Summary of Findings of Impact Study of Special Olympics on Participants, Parents and the Community

1. Special Olympians, especially those in full-year training programs, demonstrated a significant increase in physical fitness performance when compared to the control group that received no Special Olympics training.

2. The greatest improvement measured was in the softball throw and the broad jump.

3. According to teachers' ratings, Special Olympics participants, more than a control group of non-participants, improved in their attitudes toward school and physical education activities and improved in their physical skills.

4. Most of the measures described above showed greater improvement associated with the full-year Special Olympics program than with the half-year program.

5. According to responses collected from parents, participation in Special Olympics programs appeared to be associated with greater progress in physical skills, interest in sports, and self-esteem on the part of their children, and a greater improvement in the degree to which the parents viewed themselves as good parents.

6. Members of the general public in communities having a special Olympics program were more likely to know about special Olympics and to have a number of positive attitudes toward retarded children and their potential.

7. Newspapers in communities having a full-year Special Olympics program had twice as many articles on the Special Olympics and on retardation in general than did newspapers in control communities.

These results provide objective evidence that Special Olympics programs benefit the children who participate in them and their parents, and promote enlightened attitudes among members of the general community.

160

Bibliography

Cull, John G. and Richard E. Hardy. *Volunteerism: An Emerging Profession.* Springfield, Ill.: Charles C. Thomas Publisher, 1974.

Bannon, Joseph J. *Leisure Resources: Its Comprehensive Planning.* Englewood Cliffs, New Jersey: Prentice-Hall, Inc., 1976.

Farrel, Patricia and Herberta M. Lundegren. *The Process of Recreation Programming: Theory and Technique.* New York: John Wiley and Sons, 1978.

Friedberg, M. Paul and Ellen Perry Berkley. *Play and Interplay: A Manifesto for New Design in the Urban Recreational Environment.* New York: The Macmillan Company, 1970.

Schaefer, Charles E. (Ed.). *The Therapeutic Use of Child's Play.* New York: Jason Aronson, Inc., 1976.

Gunn, Scout Lee and Carol Ann Peterson. *Therapeutic Recreation Programming: Principles and Procedures.* Englewood Cliffs, New Jersey: Prentice-Hall, Inc., 1978.

Overs, Robert P., O'Connor, E.O., and B. Demarco. *Avocational Activities for the Handicapped.* Springfield, Ill.: Charles C. Thomas, 1974.

Berryman, Doris L., et al. *Prescriptive Therapeutic Recreation Programming: A Computer Based System,* New York: New York University Press, 1976

Alpern, Gerald D., and Thomas J. Boll, *Education and Care of Moderately and Severely Retarded Children,* Seattle, Washington: Special Child Publications, Inc. (4535 Union Bay Place N.E.), 1971.

Drowatzky, John N., *Physical Education for the Mentally Retarded,* Philadelphia: Lea & Febiger, 1971.

Hollander, H. Cornelia, *Creative Opportunities for the Retarded Child at Home and in School,* Garden City, New York: Doubleday & Company, 1971. $10.00

Laskin, Joyce Novis, *Arts and Crafts Activities Desk Book,* West Nyack, New York: Parker Publishing Company, Inc., 1971.

Tooper, Virginia O., *A Graded Activity Handbook for Teachers of the Mentally Retarded,* Columbus, Ohio: Ohio Department of Mental Hygiene and Correction, Division of Mental Retardation (State Office Building, Room 1210), 1971.

Voss, Donald G., *Physical Education Curriculum for the Mentally Retarded,* Madison, Wisconsin: Wisconsin Department of Public Instruction (126 Langdon Sreet), September, 1971. $1.50.

Williams Beverly S., *Your Child Has A Learning Disability . . . What Is It? A Guide For Parents and Teachers of Children with a Hidden Handicap,* Chicago: National Easter Seal Society for Crippled Children and Adults, (2023 West Ogden Avenue), 1971.

Frostig, Marianne, and Phyllis Maslow, *Frostig MGL (Move-Grow-Learn) Movement Education Activities,* Chicago, Illinois: Follett Educational Corporation, 1970.

Frostig, Marianne, and Phyllis Maslow, *Movement Education: Theory and Practice,* Chicago, Illinois: Follett Education Corporation, 1970.

Trends for the Handicapped, Arlington, Virginia: National Recreation and Park Association, Park Practice Program (1601 North Kent Street). July/August/September, 1974.

The Winter Park Amputee Ski Teaching System, 2nd edition, Hal O'Leary, P.O. Box 76, Hideway Park, Colorado, 1974.

Playscapes, Washington, D.C.: Association for Childhood Education International, 3615 Wisconsin Ave., NW, 1973.

Adams, Ronald C., A.N. Daniels, and L. Rullman, *Games, Sports, and Exercises for the Physically Handicapped,* Philadelphia: Lea & Febiger (Washington Square), 1972. $11.00.

Bates, Barbara J., Curtic C. Hansen, Larry L. Neal, and John A. Nesbitt, *Training Needs & Strategies in Camping for the Handicapped,* Eugene, Oregon: Center of Leisure Studies (1587 Agate Street), 1972. $3.50.

Bauer, Joseph J., *Riding for Rehabilitation: A Guide for Handicapped Riders and Their Instructors,* Toronto, Ontario, Canada: Canadian Stage and Arts Publications Limited (49 Wellington Street East), 1972.

Beter, Thais R., and Wesley E. Cragin, *The Mentally Retarded Child and His Motor Behavior: Practical Diagnosis and Movement Experiences,* Springfield, Illinois: Charles C. Thomas Publisher (301-327 East Lawrence Avenue), 1972. $7.00.

Fredericks, H.D. Bud, V. Baldwin, P. Doughty, and L.J. Walter, *The Teaching Research Motor-Development Scale for Moderately and Severely Retarded Children,* Springfield, Illinois: Charles C. Thomas, Publisher (301-327 East Lawrence Avenue), 1972. $7.00

Frye, Virginia, and Martha Peters, *Therapeutic Recreation: Its Theory, Philosophy, and Practice,* Harrisburg, Pennsylvania: The Stackpole Company (Cameron and Kelker Streets), 1972. $12.50.

Griswold, Patricia A., *Play Together, Parents and Babies,* Indianapolis, Indiana. (615 North Alabama Street), 1972. $3.00

Hirst, Cynthia C., and Elaine Michaelis, *Developmental Activities for Children in Special Education,* Springfield, Illinois: Charles C. Thomas Publisher (301-327 East Lawrence), 1972. $15.75.

Miles, Nancy R., *Learning Through Individualized Trampoline Activities,* Chicago, Illinois: Developmental Learning Materials (3505 North Ashland Avenue), 1972.

Alkema, Charles J., *Art for the Exceptional,* Boulder, Colorado: Pruett Publishing Company, 1971.

Creative Crafts, Englewood Cliffs, New Jersey: Best Foods (Consumer Service Department, A Division of CPC International Inc.).

Growing Places, New York, New York: Schoolworks, 22 E. 89th Street, $1.00

Guide to Special Camping Programs, Chicago, Illinois: The National Easter Seal Society for Crippled Children and Adults (2023 West Ogden Avenue), $1.50.

National Amputee Ski Technique, National Inconvenienced Sportsman's Association/National Amputee Skiers Association, 3738 Walnut Avenue, Carmichael, California, 95608.

Special Olympics Poly Hockey, Massachusetts Special Olympics, 63 Winslow St., Marshfield, Massachusetts, Jim Morrison.

Teaching the Blind to Ski, National Inconvenienced Sportsman's Association, 3738 Walnut Avenue, Carmichael, California, 95608.

Annotated Research Bibliography in Physical Education, Recreation, and Psychomotor Function of Mentally Retarded Persons, American Alliance for Health, Physical Education, and Recreation Publications Sales, 1201 16th Street, N.W. Washington, D.C., 20036, 1975. $7.00

Lawrence, Connie C., and L.C. Hackett, *Water Learning: A New Adventure,* Palo Alto, California: Peek Publications, 1975.

Motor Fitness Testing Manual for the Moderately Mentally Retarded, American Alliance for Health, Physical Education, and Recreation Publication Sales, 1201 16th Street, N.W. Washington, D.C., 20036, 1975. $3.95.

Testing for Impaired, Disabled, and Handicapped Individuals, American Alliance for Health, Physical Education, and Recreation Publication Sales, 1201 16th Street, N.W. Washington, D.C., 20036, 1975. $3.95.

Integrating Persons with Handicapping Conditions Into Regular Physical Education and Recreation Programs, Washington, D.C.: American Alliance for Health, Physical Education, and Recreation, December 1974, $2.00.

One Out of Ten: School Planning for the Handicapped, New York, New York: Educational Facilities Laboratories, (850 3rd Avenue), 1974.

Remy Charlip, and Mary Beth, *Handtalk: An ABC of Finger Spelling & Sign Language,* New York, New York: Parents' Magazine Press, (52 Vanderbilt Avenue), 1974. $4.95.

Periodicals and Pamphlets

A Glossary of Recreation Terms for the Public and Medical Setting. Bulletin Number 20, June, 1962. The North Carolina Recreation Commission, Mansion Park Building, Raleigh, North Carolina.

Challenge. (Five times yearly) Recreation and Fitness for the Mentally Retarded. A.A.H.P.E.R. Unit on Program for Handicapped, 1201 16 Street, N.W., Washington, D.C. 20036.

Communique'. (Monthly) National Recreation and Park Association, 1601 North Kent Street, Arlington, Virginia 22209.

Day Camping for the Trainable and Severely Retarded. Guideline for Establishing Day Camp Programs, 1970. Illinois Division of Mental Retardation, 401 South Spring Street, Springfield, Illinois 62706.

Design for All Americans. National Commission on Architectural Barriers to Rehabilitation of the Handicapped. Rehabilitation Services Administration, U.S. H.E.W., Washington, D.C., 1967.

Diversified Games and Activities of Low Organization for Mentally Retarded Children. Little Grassy Facilities. Southern Illinois University, Carbondale, Illinois.

Easter Seal Directory of Resident Camps for Persons with Special Needs (Annually) National Easter Seal Society for Crippled Children and Adults, 2023 West Ogden Avenue, Chicago, Illinois 60612.

Expanding Horizons in Therapeutic Recreation, Vol. I and II. University of Missouri, Columbia, Missouri.

Guide to the National Parks and Monuments for Handicapped Tourists. President's Committee on Employment of the Handicapped. U.S. Government Printing Office, Washington, D.C. 20402.

IRCH Newsletter. (Monthly) Recreation for the Handicapped. Outdoor Laboratory, Southern Illinois University, Carbondale, Illinois 62901.

Journal of Leisurability. (Quarterly) The Leisure and Disability Publications, Steering Committee, Box 281, Station A., Ottawa, Ontario KIN 8V2 Canada.

Journal of Leisure Research. (Quarterly) National Recreation and Park Association, 1601 North Kent Street, Arlington, Virginia 22209.

Journal of Physical Education and Recreation. (Monthly) American Alliance for Health, Physical Education and Recreation, 1201 16th St., N.W., Washington, D.C. 20036.

Leisure Today: Selected Readings. American Association for Leisure and Recreation, 1201 16th St., N.W., Washington, D.C. 20036.

Outdoor Recreation Planning for the Handicapped. Department of the Interior, Bureau of Outdoor Recreation. U.S. Department Printing Office, Washington, D.C. 20402.

Parks and Recreation. (Monthly) National Recreation and Park Association, 1601 North Kent Street, Arlington, Virginia 22209.

Performances. The President's Committee on Employment of the Handicapped, Washington, D.C. 20210.

Physical Education and Recreation for the Visually Handicapped. Charles E. Buell, A.A.H.P.E.R., 1973. 1201 16th St., N.W., Washington, D.C. 20036.

Physical Education and Recreation for Handicapped Children. A.A.H.P.E.R National Recreation and Park Association, 1601 North Kent Street, Arlington, Virginia 22209.

Physical Education and Recreation for the Visually Handicapped. Charles E. Buell, A.A.H.P.E.R., 1973. 1201 16th St., N.W. Washington, D.C. 20036.

Recreation Digest. (Monthly) Periodical on Recreation for the Ill, Handicapped and Aged. National Research Institute, 258 Broadway, N.Y., N.Y.

Recreation in Treatment Centers. Vol. III-VII. National Therapeutic Recreation in Society, 1601 North Kent Street, Arlington, Virginia 22209.

Rehabilitation Literature. (Monthly) National Easter Seal Society for Crippled Children and Adults, 2023 West Ogden Ave., Chicago, Illinois 60612.

Supervisor's Guide: A Handbook for Activities Supervisors in Long-Term Care Facilities U.S Department H.E.W. Public Health Services, U.S. Government Printing Office, Washington, D.C. 20402.

The Best of Challenge. Vol. I & II. American Alliance for Health, Physical Education and Recreation, 1201 16th St., Washington, D.C. 20036.

Films

Tools for Learning, (16mm, color, sound, 27-minutes), Kingsbury Center, 2138 Bancroft Place, Washington, D.C., (Rental $25.00; purchase $250.00)

Let Me Live In Your World. (16mm, color/sound, 24-minutes, $450.00 purchase), Premru Productions, #13831 Cherry Creek Drive, Tampa, Florida, 33618. Also available in 8mm color/sound cassette for $99.95.

Free, (16mm, sound, color, 18-minutes), Hawaii Association for Retarded Children, 245 North Kukui Street, Honolulu, Hawaii, 96815. Purchase $150.00.

Specific Sports Skills, (16mm, sound, color, 20-minutes), Documentary Films, 3217 Trout Gulch Road, Aptos, California.

Why Billy Couldn't Learn (16mm, sound, color, 40-minutes), California Association for Neurologically Handicapped Children, P.O. Box 604, Main Office, Los Angeles, California, 90053.

Mental Retardation Films, Parsons, Kansas: Audio-Visual Department, Parsons State Hospital and Training Center, (P.O. Box 738).

Focus on Ability, (16mm, color/sound, 22 minutes), American National Red Cross, Washington, D.C.

Aqua Dynamic Conditioning, (16mm, color/sound, 18-minutes), President's Council of Physical Fitness and Sports and National Varsity Club, Washington, D.C.

Water Play for Teaching Young Children, (16mm, color/sound, 16 minutes), New York University Film Library, 25 Washington Place, New York, New York, 10003.

A Matter of Inconvenience, Stanfield House. 900 Euclid Ave., Santa Monica, California, 90403, (16mm, color, sound, 10 minutes).

. . . Two, Three, Fasten Your Ski, Children's Hospital, 1056 East 19th Ave., Denver, Colorado, 80218. (16mm, color, sound, 17 minutes).

Thursday's Children, (16mm, color, sound, 20-minutes), Swank Motion Pictures, Inc., 201 South Jefferson Avenue, St. Louis, Missouri, 63166.

Playground, (16mm, sound/color, 7 minutes), ACI Films, 35 West 45th St., New York, New York, 10036. Purchase $110.00.

Coming Home, (16mm, sound/color 27 minutes), The Stanfield House, P.O. Box 3208, Santa Monica, California, 90403. Purchase, $300.00, rental $25.00.

1975 International Special Olympics Games, (16mm, sound/color, 23 minutes), The Joseph P. Kennedy, Jr. Foundation, 1701 K Street, N.W., Suite 205, Washington, D.C., 20006.

A Dream to Grow On, (16mm, sound, color, 28 minutes), Bone Film Service (3132 M Street, N.W., Washington, D.C.), Purchase, $125.00; rental, $9.00.

Heart of Winning, (12 minutes, 16mm, color), The Joseph P. Kennedy, Jr. Foundation, 1701 K Street, N.W., Suite 205, Washington, D.C., 20006.

Floor Hockey Training, (15 minutes, 16mm, color), The Joseph P. Kennedy, Jr. Foundation, 1701 K Street, N.W., Suite 205, Washington, D.C., 20006.

A New Kind of Joy, (11-minutes, 16mm, color), The Joseph P. Kennedy, Jr. Foundation, 1701 K Street, N.W., Suite 205, Washington, D.C., 20006.

1972 International Games, (20 minutes, 16mm, color), The Joseph P. Kennedy, Jr. Foundation, 1701 K Street, N.W., Suite 205, Washington, D.C., 20006.

Medals, (22-minutes, 16mm color), The Joseph P. Kennedy, Jr. Foundation, 1701 K Street, N.W., Suite 205, Washington, D.C., 20006.

Maybe Tomorrow, (16mm, color, sound, 28-minutes), AIM for Handicapped, 945 Danbury Road, Dayton, Ohio, 45420.

Dance With Joy, (16mm, color, sound, 13-minutes). Documentary Films, 3217 Trout Gulch Road, Aptos, California, (Rental, $17.50 per day; purchase, $155.00).

A Walk in Another Pair of Shoes. (35mm filmstrip or 35mm slide with synchronized cassette tape; color, 18 1/2 minutes). California Asociation for Neurologically Handicapped Children, Film Distribution, P.O. Box 604, Main Office, Los Angeles, California, 90053. Filmstrip set, $6.90; slide set, $21.00.

Looking for Me, (16mm, black and white, sound, 29-minutes). New York University Film Library, 26 Washington Place, New York, New York, 10003.

The Proud Ones, (16mm, sound, color, 13 1/2 minutes). Montana Film Productions, 1236 Helena Avenue, Helena, Montana, 59601.

A Song for Michael: A Demonstration of How Music Therapy Is Used To Develop Language in a Multiply Handicapped Boy of Fourteen, (16mm, sound, black and white, 22-minutes), Music Therapy Center, 810 Eighth Avenue, New York, New York, 10019.

Splash, (16mm, sound color, 21-minutes), Documentary Films, 3217 Trout Gulch Road, Aptos, California, 95003.

HAP- America At Its Best, (16mm, sound, color, 27-minutes), Columbia Forum Productions, 10621 Fable Row, Columbia, Maryland, 21043.

In-Out-Up-Down-Over-Under-Upside Down, (16mm, color, sound, 9-minutes), ACI Films, 35 West 45th Street, New York, New York, 10036.

Community Adoptive Recreation Program for the Handicapped, (16mm, color, sound, 7-minutes). Recreation and Adult Division, Milwaukee Public Schools, P.O. Box Drawer 10K, Milwaukee, Wisconsin.

Beginnings - A Film About Play, (16mm, color, sound, 14-minutes). Produced by Toy Manufacturers of America and distributed through Modern Talking Picture Service.

Madison School Plan, (16mm, color, sound, 18-minutes), Aims Instructional Media Services, Inc., P.O. Box 1010, Hollywood, California, 90028.

The Santa Monica Project, (16mm, color, sound, 28-minutes), AIMS Instructional Media Services, Inc., P.O. Box 1010, Hollywood, California, 90028.

Challenge: A Camp For All Seasons, (16mm, sound, color, 12-minutes), Easter Seal Society of Florida, 231 East Colonial Drive, Orlando, Florida, 32801.

Therapeutic Recreation   Textbooks

Annotated Bibliography in Physical Education, Recreation, and Psychomotor Functions of Mentally Retarded Persons. American Alliance for Health, Physical Education, and Recreation, 1975.

McClenaghan and David L. Gallahue. *Fundamental Movement: A Developmental and Remedial Approach.* Philadelphia, Pa.: W.B. Saunders, Co., 1978.

Vodola, Thomas A. *Individualized Physical Education Program For The Handicapped Child.* Englewood Cliffs, New Jersey: Prentice-Hall, Inc., 1973.

Chabner, Davi-Ellen. *The Language of Medicine.* Philadelphia, Pa.: W. B. Saunders, Co., 1976.

Winnick, Joseph P. *Early Movement Experiences and Development: Habilitation and Remediation.* Philadelphia, Pa.: W.B. Saunders, 1979.

Ball, Edith L., and Robert E. Cipriano. *Leisure Services preparation: A Competency Based Approach.* Englewood Cliffs, New Jersey: Prentice-Hall, Inc., 1978.

Curtis, Joseph E. *Recreation Theory and Practice.* St. Louis: C.V. Mosby Company, 1979.

Therapeutic Recreation Annual. (Annually) National Therapeutic Recreation Society, 1601 North Kent Street, Arlington, Virginia 22209.

Therapeutic Recreation Journal. (Quarterly) National Therapeutic Recreation Society, 1601 North Kent Street, Arlington, Virginia 22209.

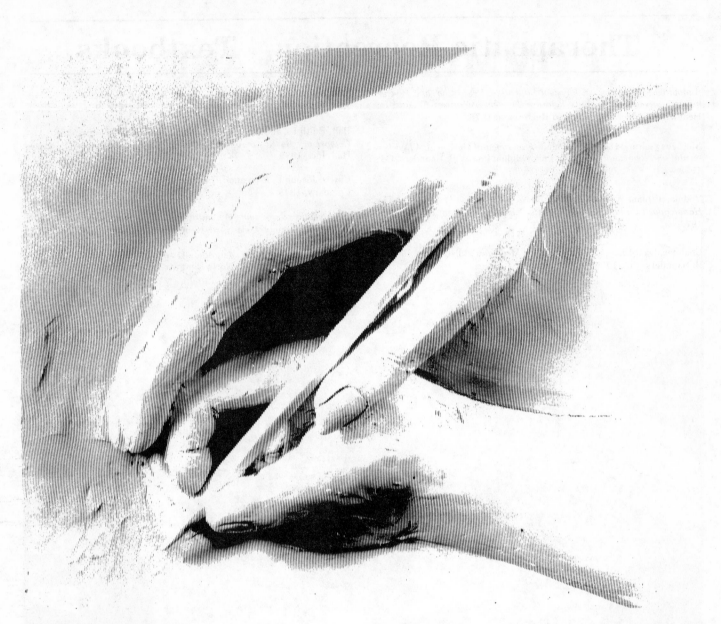

STAFF

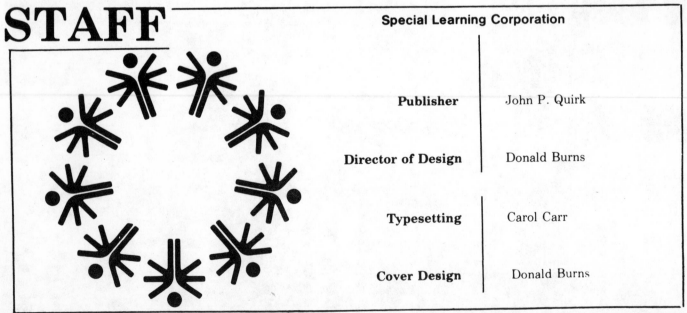

Special Learning Corporation

Publisher	John P. Quirk
Director of Design	Donald Burns
Typesetting	Carol Carr
Cover Design	Donald Burns

COMMENTS PLEASE:

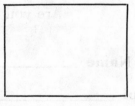

SPECIAL LEARNING CORPORATION

COMMENTS PLEASE ! ! !

1. Where did you use this book?

2. In what course or workshop did you use this reader?

3. What articles did you find most interesting and useful?

4. Have you read any articles that we should consider including in this reader?

5. What other features would you like to see added?

6. Should the format be changed, what would you like to see changed?

7. In what other area would you like us to publish using this format?

8. Did you use this as a
( ) basic text?   ( ) in-service?
( ) supplement?   ( ) general information?

———————————————— Fold Here ————————————————

Are you a ( ) student   ( ) instructor   ( ) teacher   ( ) parent

Your Name _____

School _____

School address _____

_____

Home Address _____

City _____ **St.** _____ **Zip** _____

Telephone Number _____

☐   **ORDER PLACED ON REVERSE SIDE**